Foundation HTML5 Canvas

Rob Hawkes

DESIGNER TO DESIGNER™

an Apress® company

Foundation HTML5 Canvas

Copyright © 2011 by Rob Hawkes

ISBN-13 (pbk): 978-1-4302-3291-9

ISBN-13 (electronic): 978-1-4302-3292-6

Printed and bound in the United States of America (POD)

Distributed to the book trade worldwide by Springer Science+Business Media LLC., 233 Spring Street, 6th Floor, New York, NY 10013. Phone 1-800-SPRINGER, fax (201) 348-4505, e-mail orders-ny@springer-sbm.com, or visit www.springeronline.com.

For information on translations, please e-mail rights@apress.com or visit www.apress.com.

Apress and friends of ED books may be purchased in bulk for academic, corporate, or promotional use. eBook versions and licenses are also available for most titles. For more information, reference our Special Bulk Sales– eBook Licensing web page at www.apress.com/info/bulksales.

The source code for this book is freely available to readers at www.friendsofed.com in the Downloads section.

Credits

To Lizzy, whose love and support stopped me from going too crazy while writing this.

To my family, who nurtured my interest in technology and the Web as a child, even if they didn't fully understand them (and probably still don't).

— Rob Hawkes

Contents at a Glance

Contents

CONTENTS

CONTENTS

About the Author

Rob Hawkes thrives on solving problems through code. He's addicted to visual programming and can't get enough of HTML5, alongside other exciting new features of the Web. Most of his waking life is spent working on crazy projects involving all sorts of new and exciting technologies, both online and off. Rob is originally from London, but now lives in Bournemouth on the South coast of the UK. He studied Interactive Media Production at Bournemouth University, which is how he fell in love with the seaside town and is the reason why he still lives there today.

You can find out more about Rob and his crazy experiments with technology by visiting his website (`http://rawkes.com`), or adding him on Twitter (`@robhawkes`).

About the Technical Reviewer

Doug Swartzendruber, after earning a bachelor's degree in Computer Science from the Colorado School of Mines in 1996, went to work in the aerospace industry as a software engineer for Raytheon. Most of his career there was spent developing satellite command and control software in the C++ language.

An avid video and board game player, Doug's hobbyist work with web development continues to have an emphasis on games. Excited by the new possibilities offered by HTML5, he began working with the canvas and audio objects in late 2009. His web site, DougX.net, showcases some of his applications.

About the Cover Image Designer

Corné van Dooren designed the front cover image for this book. After taking a brief hiatus from friends of ED to create a new design for the Foundation series, he worked at combining technological and organic forms, with the results now appearing on this and other books' covers.

Corné van Dooren spent his childhood drawing on everything at hand and then began exploring the infinite world of multimedia—and his journey of discovery hasn't stopped since. His mantra has always been, "The only limit to multimedia is the imagination"—a saying that keeps him constantly moving forward.

Corné works for many international clients, writes features for multimedia magazines, reviews and tests software, authors multimedia studies, and works on many other friends of ED books. You can see more of his work at and contact him through his website, at www.cornevandooren.com.

Acknowledgments

First and foremost, I'd like to thank my girlfriend, Lizzy, for her unbelievable patience and support throughout the past six months. I can't even begin to understand how frustrating I must have been during the writing of this book, particularly when locking myself away and stressing over the smallest of details. I'm very much looking forward to being there for you, just as you have been for me.

I wouldn't even be here today without my parents (quite literally). I'd like to thank them for supporting my unhealthy obsession with technology and computers as a child, and for nurturing that obsession as I grew up. I'll never forget the sheer amazement I experienced spending time at my dad's Internet cafe back in the day, particularly playing Doom with awesome virtual reality goggles. It's weird, virtual reality never seemed to take the world by storm as it promised to. Back to the point, you guys may not have fully understood how all this technology worked and why I was so interested in it, but I'm so glad that you continued to let me play with and learn about it. Thank you so much.

My sibling, Laura, has been an inspiration to me. We've been through a lot together, and being able to see how well she is doing in her life and work is plenty enough to keep me happy. We may bicker, we may fight, but I couldn't have asked for a better sister.

On a more technical note, I'd like to thank David Burton and the rest of the guys at Redweb for letting me work on some crazy stuff in the Innovation Department for the past two summers. David was the person who gave me the time and encouragement to really push HTML5 canvas and to learn exactly how it works. For this I thank you, as without those few weeks of solid experimentation, I probably wouldn't have written this book!

John and Hannah, two of my closest friends, have kept me grounded and have not been afraid to question me about my opinions and work. Not many people have the guts to do that, and for that I am eternally grateful; you've both prevented me from looking like a fool on multiple occasions. I also want to thank you both or the spirited and humorous debate on the ExplicitWeb podcast; I don't think I've ever laughed so hard as I do when we record the show together.

Finally, I'd like to thank the whole team at Apress and friends of ED. Particularly, I'd like to thank my editors, Ben and Corbin, for their immense patience and help throughout the writing process. You have both helped keep my stress levels below critical. This book wouldn't have even happened without Ben and his trust in me, and for that I owe you one. And I can't forget Doug, my technical reviewer, who sifted through all of my code and technical content with amazing precision. The accuracy and experience that you've shown me is truly inspirational. Thank you.

I'm sure that there are plenty more people that have helped me throughout the development of this book, like my friends on Twitter who showed immense enthusiasm about the book and helped test all the games for me. I could go on forever if I listed you all (so I won't). Just rest assured that I appreciate each and every one of you who have supported and encouraged me. You're all awesome.

Preface

If you asked me a year ago if I could imagine myself writing a book, I'd probably have said no. Yet here I am as the author of one of just a handful of books on HTML5 canvas. My aim has been to create the book that I wished existed two years ago when I first started to learn about canvas. Back then there were barely any resources on canvas. Fortunately that has now started to change for the better.

Over those past two years, I've spent much of my time experimenting with canvas and other new Web technologies that are only just starting to see the light of day. These experiments range from recreating the interactive Google balls logo in September 2010, to creating a fully-fledged multiplayer game with HTML5 canvas and WebSockets. It is these experiments that armed me with the knowledge and experience to write this book and to teach others the lessons I've learned.

I'm absolutely fascinated by animation and games development with technologies like canvas and JavaScript. I truly hope that this book gets across some of that enthusiasm, and I hope that it helps you on your journey to becoming a master of HTML5 canvas.

Who is this book for?

Foundation HTML5 Canvas has been written in a friendly way that makes it approachable to beginners and experts alike. It is predominantly for Web designers who are new to HTML5 and JavaScript, and covers the absolute basics of creating interactive games and applications using the HTML5 canvas element. Experienced Web designers and programmers will also learn about all the features of canvas and how to use them in their own projects. Flash and Silverlight developers wanting to broaden their reach across the Web and mobile devices will also benefit from the information in this book.

How is this book structured?

The book starts off with a short introduction, easing you into HTML5 and the awesome new functionality that it brings to the Web. The purpose of this first chapter is to arm you with the necessary background knowledge about HTML5 and the surrounding technologies.

Once the basics of HTML5 are sorted, you'll move on to learning all about JavaScript. The purpose of this second chapter is to teach you everything you'll need to know to start utilizing HTML5 canvas and creating amazing animations and games with it.

Chapter 3 is where you're properly acquainted with the canvas element, learning how to utilize it to draw basic shapes and text. It is at this point I hope that you will begin to fall in love with canvas and its simplicity.

Next up is Chapter 4, where you're introduced to the more advanced functionality of canvas. You'll learn how to perform transformations as well as how to draw complex shapes. You'll also learn how to save drawings in the canvas as images.

Chapter 5 takes the knowledge from previous chapters and uses it to let you manipulate images and video with canvas. This is where things start to get really interesting, and it is where I hope you'll start to really see the practical uses of canvas.

The following chapters, 6 and 7, step up a gear and teach you how to animate with JavaScript and canvas. It is in these chapters that you'll learn the fundamentals of animation, as well as how to use physics to make your animations look realistic.

Chapters 8 and 9 are the culmination of the book. These two chapters each walk you through the creation of an HTML5 game, from the core aspects of creating a game with canvas, to user input, to adding sound with HTML5 audio. Everything you learn in these chapters will be useful to the creation of your own HTML5 games.

The book ends with a look at the future of canvas and how you can take things further. This final chapter will hopefully inspire you to take everything that you've learned and really push it to another level.

I've tried to keep this book structured so that you can read it from front to back, or jump in and read about just a specific topic. The purpose of this book is to act as a learning resource, as well as a point of reference for working with canvas and animation in JavaScript.

All the code for this book can be downloaded from the book's page on the friends of ED website [http://www.friendsofed.com].

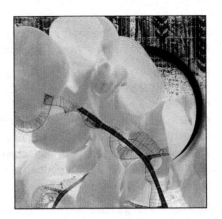

Chapter 1

Introducing HTML5

We're going to start right at the beginning. In this chapter, we'll look at the history of HTML, to understand where we've come from and where we're headed. Next, we'll explore the new features that HTML5 brings to the table, detailing how and when they should be used. We'll then deconstruct an example web page created using HTML5 to better understand how it could be applied in authentic situations. And lastly, we'll clear up some of the confusion surrounding HTML5 and other new web technologies. Ultimately, this chapter will give you a better understanding of HTML5, providing you with the knowledge necessary to progress further into the book.

A brief history of HTML

In December 1997, the World Wide Web Consortium (W3C) officially announced HTML 4.0 as a W3C recommendation.[1] HTML 4.0 was very different to its predecessors, and brought with it new and exciting functionality, like cascading style sheets (CSS) and client-side scripting. These features alone dramatically changed the way people created websites, moving away from the reliance on tables for presentation, and allowing for dynamic websites using scripting languages like JavaScript. Before this, HTML was mostly a static and limiting environment that lacked most of the features you would normally now associate with the Web: it was basically just text and images.

HTML 4.01 was released in December 1999, but didn't bring with it any major new functionality.[2] Its main purpose was to correct some errors in the specification and apply a few minor changes. After all, by this time HTML 4 had only been around for a couple of years, so there wasn't much need to muck around with it. For the next five years things chugged along fairly smoothly. During that time there were attempted updates to CSS, XHTML 1.0 was released, and the infamous browser Internet Explorer 6 was launched. It

---

[1] http://www.w3.org/html/wg/wiki/History
[2] http://www.w3.org/TR/html4/

1

was in 2005 when the draft specification for Web Applications 1.0 was released, by the Web Hypertext Application Technology Working Group (WHATWG),[3] that the story begins to get interesting.

Both HTML 4.0 and XHTML 1.0 (with 2.0 in draft) were created before today's concepts of blogs, online shops, and forums really took hold. The problem with these versions was that they were built to mark up static documents, which blogs and online shops are not – they are essentially applications. Web Applications 1.0 was created to solve this problem – to provide an extension to HTML that accommodated these types of websites by adding new elements (the tags used to mark up content) and functionality. By 2008, Web Applications 1.0 blossomed, was adopted by the W3C, and turned into the first draft of the HTML5 specification. It introduced a raft of new and powerful features that we'll discuss in more detail throughout this book.

So after a brief glimpse into the past, we arrive at the present. HTML5 is now in a working draft form and is changing as we speak. It's technically unfinished and will stay that way for some time to come; a working draft is one step above a draft, but it's only the third step out of six.[3] However, the good news is that parts of HTML5 are already being built into a variety of browsers, allowing us to use these exciting features right now. There is really no reason for any decent Web designer or programmer not to look at HTML5. It is, put simply, the future of the Web. Do you really want to be left behind while everyone else is having such good fun?

Why is HTML5 needed?

As we've discussed, HTML5 has been created to scratch the proverbial itch. But what exactly *is* the itch? And how does HTML5 scratch it? Let's find out.

The itch

In HTML 4.01, and earlier versions, we know that there was a document-oriented approach to things. The Web was originally created to display and share scientific documents. That concept of documents continued through the Web's early life, albeit with more generic information rather than just scientific data. However, in the years after HTML 4.01 there began a rise in dynamic websites and online applications, supported in part by the adoption of Adobe Flash and other third-party plugins that allowed you to create applications full of rich, interactive media. Content management systems (CMS) and services like WordPress started to crop up, offering anyone the ability to create a blog or manage large quantities of content using templates. Flickr allowed for the sharing of photographs, with YouTube doing the same for video. And, once faith was restored in the Internet after the dot com bubble went pop, online stores and auction sites started cropping up all over the place, selling items from books to the unwanted crap in your attic. The Web was becoming less and less static, with more content being user-generated and inherently dynamic.

In essence, the Web grew away from its roots in individual static documents, focussing now on large quantities of dynamic data being displayed using templates. It would be wrong to describe the Web in its entirety using this definition, of course, but it highlights a fundamental shift in how the Web was being

---

[3] http://wiki.whatwg.org/wiki/FAQ#When_will_HTML5_be_finished.3F

used. The problem was that HTML was never built to deal with this kind of use; it was built to deal with fairly strict types of document-based content (paragraphs, images, headings, and so on). Anything more exotic, like media or CMS content, required the use of external plugins, like Adobe Flash, and ill-fitting code. Something else was needed that brought HTML up to speed, allowing it to accommodate media and allow for better, more semantic code.

Scratching the itch

HTML5 brings with it a massive amount of improvements over the old document-oriented Web. New elements have been created to mark up dynamic, templated content. Other elements have been created with the sole purpose of ending our reliance on external plugins to experience audio-visual content. These elements alone solve many of the problems, but the W3C (with credit to the WHATWG) hasn't stopped there. For example, form validation, previously something only achieved via JavaScript, is also part of HTML5. With practically all user-generated content on the Web being created, in part, using some kind of input form, validation within the browser is more important than ever.

As well as HTML5, and intrinsically tied to its development, are other technologies that hope to solve related issues. One such example is the Web today being much more mobile than it was 10 years ago – it's reckoned that 95% of mobile phones have some sort of Internet browser.[4] With more and more people wanting to access content specific to their location, would it not make sense to implement geolocation within the browser? These, among others, are technologies that are being created alongside HTML5 to scratch the itch once and for all.

HTML5 introduces a whole host of new functionality, covered in page after page of specification on the W3C and WHATWG websites. This book has been written to give you a foundation for understanding the specification; it will take you through the important new features of HTML5 in detail – in plain English.

> Note: It's not easy to define exactly what is and isn't HTML5. The specification is in a state of flux at the moment, particularly as it's split between the W3C and WHATWG. Also, many features that started life as HTML5 have since grown up and moved into their own separate specifications, like geolocation and scalable vector graphics (SVG). The definition of HTML5 in this book is based solely on the specification found at the WHATWG.[5]
>
> As we'll discuss at the end of this chapter, many people lump other technologies into the HTML5 category (like CSS3) that are not actually part of the specification. Fortunately for us, the canvas element is firmly attached to the HTML5 specification, so we need not worry about referring to it as HTML5.

---

[4] TomiAhonen: Mobile Industry Numbers 2010
[5] http://www.whatwg.org/specs/web-apps/current-work/multipage/

What's new in HTML5?

By now we already know that HTML5 brings with it a variety of new elements, both for content structure and media. HTML5 also brings with it a raft of new and improved features, like with forms. But what are these new features, and what do they do? You could write an entire book covering everything new in HTML5, but the next few sections will provide an overview of the most interesting and important features.

> *Note: Explaining every single detail of HTML5 is beyond the scope of this book. If you'd like to learn more about the new features, then have a read through the HTML5 specification. It can be a bit of an eyeful, but it's well worth it if you want to truly understand how everything works.*

Structural and content elements

It's safe to say that every website ever created uses structural and content elements in one way or another. From paragraphs (`<p>`) to divisions (`<div>`), these types of elements are the bread and butter of the Web. However, the problem with HTML as it existed previously was that it didn't support content that falls outside of the concept of documents. Fortunately, HTML5 introduces a huge list of new elements that aim to solve this issue and give content much more semantic meaning.

Structure in HTML5

The new structural elements in HTML5 give us a whole host of ways to describe the various sections within our Web pages. Normally you would be limited to using copious amounts of `div` elements with a splattering of `span` elements for good measure. Not anymore! We now have access to elements like `section`, `header`, `hgroup`, `footer`, `nav`, `article`, and `aside`. Each of these new elements has a unique purpose to help differentiate the most common areas on a modern Web page.

The section element

Arguably the `div` of the HTML5 world is the `section` element. The HTML5 specification describes it as a generic section of a website. Specifically, its purpose is to group content thematically; that is, grouping content into areas that are distinguishable from the rest in theme or focus. An example would be chapters in a large body of writing, or areas on the same page of a website, like an introduction, gallery of portfolio work, and a contact form.

> *Note: The important rule with the `section` element is not to think of it as a replacement for the `div` element. A `section` is to be used for defining specific, distinguishable areas of a website. A `div` element should be used only as a last resort, usually when no other element would make sense.*

The header element

Whether it holds a logo or the name of a company, most websites have a header of some sort. Before now, a header, like most areas of a website, would likely be constructed using a div element, or some other generic element not suited to the task. The new header element essentially saves our sanity by allowing us to define a specific area of a website that contains headings, logos, navigation, and any other content you'd normally associate with a header. You can also have more than one header on a website; it works just as well for containing the headings within content.

The hgroup element

Separate to heading is the hgroup element, which is used to contain a set of multiple heading elements (h1-h6). The most common use for hgroup is with content that has both a heading and subheading. Previous to HTML5, the only way to contain a group of headings would be with generic HTML 4 elements, like div, which isn't ideal as there is no semantic meaning. It is normal for an hgroup element to be included within a heading element.

The footer element

Copyright notices and details about who made the site are commonly associated with the bottom of a website. The footer element has been created to give these types of content a place to live, because most websites have a footer of some sorts. A footer can also contain things like links to related content, which means they're perfect for use within sections and articles. Like the header element, there is nothing to stop you having more than one footer per page.

The nav element

As you've probably guessed by now, all the new HTML5 elements have come about because people are trying to do things with HTML 4 that it was never intended to do. Navigation is no different. The nav element has been created with the sole purpose of containing navigational links to sections of a page and other pages of a website. The most common use for the nav element is to contain the main navigation menu of a website. It's often found in a header element alongside a logo or other content typically seen within a header.

The article element

Any content that is self-contained and potentially reused in other formats (for example, distribution through RSS) should be placed within an article element. A perfect example of such content would be a blog post. You could remove every other piece of content surrounding a blog post and it should still make sense and retain its meaning. Blog posts are also commonly reused and distributed in formats like RSS. Other examples would be comments, forum posts, and news articles.

> Note: There is a lot of confusion about when to use the article element. Bruce Lawson has written an excellent post attempting to clarify the issue.[6] A good rule of thumb is to use article if the content would make sense on its own in a RSS feed reader.

The aside element

Our last structural element is the aside element. Its purpose is to contain content that is related to the content surrounding it. A typical example of this would be pull quotes and sidebars.

Content in HTML5

So, as we can see, there are plenty of new elements that help us structure our website in ways that make sense. Fortunately we're a lucky bunch, as we have some more elements to cover. This time the focus is on the new elements that help us group and mark up bodies of content. Elements like figure, figcaption, mark, and time.

The figure element

A typical use of the figure element is for annotating content with things like images, code, and anything else that helps explain the content in some way. The content within a figure element should be able to be moved outside of the main content without disrupting the flow. In other words, you should be able to remove a figure element and still understand the original content.

```
<figure>
        <img src="example.jpg" alt="An example image">
</figure>
```

The figcaption element

Some annotated content requires a short caption to explain what it is, usually because it is shown outside of the context of the original content. To include a caption within a figure element you should use the figcaption element. Simple!

```
<figure>
        <img src="example.jpg" alt="An example image">
        <figcaption>This example image will help you understand.</figcaption>
</figure>
```

---

[6] http://www.brucelawson.co.uk/2010/html5-articles-and-sections-whats-the-difference/

The mark element

Content that is highlighted for the purpose of referencing should be included within the mark element. An example would be highlighting a sentence within a quotation that the author of the quote didn't consider important at the time. Another use for the mark element would be highlighting areas of content relevant to a user's current activity. For example, if a user came from a search engine, you could wrap words in your content related to the user's search terms in mark elements.

```
<p>This is a great example of <mark>HTML5 canvas</mark>.</p>
```

> Note: The mark element is not to be confused with the em or strong elements. The latter denote content that is felt important or worthy of emphasis by the original author. A mark element denotes content deemed relevant in some other context by a different author or as a result of user activity.

The time element

When you need a time or date in your content, it's advisable to use the time element. It's important to remember that any time used must be in a 24-hour format, and dates must be in the proleptic Gregorian calendar – the calendar most people in the West use. The time element can also include a couple of attributes: datetime, which indicates the exact date and time specified within the element, and pubdate, which indicates that the date and time given by the element indicates when an article (or the document as a whole) was published. Both attributes take a date in the format YYYY-MM-DD, like 2010-12-25. The datetime attribute is particularly useful when the date inside the time element is represented in a string format that could be misunderstood (such as 24 October, which has no year attached).

```
<time datetime="2011-09-06">My birthday this year</time>
```

Forms

If you've ever had the luxury of dealing with forms, then you'll understand the pain that is associated with making sure everything is validated and safe. You'll also be aware of the severe lack of control you have when constructing forms. Want a special input that only accepts emails? Tough, have a generic text input instead. Want an input that pops up a calendar so users can choose a date? Sorry pal, you'll need to spend half your life in JavaScript for that. Okay, so perhaps the world of forms isn't quite as grim as that, but there's no denying that the only way you can validate forms and provide intelligent functionality is through JavaScript. However, thanks to what started out as Web Forms 2.0, HTML5 has come to save our collective souls (and our sanity to boot!)

Validation in the browser

One of my favourite features of HTML5 forms is validation built right into the browser. That means no JavaScript, which means happy Web designers and developers! The problem with the current JavaScript-only system is that you can't guarantee that everyone will have JavaScript enabled. This is why you should always use server-side validation, like PHP, alongside client-side validation, like JavaScript. Having validation baked directly into the browser would not only bring it to everyone that uses the browser, it also means you save a whole bunch of time that you'd normally have spent cooking up validation in JavaScript.

By default, HTML5 form validation is turned on in browsers that support it, although you can turn it off by placing the novalidate attribute in your form element. At the time of writing the only browser to support HTML5 forms fully is Opera (9.5 and later), which displays lovely warning messages if validation fails. Other browsers like Safari and Chrome have a haphazard implementation that is effectively useless – there is no visual feedback for validation errors. Fortunately, browser support is changing at a rapid pace, so it's possible that form validation will work in all browsers by the time you read this.

Input types

Anyone who's made a form in the past will know about input types. For those who haven't, an input element is generally used for user input in forms (alongside other elements, like select, textarea, and so on). By setting the type attribute within the input element you're able to make that form input do interesting things; like looking different if someone is entering a password (type = "password"), giving users a selection of checkboxes to tick (type = "checkbox"), or turning it into a submission button (type = "submit"). Input really is the powerhouse behind HTML forms.

The new input types in HTML5 allow you to extend forms beyond things like buttons, checkboxes, and text input. We now have types at our disposal that let us define inputs for email addresses, telephone numbers, URLs. Some of the cooler input types, like datetime, let us select dates using something like a calendar interface. Others, like range, allow us to limit users to choosing a number between a minimum and maximum value. Then you have the color type that lets us choose a colour value using something akin to a colour picker you'd normally associate with a graphics application. A weird choice for inclusion in the HTML5 specification, but most definitely cool!

Input attributes

Alongside input types there are a range of other attributes that can be used in input elements. These range from attributes like placeholder, allowing you to pre-fill an input with a hint for the user, to autocomplete, which lets you toggle whether you want the user's data to be auto-filled based on previous data.

There are numerous other input types, attributes, and other cool features of forms. However, although forms are admittedly very interesting, our time is probably best spent looking at the meatier aspects of HTML5 that are related to this book. Yup, that means it's time for the really cool stuff, media elements!

Media elements

Before HTML5 came on the scene, external plugins and applications were required to play media in the browser—it was just the way things were done. There was also no built-in support for manipulating graphics—you could only embed images that had already been constructed. One of the core aims of HTML5 is to improve media support, and boy is it doing that. New elements such as audio and video have been introduced that allow media to be played in the browser without the need for any external plugins, like Adobe Flash and Microsoft Silverlight. The canvas element has been brought in so images and graphics can be constructed and manipulated directly within the browser.

The coolest thing about all of these new media elements is that they have open JavaScript APIs that let us take control of media in a really simple way. Want to rewind a video with a custom button? No problem. What about animating some canvas graphics on the fly? Easy peasy. Media in HTML5 is both powerful and exciting, and you don't need to rely on proprietary technology to create it. Never before has this kind of control been implemented at the browser level.

The audio element

How often do you need an audio player when building a website? For most people the answer to this question is either never or rarely. There's no denying that audio players are a pretty niche requirement on the Web or, at least, they are in their current Flash-based format. On top of that there is a slight hatred of audio on the Web after the influx of websites with auto-playing background music in the 90s. So why then is there a dedicated audio element in HTML5? Because the current methods require you to use a third-party plugin, silly! A cool thing about the audio element is that can be used without rendering it to the page. The beauty of this is that it can be used to complement other features of a website without causing visual mess. For example, you could use an audio element without a user interface for the sound effects of a game – just like what we'll be doing later in this book.

Currently there is no consistent support for the audio element across all the major browsers. There are a grand total of five audio codecs available across these browsers, with none of them all supporting the same codec. The most common of the formats are MP3, and OGG (an open source and free codec). At the moment the best way to implement HTML5 audio cross-browser is to provide an audio source for two or more different codecs. It's not ideal, but it's easy enough to do – you just replace the single src attribute for one or more source elements within the audio element:

```
<audio controls>
        <source src="http://yourwebsite.com/sound.ogg">
        <source src="http://yourwebsite.com/sound.mp3">
        <!- Insert fallback audio content here, perhaps a Flash player ->
</audio>
```

Hopefully over time a single codec will be supported by all the major browsers. For now we'll just have to put up with this minor hassle.

The great thing about these new media elements is that you can easily provide fallback content, like a Flash player, for browsers that don't support them. Fallback content is provided by placing normal HTML elements within the media element.

For some fine-grained control over the audio element there are a few attributes you can use, other than src, which we've already covered. First up is the controls attribute that, if used, tells the browser to provide a default user interface for controlling audio content (see Figure 1-1).

```
<audio src="http://yourwebsite.com/sound.ogg" controls>
        <!- Insert fallback audio content here, perhaps a Flash player ->
</audio>
```

Figure 1-1. HTML5 audio controls in Google Chrome

If you want audio to loop once, it finishes then there is the `loop` attribute. But it's worth mentioning that each browser seems to implement looping in a slightly different way.

```
<audio src="http://yourwebsite.com/sound.ogg" controls loop>
        <!- Insert fallback audio content here, perhaps a Flash player ->
</audio>
```

All pretty straightforward so far. `Preload` tells the browser how you'd like the audio preloaded, if at all.

```
<audio src="http://yourwebsite.com/sound.ogg" controls preload="auto">
        <!- Insert fallback audio content here, perhaps a Flash player ->
</audio>
```

And lastly you have the `autoplay` attribute, which allows you to have audio content play automatically when the browser loads (please keep the sanity of your users in mind before implementing this).

```
<audio src="http://yourwebsite.com/sound.ogg" controls autoplay>
        <!- Insert fallback audio content here, perhaps a Flash player ->
</audio>
```

> *Note: Mozilla has put together an Audio Data API that allows for direct manipulation of audio data. With it you can read and write raw audio content through code. Examples of its use are audio synthesizers and visualizations, like you get in iTunes. Currently only Firefox supports this, but it's a very cool sign of what can be done now media is built into the browser.[7]*

The video element

Audio is cool and all, but combining audio and moving pictures (video) is even cooler. Unlike audio, video content is extremely widespread on the Web, and you'd be hard pushed not to stumble across it somewhere on your travels. However, like audio, the current methods for implementing video content involve external plugins like Flash. And again, like audio, the current methods are bloated and confusing, so it's no surprise that a dedicated `video` element has been introduced with HTML5 to save the day.

You'd be forgiven for thinking video is harder to implement in HTML5 than audio. Fortunately for us, these two media elements stem from the same guidelines, meaning that they use similar attributes and are implemented in similar ways. A simple `video` element would look something like this (see Figure 1-2).

---

[7] https://wiki.mozilla.org/Audio_Data_API

```
<video src="http://yourwebsite.com/video.ogv" controls>
        <!-- Insert fallback video content here, perhaps a Flash player -->
</video>
```

Looks mighty similar to the audio example doesn't it? HTML5 consistency win!

Figure 1-2. HTML5 video and controls in Google Chrome

There are a variety of video codecs available for you to use, but unfortunately, like audio, none of the codecs are supported by all browsers. To get around this we can use the source element just like we did with the audio element.

```
<video controls>
        <source src="http://yourwebsite.com/video.ogv">
        <source src="http://yourwebsite.com/video.mp4">
        <!- Insert fallback video content here, perhaps a Flash player ->
</video>
```

Again, like with the audio codecs, I very much hope a single codec will be supported by all browsers in the future. It would certainly make things easier for us.

Because media in HTML5 is awesome, the video and audio elements both share common attributes like src, autoplay, loop, preload, and controls. The video element also brings with it a few special attributes only applicable to video content.

To display an image when the video isn't being played you can use the poster attribute.

```
<video src="http://yourwebsite.com/video.ogv" controls
poster="http://yourwebsite.com/video_poster.jpg">
        <!- Insert fallback video content here, perhaps a Flash player ->
</video>
```

To mute audio on a video by default you can use the audio attribute.

```
<video src="http://yourwebsite.com/video.ogv" controls audio="muted">
        <!- Insert fallback video content here, perhaps a Flash player ->
</video>
```

And to define a specific width and height for the video you can use the width and height attributes.

```
<video src="http://yourwebsite.com/video.ogv" controls width="1280" height="720">
        <!- Insert fallback video content here, perhaps a Flash player ->
</video>
```

Due to codec juggling and support in older browsers, video in HTML5 isn't *quite* ready for the mainstream just yet, but that doesn't mean you can't start using it. Some big video providers like YouTube and Vimeo are already rolling out experimental HTML5 video support in preparation for the maturing and future uptake of HTML5. In any case, you can always use a traditional Flash video as fallback for a HTML5 video if you really want to use it on your website.

> *Note: A major reason why HTML5 media is so important is that it provides a completely open way of implementing audio and video. Before this you were limited to closed systems like Flash, which, although functionally sound, make it difficult to control media outside of the plugin. HTML5 doesn't place these restrictions on you and allows you to control and manipulate media in any way you like, anywhere you want. See* The Definitive Guide to HTML5 Video *by Silvia Pfeiffer (Apress) for a detailed examination of video in HTML5.*

The canvas element

Easily my favorite feature of HTML, the canvas element is the reason behind writing this book and, in some part I hope, the reason why you're reading it. This element is very different from the others as its main purpose is to manipulate 2d graphics or create them from scratch, rather than simply embedding existing media like with the audio and video elements. I suppose you could imagine it like Microsoft Paint built into the browser. But don't despair, as I can assure you it's much, *much* better than and, in reality, nothing like Microsoft Paint! My point is to look at it as a 2d graphics environment instead of a simple container for embedding media.

> *Note: Did you know: Apple originally invented the* canvas *element for creating Dashboard widgets, but it quickly caught on with other browser manufacturers and eventually made its way directly into the HTML5 specification.*

I'd be doing canvas an injustice if I didn't give you a better insight into its possibilities. Yes, it may only be a 2d platform (for now), but that doesn't mean it can't do some pretty amazing stuff. For example, by manipulating the canvas element with the JavaScript API you can create dynamic graphics and animations that react to user interaction (like games – some genii at Google even ported the first-person

3D shooting game Quake II into canvas). You can use it to create data visualizations and graphs based on data in a HTML table, which updates on the fly. You can use it to construct a UI for a Web application, although I'd probably advise using traditional HTML and CSS for that. What I'm getting at here is that the canvas element is simple and benign but, together with the JavaScript API and a bit of imagination, canvas as a whole is a massively potent tool for creating dynamic graphics and interactive experiences. In a nutshell, canvas is really exciting!

> Note: You may have noticed that I refer to both the canvas element and canvas. There is a subtle distinction. I will refer to the canvas element when directly talking about the HTML5 element and its features, not including the JavaScript API. I will refer to canvas (without the emphasis) when talking about the whole family of canvas-related features as a whole (the canvas element, the JavaScript API, the sense of awe you receive while using it, and so on).

So that's all you need to know about the canvas element. Now you can go off and create these amazing graphics and games. *But, isn't there more?* I hear you ask. Well, you've got me. I lied. There is *so* much more to say about canvas and what can be done with it. We've not even scratched the surface yet! Future chapters are dedicated to learning more about this powerful element and how to control it. You'll be a master of canvas in no time.

Deconstructing an example HTML5 page

It's all well and good learning about the new elements in HTML5, but until you see them in context it's hard to imagine how they're used. So that is exactly what we're going to do now. I'm going to show you an example HTML5 Web page and then we'll dissect it line by line and learn how the new elements are used in a real environment. The example page we're going to look at is for an imaginary blog homepage, which will include a header, some blog posts, a sidebar, and a footer. We won't be styling the page so I've left out things like CSS and presentational attributes. We're concentrating purely on how a HTML5 website is structured.

Here is the full code for our HTML5 blog homepage. Don't worry if it's all a bit much right now.

```
<!DOCTYPE html>

<html>
        <head>
                <title>A basic HTML5 blog homepage</title>
                <meta charset="utf-8">
                <!-- CSS and JavaScript to go here -->
        </head>

        <body>
                <header>
                        <!-- Website name and navigation -->
                        <h1>My amazing blog</h1>
```

```
                                <nav>
                                    <ul>
                                        <li><a href="/">Home</a></li>
                                        <li><a href="/archive/">Archive</a></li>
                                        <li><a href="/about/">About</a></li>
                                        <li><a href="/contact/">Contact</a></li>
                                    </ul>
                                </nav>
                        </header>

                        <section>
                            <!-- Blog articles - repeat as many times as required -->
                            <article>
                                <header>
                                    <hgroup>
                                        <h1><a href="/blog/first-post-
link/">Main↪
 heading of the first blog post</a></h1>
                                        <h2>Sub-heading of the first blog
post</h2>
                                    </hgroup>
                                    <p>Posted on the <time pubdate datetime=↪
"2010-10-30T13:08">30 October 2010 at 1:08 PM</time></p>
                                </header>

                                <p>Summary of the first blog post.</p>
                            </article>

                            <article>
                                <header>
                                    <hgroup>
                                        <h1><a href="/blog/second-post-
link/">Main↪
 heading of the second blog post</a></h1>
                                        <h2>Sub-heading of the second blog
post</h2>
                                    </hgroup>
                                    <p>Posted on the <time pubdate datetime=↪
"2010-10-26T09:36">26 October 2010 at 9:36 AM</time></p>
                                </header>

                                <p>Summary of the second blog post.</p>
                            </article>

                            <article>
                                <header>
                                    <hgroup>
```

```
                                        <h1><a href="/blog/third-post-
link/">Main↪
 heading of the third blog post</a></h1>
                                        <h2>Sub-heading of the third blog
post</h2>
                                    </hgroup>
                                    <p>Posted on the <time pubdate datetime=↪
"2010-10-21T17:13">21 October 2010 at 5:13 PM</time></p>
                                </header>

                                <p>Summary of the third blog post.</p>
                        </article>

                        <!-- Blog sidebar -->
                        <aside>
                                <h2>Subscribe to the RSS feed</h2>
                                <p>Make sure you don't miss a blog post by↪
 <a href="/rss">subscribing to the RSS feed</a>.</p>
                        </aside>
                </section>

                <footer>
                        <!-- Copyright and other stuff -->
                        <p>My amazing blog &copy; 2010</p>
                </footer>
        </body>
</html>
```

Line by line analysis

Still with me? Let's start from the top.

```
<!DOCTYPE html>
```

This is the new spangly HTML5 doctype declaration and, although it may look like it, it's not an element. The purpose of the doctype is to tell the browser which version of HTML (or XHTML) we're using – how to render it and what kind of validation to use. In HTML 4.01 the doctype looked much different and involved you knowing if you were using a strict, transitional, or frameset document type. Like so:

```
<!DOCTYPE HTML PUBLIC "-//W3C//DTD HTML 4.01//EN"
"http://www.w3.org/TR/html4/strict.dtd">
```

A bit much, don't you think? Fortunately the HTML5 doctype is much simpler and doesn't require anything further than the text, "html". What's even better about the new doctype is that it doesn't break browsers that don't support HTML5, they just revert to something called standards mode – rendering the page as close to W3C standards as possible. So there really is no reason why you can't start using the HTML5 doctype today.

```
<html>
```

The `html` element is the root of our page; everything else is placed within it. There should only ever be one of these elements per page.

```
<head>
```

All of the `meta` elements for our page are contained within the head element. There should only ever be one of these elements per page.

```
<title>A basic HTML5 blog homepage</title>
```

We give our page a name with the `title` element, it will be displayed in the title bar of your browser window. There should only ever be one of these elements per page.

```
<meta charset="utf-8">
```

The `meta` element is used to represent other metadata about our page. The `charset` attribute declares the method of character encoding that we want to use. Unless you have a legitimate reason for doing otherwise, stick with UTF-8 character encoding.

```
<!-- CSS and JavaScript to go here -->
```

This is a HTML comment. You should replace it with links to your CSS and JavaScript files.

```
</head>
```

We're finished setting metadata for our page, so we can close the head element.

```
<body>
```

The main content of our page goes within this body element. There should only ever be one of these elements per page.

```
<header>
```

Everything related to the header of our page, including a website name and some navigation, is contained within this HTML5 header element.

```
<h1>My amazing blog</h1>
```

This h1 element displays the name of the website on our page.

```
<nav>
```

The website navigation is stored in this HTML5 nav element.

```
<ul>
```

We're using an unordered list to structure the navigation menu.

```
<li><a href="/">Home</a></li>
<li><a href="/archive/">Archive</a></li>
```

```
<li><a href="/about/">About</a></li>
<li><a href="/contact/">Contact</a></li>
```

Each part of the navigation is stored as a link (an `href` element) within a list item (an `li` element). Without styling, this will list the navigation items one-by-one, one under the other.

```
</ul>
```

We're finished with the navigation items, so we can close the unordered list.

```
</nav>
```

The website navigation is finished, so we can close that as well.

```
</header>
```

And the same with the header.

```
<section>
```

We're using a HTML5 `section` element to contain our blog posts. This isn't entirely necessary; if we know there is only blog content on the page, we can remove the `section` element entirely.

```
<article>
```

To distinguish each blog post, we contain them within a HTML5 `article` element. Remember, we use the `article` element for content that would make sense on its own in an RSS reader.

```
<header>
```

Here we open up the header of the blog post.

```
<hgroup>
```

As we're using multiple headings in our blog posts, we're containing them within a HTML5 `hgroup` element.

```
<h1><a href="/blog/first-post-link/">Main heading of the first blog post</a></h1>
<h2>Sub-heading of the first blog post</h2>
```

Here we declare the main heading for the blog post, with link, as well as the subheading.

```
</hgroup>
```

We're done with the headings, so we can close the `hgroup` element.

```
<p>Posted on the <time pubdate datetime="2010-10-30T13:08">30 October 2010 at 1:08
PM</time></p>
```

Still in the header, we output the data and time the blog post was published using a HTML5 `time` element. Notice how we set the pubdate attribute, as this is the date a piece of content was published. Also, note the use of the `datetime` attribute to give a correctly formatted version of the date and time.

```
</header>
```

The blog post header is complete so we can close the header element.

```
<p>Summary of the first blog post.</p>
```

A simple paragraph giving a summary of the blog post.

```
</article>
```

We're done with the first blog post so we can close the article element. The process for the other blog posts is exactly the same, so I've removed them for brevity.

```
<aside>
```

To create related content we use a HTML5 aside element. We use this instead of something else, like a section element, because the sidebar is directly related to the content around it – the blog posts.

```
<h2>Subscribe to the RSS feed</h2>
```

The heading of the sidebar. Notice how we're using an h2 element here, as the heading is less important than the others on this page.

```
<p>Make sure you don't miss a blog post by <a href="/rss">subscribing to the RSS feed</a>.</p>
```

A simple paragraph with a link to subscribe to the imaginary RSS feed.

```
</aside>
```

We're done with the sidebar, so we can close the aside element.

```
</section>
```

Everything related to the blog posts is finished, so we can close the section element.

```
<footer>
```

We contain all of our footer content, like the copyright statement, within a HTML5 footer element.

```
<p>My amazing blog &copy; 2010</p>
```

A simple paragraph with the copyright statement for our page.

```
</footer>
```

That's all for the footer, so we can close the footer element.

```
</body>
```

We're done with all the content for our page, so we can close the body element.

```
</html>
```

We've reached the end of our page, so the last thing left to do is to close the html element.

That wasn't too bad, was it? As I hope you can see, using HTML5 isn't all that hard. The main issues are understanding what all the new elements do, when to use them and, most important, why you'd use one element instead of another. The best way to get to grips with HTML5 is by constructing a proper website using the new elements. Try it on your own website. You don't even need to put it online; just converting it into HTML5 is good enough to get something out of it.

Misconceptions about HTML5

As with any new technology, a lack of understanding often leads to misconceptions about what it is and what it does. HTML5 is no different, and it suffers from a massive lack of understanding and confusion regarding its features and those of other technologies. So prevalent is the issue that it's no wonder people find it hard to work out what is HTML5 and what isn't. Even I find it hard sometimes. So I've made it my personal duty to clear up the most common misconceptions about HTML5. My hope is that, armed with this information, you can go forth and not only sound intelligent, but help the Web community as a whole.

The CSS3 misconception

CSS has been around for HTML since 1996 – it's an old technology. The latest version, CSS3, has been in development since 2005 and is still nowhere near full recommendation by the W3C. In fact, it's not even being developed and recommended as one big specification. It has been split into individual modules that are being implemented by browsers as they are worked on. Because of this it's hard to say when CSS3 will be classed 100 percent complete, although, like HTML5, parts of it are already usable in most browsers.

The important thing to note with CSS is that it is *separate to HTML* in both development and use. CSS3 is not part of the HTML5 specification (it never was, and never will be). They are two completely different technologies – one for structure and layout, the other for presentation – that, because of their close proximity in use, have been bundled together for some reason. The bottom line? Don't refer to CSS3 as HTML5.

Is CSS3 part of HTML5?

No – it's a styling technology; it has nothing to do with content or structure. You can find out more about CSS3 at www.w3.org/Style/CSS/current-work.

The Web Fonts misconception

One of the massive drawbacks with Web design has been that it's incredibly hard to use custom fonts. Up until recently the only way you could do that was by constructing static images depicting the words you want to use, or by using convoluted systems like sIFR or cufon. Web Fonts solves this issue by introducing the @font-face rule to CSS, which allows you to use custom fonts with just a couple lines of code. Much easier!

Is Web Fonts part of HTML5?

No – it's part of CSS3, and isn't technically referred to as Web Fonts any longer. You can find out more about CSS Fonts at http://dev.w3.org/csswg/css3-fonts/.

The Geolocation misconception

Imagine if you could automatically get information on the Web related to your current location, wherever you are. The Geolocation API is doing just this by providing Web developers with a way of knowing where a user is by using some simple JavaScript. A user has to allow this location information to be shared, but the implications of doing so are profound – like related advertisements, useful search results, and relevant website content. All of this is provided without you having to type in or select your current location.

Is the Geolocation API part of HTML5?

No – it's a JavaScript API that is designed to be implemented by browsers that want to support it. You can find out more about the Geolocation API at http://dev.w3.org/geo/api/spec-source.html.

The SVG misconception

Scalable vector graphics (SVG) is a language that allows you to create 2d vector graphics using XML. It is very much similar to canvas in its functionality and purpose, but differs substantially in other areas (which I'll discuss in Chapter 10).

Is SVG part of HTML5?

No – it's a completely separate technology that describes graphics using XML. You can find out more about SVG at www.w3.org/TR/SVG/.

The Web Storage misconception

Cookies. Everyone's favorite snack and, coincidently, the method of choice for storing small pieces of information on a user's computer. Until now it has been the only viable method of storing data on the client-side (the user's computer), but it has a few flaws that can potentially cause a lot of pain. Web Storage, a set of JavaScript APIs, has been created to offer a powerful selection of new storage options that solve the inherent downsides of using cookies. They don't sound as cool, but they open the door to things like viewing your browser-based email inbox offline. Cool!

Is Web Storage part of HTML5?

No – it's a JavaScript API that is designed to be implemented by browsers that want to support it. You can find out more about Web Storage at http://dev.w3.org/html5/webstorage/.

The Web Workers misconception

Web Workers are essentially tireless JavaScript slaves ready to do your bidding. Their sole purpose is to perform heavy calculations and other intensive tasks in the background, without causing the Web page to slow and disrupting the user's experience. There aren't a huge number of use-cases for Web Workers, but it's good to know that they're there in case you do need them.

Are Web Workers part of HTML5?

No – they are a JavaScript API that is designed to be implemented by browsers that want to support it. You can find out more about Web Workers at www.whatwg.org/specs/web-workers/current-work/.

The WebSockets misconception

Normal communication over the Web is done via HTTP, a method that only allows communication in one direction at a time, and requires a Web page to be requested each and every time you want new data. To get around this Web developers have been using a whole host of options to circumvent the requirement for having to request a new page. Technologies like Ajax and Comet were invented for this very purpose. However they still weren't truly bi-directional methods of communication – information still only travelled in a single direction at any one time.

WebSockets are different; they use TCP which allows for true bi-directional communications between a client (your computer) and a server. This means you never have to make a request for new data from the server, as information is literally streamed to your computer in real-time as and when new data arrives. It's a complicated concept, but a very powerful one once you get to grips with it.

Is the WebSocket API part of HTML5?

No – it's a JavaScript API that is designed to be implemented by browsers that want to support it. You can find out more about the WebSocket API at http://dev.w3.org/html5/websockets/.

Although all of these technologies aren't part of the HTML5 umbrella, they all solve a distinct purpose and they should be embraced and used together with HTML5 whenever possible. The point of this section is to highlight the reason why these technologies aren't part of HTML5, not to put you off using them altogether. For example, by combining WebSockets with HTML5 canvas you can create amazing real-time multiplayer games. Now that's a cool combination of two different technologies!

Summary

This chapter has taken you on a journey through the history of HTML. You've travelled a great distance, from the recommendation of HTML 4.01 in 1999, right up to the development of HTML5, which is still ongoing to this day. I explained the reasons why HTML5 is needed, and how it is going to meet those needs. We've taken a look at all of the major new elements and and features of HTML5, learning their purpose and the ways they can be used. You've learned how to put all of this together to construct a Web page in HTML5. Lastly, I've made clear the confusion surrounding HTML5 and other new Web technologies.

It's been a very wordy chapter (well done for sticking with it) and I promise you that now we have the basics out of the way, future chapters will be much more hands-on. After all, you've come here to learn stuff, not listen to me drone on about the history of HTML5!

Next up, the fundamentals of JavaScript.

Further HTML5 resources

For those of you who did enjoy learning the history of HTML5, or those of you who'd like to know more about the elements and features we aren't discussing further, here are a few resources for you to consume at your leisure.

- Introducing HTML5, by Bruce Lawson and Remy Sharp [http://introducinghtml5.com/]

- HTML5 Doctor [http://html5doctor.com/]

- Dive Into HTML5, by Mark Pilgrim [http://diveintohtml5.org/]

- WHATWG HTML5 Specification [www.whatwg.org/specs/web-apps/current-work/multipage/]

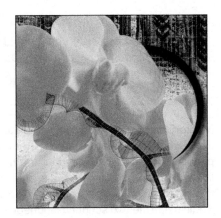

Chapter 2

Foundation JavaScript

In this chapter we delve into the realm of JavaScript. We review its history and the differences with its implementation. We also look into the jQuery code library and how it can save us a lot of time. The rest of the chapter is dedicated to learning the fundamental features of JavaScript, including everything you'll need to know to create amazing games in HTML5 canvas. I'm not going to lie, this is a big chapter; but it's all explained in as much detail as possible to help make your transition into JavaScript an easy one.

An overview of JavaScript

In Chapter 1 we stumbled across JavaScript. Now, we know it's a scripting language, but what *exactly* is it? And, what does it do? I'll answer those questions and others now. In this chapter, I put things in context and take a look at how JavaScript has evolved.

JavaScript was created way back in 1995 by Brendan Eich of Netscape, a browser company (remember it?), with cooperation from Sun Microsystems. When it started out it was actually called Mocha, eventually being renamed to LiveScript, then JavaScript in December of 1995. It was originally created to make the lives of web developers a little easier, as the only real option for adding animations or anything vaguely cool at the time was to use something like Java – a pretty complex programming language. The problem with Java is that the only way you can get it into the browser is by compiling the code (packaging it up) into something called an applet. This is great, but it means everything inside your applet is pretty much cut off from the outside world –it's in a walled garden, or however you want to put it.

JavaScript is much different in that the code is not compiled; it's embedded and interpreted by the browser. This means you don't have to construct huge, complete pieces of code to get it working. Just a few short snippets of code is all it takes, at least get you started. In short, JavaScript was created to be simpler and more forgiving than the stricter programming languages like Java. It was designed to be picked up by web developers who may not have any experience with traditional programming, and who just want to quickly add a bit of shine to their website. It's important to point out that JavaScript is in no way related to Java, apart from sharing a similar name.

> Note: JavaScript code is interpreted by the browser, which means that each part of the code is analyzed by the browser when it's run. In comparison, compiled code is typically converted into an application that can be executed directly, without any interpretation of the code.

No story on the Web would be complete without a legal wrangle between two tech companies. The story of JavaScript is no different. Soon after it was released by Netscape, Microsoft was eager to implement the popular scripting language in its Internet Explorer browser. Unfortunately for Microsoft, it failed to get a license from Sun Microsystems, the owners of the JavaScript trademark, so it were forced to call its implementation JScript. This has caused a bit of confusion with some developers, as at first glance it would seem the two scripting languages, JavaScript and JScript, are completely different things. In reality the two are very much the same, although each provides some functionality that the other doesn't. It should probably be mentioned that all the major browsers other than Internet Explorer (Firefox, Chrome, and so on) use JavaScript, not JScript. However, for the sake of our sanity, when I mention JavaScript in this book I'm referring to both Netscape's version and Microsoft's JScript.

> Note: You may have heard of ECMAScript on your travels around the Web. There is a reason why it has a name so similar to JavaScript; ECMAScript is the standardized scripting language that originated from Netscape's JavaScript. The ECMA specifications are what both JavaScript and JScript aim to support.

jQuery

If you've never heard of jQuery then you're probably a little perplexed right now. Jay what?! But don't fret, it's something that is going to make your life much easier in the long run. Let me explain.

What is jQuery?

jQuery is a JavaScript library. No, it isn't a giant building full of JavaScript books (who would even go to such a place?) It is effectively a simple wrapper around the most complicated and time-consuming tasks performed in JavaScript – things like traversing the document object model (DOM), event handling, and animation. Don't worry about what those things are just yet; I'll cover them in detail later. The official line from jQuery sums it up quite nicely: "jQuery is designed to change the way that you write JavaScript." It sounds pretty profound doesn't it? To put it another way: jQuery allows you to write less, do more. That's good enough for me!

Why are we using it?

Writing in pure JavaScript without the help from libraries like jQuery isn't quite as simple as it should be. Most of the core features are apparent in all the major browsers, which is fantastic. What isn't fantastic is that a lot of these browsers implement other features in slightly different ways. One example is detecting when a HTML document has finished loading, which is very important (we'll look into it later).

Unfortunately, there is no single way to do this across all the major browsers, which can make it a nightmare to get your JavaScript working the same for all your users. jQuery provides its own functionality for tasks like this, which works consistently across all the major browsers. For example, with one line of jQuery you can make that check to see if a HTML document has finished loading, something that would take tens of lines to cover all browsers if written in pure JavaScript. jQuery isn't doing anything magic here (it still uses the pure JavaScript behind the scenes), it just wraps everything up and does all the laborious browser checks for you. It lets you get on with what you're making, safe in the knowledge that it will work across all the major browsers.

> Note: There is no specific reason behind choosing the jQuery library over other JavaScript libraries, like Prototype and YUI. On a personal level, I find jQuery very easy to use and, most important, easy to teach. There would be no point me teaching you how to use a JavaScript library that I'm not 100 percent comfortable with. If you already use another library then feel free to ignore the jQuery code and replace it for the equivalent code in your chosen library.

Isn't this cheating?

Some people, particularly those who have already learned pure JavaScript, believe it's a bad idea to learn JavaScript with the help of libraries like jQuery. Their argument is that if you only learn the jQuery way then you won't have a proper understanding of how JavaScript works, like what to do if things go wrong. While I partly agree with this argument (it *is* wrong not to have an understanding of how JavaScript works), I don't see an issue with learning a library like jQuery at the same time. Let me put it this way: in reality, web developers are pushed for time and are much more interested in getting something working than worrying about if it's going to break in other browsers. Because of this, most people who work with JavaScript will use a library of some sort to make their lives that little bit easier. So why should I teach you a way of using JavaScript that deliberately complicates matters and is different to the way people work in the real world?

Does this mean I won't understand pure JavaScript?

Not at all. My aim in this book is to use jQuery only when it's appropriate. I'll be teaching you the foundations of pure JavaScript with jQuery added in to make things easier. Whenever we use a new feature of jQuery, I will explain what it does, and show you the equivalent way of doing it in pure JavaScript. I'll be doing this not only for the sake of comparison, but to help you understand how JavaScript works, and to enforce the reasons why jQuery makes things simpler. At the end of the day, jQuery is JavaScript, but instead of giving you the individual flour, eggs, butter, and sugar of JavaScript, jQuery just gives you cake. So by using jQuery you're actually using and learning parts of pure JavaScript at the same time.

How do I start using jQuery?

Getting jQuery into your project is really easy – like, one line of code easy. All you have to do is link the jQuery file into your HTML document. Something like the following would do:

```
<script type="text/javascript" src="jquery.js"></script>
```

Now, to do this you would need to go to the jQuery website, download the library, and add it into the same folder as your HTML page. Not an amazingly difficult task. Or, you could let Google do all the legwork and host the jQuery library for you. The second option sounds a little weird, but it makes sense really. If web developers use the library that Google hosts, by using the Google Libraries API, then the users of those websites will have that version of the jQuery file cached on their computer. This means that they won't have to re-download the library if they visit another site that also uses the Google-hosted jQuery. In short, it makes things quicker for the user, and that's a good thing. However, heed this warning: if you do use the Google-hosted file you will need to be connected to the Internet when testing your JavaScript. If you want a method that works offline you'll need to download jQuery and use the method described in the previous example.

To use the Google-hosted version you simply change the `src` attribute of the example above:

```
<script type="text/javascript" src="http://ajax.googleapis.com/ajax/libs/jquery/1↩
/jquery.min.js"></script>
```

You may notice the jQuery file has `.min` at the end. This just means that the file has been minified – that is, it's been shrunk to be as small as possible. Using the minified version of jQuery is always a good idea once you've finished developing your website, as it's much quicker to download; it's just under seven times smaller than the unminified version.

> Note: Visit the jQuery website for more information about the library. The documentation on there is particularly useful if you want to learn some of the more advanced features: http://jquery.com.

Adding JavaScript to an HTML page

You should now have an idea of what jQuery is and why you're using it, so let's put everything together and construct a basic HTML page with a bit of JavaScript goodness.

```
<!DOCTYPE html>

<html>
        <head>
                <title>Adding JavaScript to a HTML page</title>
                <meta charset="utf-8">

                <!-- CSS to go here -->

                <script type="text/javascript" src="http://ajax.googleapis.com↩
/ajax/libs/jquery/1/jquery.min.js"></script>

                <script type="text/javascript">
                        $(document).ready(function() {
```

```
                              alert("Hello, World!");
                       });
               </script>
        </head>

        <body>

        </body>
</html>
```

The first thing you'll notice is that we're using the same HTML5 code from earlier. The only difference is that we've stripped out all the content and added a couple of `script` elements into the `head` element. This is where all the JavaScript happens.

A `script` element allows us to place JavaScript, and other scripts, within a HTML page. The first `script` element we use pulls in an external file from Google:

```
<script type="text/javascript"
src="http://ajax.googleapis.com/ajax/libs/jquery/1/jquery.min.js"></script>
```

To do this we first define the kind of script we're using by setting the `type` attribute to "text/javascript." This lets the browser know that the script we're about to provide is JavaScript rather than something else. We then pull in the jQuery library by setting the `src` attribute to the Google URL. The `src` attribute tells the browser that it will need to grab the script from an external location – external being something that isn't the current HTML page file. You can also use the `src` attribute to grab scripts from the local filesystem.

The second `script` element doesn't have a `src` attribute because we're writing the JavaScript directly inside of the element. It may sound simple, but it's important to distinguish the difference. You don't use an `src` attribute if you're writing the JavaScript directly into the HTML page – sometimes referred to as internal JavaScript.

> Note: As a rule of thumb, it's always a good idea to put your JavaScript in a separate file and place it in your HTML pages using the `src` attribute. Doing so helps keep things neat and tidy, but also means that you can use the same JavaScript code on multiple pages without having to rewrite it.

Inside of the second `script` element we find our first piece of real JavaScript:

```
$(document).ready(function() {
        alert("Hello, World!");
});
```

Doesn't look too bad, does it? We'll skip the first and last lines, as I'm going to cover them in more detail in the next section. For now, just know that they are part of a jQuery function that makes sure our JavaScript doesn't run until the HTML document has finished loading.

The line we're interested in right now is the second line, the one with the weird `alert` thing. This piece of JavaScript is one of the simplest ways to make something interesting happen. The `alert` function (we'll cover functions in more detail later) is used to open a dialog box within the browser that forces the user to read it before they can continue browsing. Sounds a bit annoying really, which it is, but it's a good first example. By passing the alert function a string (a bit of text), we're able to change the message that appears inside the dialogue box. When we run our page with "Hello, World!" as the string, we should get something like what you see in Figure 2-1:

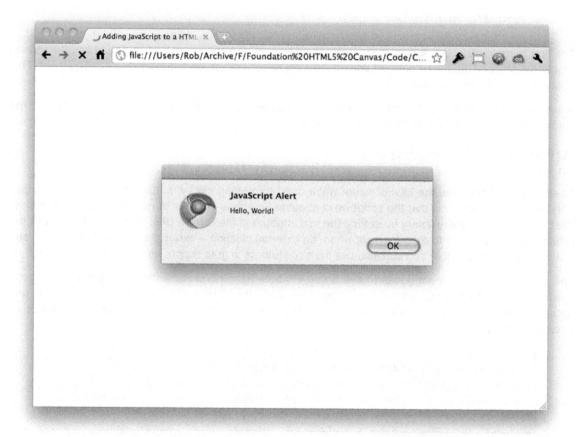

Figure 2-1. Output of the "Hello, World!" example

It works! You probably recognize the dialog box now – they used to be used for all sorts of things, like welcoming users to a website, or warning them when they submitted a form in the wrong way. Luckily for us no one really uses them any more, as they are disruptive and generally annoying. For our purposes the alert function will do as a quick and easy way to output a message in JavaScript, for testing purposes of course.

So there you have it, a basic HTML page with a bit of JavaScript thrown in for good measure. That wasn't so hard, was it?

> Note: If you ran the example and nothing happened, make sure you are online, as we're using the external Google version of jQuery. If you want to develop offline then download jQuery from the official website and use that file instead, as described in the jQuery section previous to this. If you're still experiencing issues, it's worth checking to see whether JavaScript is enabled in your browser.

Running JavaScript after the page has loaded

I've already mentioned how useful it is to run JavaScript *after* the HTML document has finished loading. But why is it so important? Why can't you just run JavaScript at any time? The answer is twofold. First, if JavaScript ran at the point you placed it in your HTML page, it would start loading and halt the rest of the HTML page from being displayed until it finished. It's generally a good idea to have the entire content load first, then let the JavaScript do its thing afterwards. That way, the user of your website can start looking at the content while the JavaScript loads in the background. Second, if JavaScript ran before the content had finished loading, it wouldn't be able to access any of the content that hadn't loaded yet. This is a massive problem if you're trying to manipulate HTML elements using JavaScript, like we will be later in the book. So we need a method of stalling the JavaScript from running until the HTML document (our page) has finished loading. We have three options available to us: the wrong way, the long way, and the easy way. Let's take a look at all three, as it's important to understand the difference.

The wrong way (the window.onload event)

Originally, developers used something called the `window.onload` event. The way this works is that after a web page has finished loading absolutely everything, it will run `window.onload`. If we converted our alert box example, it would look like this:

```
window.onload = function() {
        alert("Hello, World!");
};
```

It seems pretty clean and simple. So what makes it the wrong way? Well, the problem with `window.onload` is that it's *too* patient. It doesn't run until absolutely every piece of content has finished loading. But hang on a minute, don't we want to wait until all the content is loaded? Yes and no. We want to wait for the content to be accessible, but we don't want to wait for every single piece of content to load and become visible. For example, imagine you have a very large image in your content, one that is many megabytes in size (for your users' sakes, I hope you don't!) When you load your web page that image will take a fairly long time to load, possibly taking so long that you can sit and watch it build up line by line. Now if you were using `window.onload` on this web page, it wouldn't run until the entire image had finished downloading, which could take minutes!

We need a better option, one that runs after the browser is aware of the content, but before the content is actually loaded onto our screen. Fortunately for us there is something that allows us to do just that, the document object model (DOM).

The long way (the DOM)

The DOM is a method of representing and accessing elements of a document like, in the case of a web page, the HTML elements. This allows us to get information about and manipulate all the elements and attributes on a HTML page, directly from JavaScript. Don't worry if the DOM sounds a bit difficult; we'll be talking about it in more detail later in this chapter. The important thing to know right now is that the DOM represents the raw structure of our content, which means it has to be created before the content is displayed on the screen. If we can find out when the DOM has finished loading, we'll know when the content is accessible, regardless of whether it's visible on the screen.

Unfortunately, detecting when the DOM has loaded is a troublesome task. There's just no consistent method across all the major browsers (surprise, surprise). Even if there was, it's not exactly easy to do. The good thing for us is that a few kind souls, like freelance programmer Dean Edwards, have done the hard work for us and uncovered a method that works in each major browser. This is the result of their hard work; you'll soon see why I call this "the long way":

```
// Dean Edwards/Matthias Miller/John Resig
function init() {
        // quit if this function has already been called
        if (arguments.callee.done) return;

        // flag this function so we don't do the same thing twice
        arguments.callee.done = true;

        // kill the timer
        if (_timer) clearInterval(_timer);

        // do stuff
};

/* for Mozilla/Opera9 */
if (document.addEventListener) {
        document.addEventListener("DOMContentLoaded", init, false);
}

/* for Internet Explorer */
/*@cc_on @*/
/*@if (@_win32)
        document.write("<script id=__ie_onload defer
src=javascript:void(0)><\/script>");
        var script = document.getElementById("__ie_onload");
        script.onreadystatechange = function() {
                if (this.readyState == "complete") {
                        init(); // call the onload handler
                }
        };
/*@end @*/

/* for Safari */
```

```
if (/WebKit/i.test(navigator.userAgent)) { // sniff
        var _timer = setInterval(function() {
                if (/loaded|complete/.test(document.readyState)) {
                        init(); // call the onload handler
                }
        }, 10);
}

/* for other browsers */
window.onload = init;
```

Even for a JavaScript veteran, it's not exactly something you want to get your hands dirty with on each and every project. Surely there's an easier way to detect when the DOM has loaded? As luck would have it there is: it's called jQuery.

> Note: Going through the Dean Edwards script line-by-line is beyond the scope of this book. Visit his website for more information about it and the problems he encountered during its creation: http://dean.edwards.name/weblog/2006/06/again/

The easy way (the jQuery way)

Remember those two lines I told you to forget about in the last section? Well it's time to claw them back from the depths of your memory. Or, I could just show them to you again and save us both a lot of time:

```
$(document).ready(function() {
        // Put the JavaScript you want to run after the page loads in here
});
```

This is jQuery doing what it does best, letting us do something complex in an elegant and easy way. When broken down into its core components we can see how powerful jQuery really is.

The first part, $(document), is a jQuery selector. It allows you to select an element from the DOM to be manipulated, in our case the document object – the root of a web page that contains all of the HTML elements. We'll talk more about jQuery selectors in the DOM section of this chapter.

The second part, .ready(), is the juicy bit that does the cool stuff for you. Its sole purpose is to let you know when the DOM has finished loading. You'll notice that this is not only one line, but also really only one word, and it does the same stuff that tens of lines did the long way. However, I should make it clear that the jQuery .ready() method is not, as it would seem, magic. It's actually based on the Dean Edwards method, and has just been wrapped up in a ridiculously easy-to-use package. But behind the scenes it's practically exactly the same as what we looked at in the code for the long way.

To finish it all off we need somewhere to put the code we want to run once the DOM is loaded. The .ready() method allows us to do just that by using a callback function within the parentheses (rounded brackets) – a piece of JavaScript that is called once some particular event has happened. In our case we place an empty function in there, within which we can then add the code we want to run once the DOM has loaded. That's really as hard as it gets!

For now, I hope you can start to see the benefits that jQuery has over using pure, raw JavaScript. We aren't cheating; we're simply making things easier for ourselves by letting jQuery handle the repetitive and complex stuff that just gets in the way.

You should now have a good idea of how the jQuery way works. Let's step things up a notch and tackle the fundamental theories behind programming in JavaScript.

Variables and data types

At the most fundamental level we have variables and data types. They are the building blocks of JavaScript that allow us to do some pretty cool stuff.

Variables

If you ever want to remember something when programming, you'll probably use a variable. The sole purpose of a variable is to hold a value (a piece of data) for retrieval at a later date. In this way they are very much like what you may have encountered while learning algebra at school. Remember those crazy formulas you had to work out that had numbers assigned to letters (e.g., $x=3$)? Those letters are variables, they store a value.

Variables in JavaScript are no different; you create and name a variable (e.g., x) then assign a value to it, like a number or some text (e.g., $x=3$). To get the value back again you just refer to the variable you assigned it to; in our case, referring to x would return 3. This is particularly important in programming because it allows you to assign a value once, then refer to it again and again in the future by using the variable instead of typing out the value multiple times. You can even change the value of a variable once it has been assigned; hence, it's called a *variable*. This will make more sense soon, so don't worry if I've confused you.

Naming variables

To use a variable you first have to give it a name, something that explains its purpose in as few words as possible. For example, it would be a mistake to name a variable that holds a user's name *myVariable*, or *x*. How would you ever remember its purpose in the future? It's much better to give variables a meaningful name that explains exactly what it's for. For our example, a much better name would be something like *userName*, or even just *name*. With a name like that you'll never forget what value it holds.

> *Note: There are many ways to format the names of variables, but in our case we're going to be using something called camel case. This is when all the words of a variable are joined together, with the first character of each word being a capital letter, apart from the first letter of the entire variable. It's a fairly common method of naming variables, but there is nothing wrong with you using underscores to separate words, or anything else that you're used to.*

> *When naming variables, you should be aware that you can't use any word you want. The most important thing to remember is that a variable name can only start with a letter (a to z) or an underscore. Numbers can be used, but only after the first character of the name. Also, some words are reserved, which means they can't be used for variables, functions, or objects (more on these later). The Mozilla Developer Center has a great list of all the words you can't use: https://developer.mozilla.org/en/JavaScript/Reference/Reserved_Words*

Declaring variables and assigning values

So we now understand what variables are and why we need to use them. We also know how to name them properly so they make sense. The next step is learning how to actually use them in JavaScript or, in developer speak, how to declare them and assign values to them.

Declaring a variable is just another way of saying *creating a variable*. It is a good idea to declare a variable before we use it so we have full control over it, and also so we know that it exists. This is how you would declare a single variable:

```
var userName;
```

There are two things to notice here: the first being that a variable is declared to JavaScript by using the var keyword. This basically says that the next word after var is the variable name, and that JavaScript should declare a variable with that name. The second thing to notice is that a semi-colon is placed at the end of the line. In some programming languages it is extremely important to end each statement (a block of code) with a semi-colon. JavaScript is different in that it won't break without a semi-colon at the end of a statement, but it's good practice to do so, it looks a lot neater, and it can save you a whole world of pain when debugging code in the future.

After a variable is declared, it's usually a good idea to assign a value to it, or it will be automatically assigned a value of "undefined," which I'll cover later. Assigning a value to a variable is really simple; you just use an equals sign, otherwise known as an assignment operator, like so:

```
userName = "Rob Hawkes";
```

Notice we don't need to include the var keyword because the variable has already been declared. If we hadn't already declared the *userName* variable, everything would still work as JavaScript is pretty relaxed. But, although it is possible to declare a variable without a var keyword (by assigning a value to it), it's not very good practice and it can lead to all sorts of issues with scoping in JavaScript. In short, you should always properly declare a variable with the var keyword the first time you use it. Also notice that the name *Rob Hawkes* is enclosed within quotation marks, this is because text values (strings) require special treatment. We'll cover strings and other kinds of values in the data types section shortly.

> Note: Variables declared outside of all functions are in the global scope, and can be accessed by all further code. Variables declared inside of functions are in the local scope, and can't be accessed outside of the function in which they were created. Issues with scoping are common, so it's worth checking where your variables are being declared if you're having trouble getting them to work.

You can actually declare and assign variables all in one go, like this:

```
var userName = "Rob Hawkes";
var age = 34;
```

This is a much quicker way of doing things, and generally looks a bit neater.

You can also reassign a value to a variable by dropping the `var` keyword. In the previous example, my age is wrong, so to change it you would do this:

```
age = 24;
```

That's much better.

Accessing variables

It would be a bit pointless if you could assign a value to a variable and not be able to get that value back later on. The good thing is that accessing the value of a variable is ridiculously easy – you just use the name you gave it! For example, if you wanted to display the *userName* variable in an alert box, you'd do it like this:

```
var userName = "Rob Hawkes";
alert(userName);
```

If all went well you'd get an alert with the user's name in, as shown in Figure 2-2.

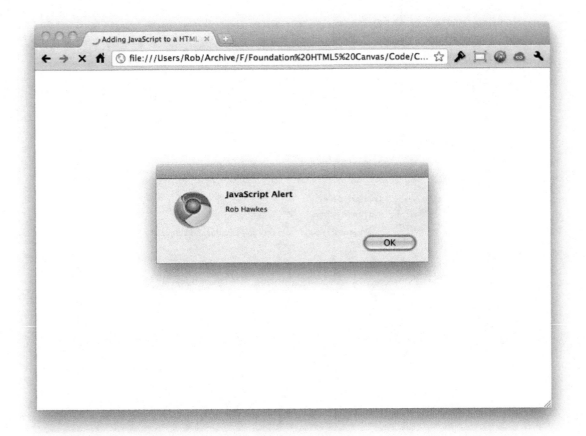

Figure 2-2. Outputting the user's name using variables

You could even display the user's age at the same time if you wanted:

```
var userName = "Rob Hawkes";
var age = 24;
alert(userName+" is "+age+" years old");
```

Which, by using something called string concatenation, will output the message shown in Figure 2-3.

Figure 2-3. Outputting the user's name and age using variables

This is the beauty of variables; they let you access values at any point in your code, and let you combine them so you can display those values in practically any way you want.

Arithmetic

Another way to use variables is with arithmetic. The great thing about JavaScript is that it includes pretty much every kind of arithmetic you'll need. For example, to add two numbers together you'd do this:

```
var myNum = 24+6;
alert(myNum); // Outputs 30
```

Wait a minute, what's that double slash thing doing there? You've just experienced a JavaScript comment, a method of adding little notes within your code that don't run or get displayed. I'll be using them from now on to give the expected output of our examples. It's important to note that everything after and on the same line as a comment will be ignored by JavaScript and treated as a comment. This can sometimes be the cause of errors, so it's something to look out for.

To subtract two numbers, you'd do this (note that you can use `alert` on its own without the need for variables):

```
alert(24-4); // Outputs 20
```

Simple stuff. To multiply, you'd do this:

```
alert(2*5); // Outputs 10
```

And to divide, this:

```
alert(100/2); // Outputs 50
```

And so on. It's all very much common sense, and uses the same mathematical symbols that would be used on a computer calculator or another programming language.

To make arithmetic more readable, you should consider using variables to store the number values. For example, consider this equation that outputs the number of seconds in a day:

```
alert(24*60*60); // Outputs 86400
```

It works, but it's not very readable. Now consider the same equation, but using variables:

```
var hoursInDay = 24;
var minutesInHour = 60;
var secondsInMinute = 60;
alert (hoursInDay*minutesInHour*secondsInMinute); // Outputs 86400
```

It's actually readable. Anyone could walk up to that code and understand what is being calculated. This is why variables are so important, and is also why you should name them properly.

Data types

It's impossible to avoid data types; you'll use them in pretty much every piece of JavaScript you write. Data types define the various kinds of data you use, placing restrictions on what can be done with them. Having knowledge of the various data types will help you avoid unnecessary errors and problems later on. One quick example is the different way the String and Number data types are dealt with when adding things together:

```
var myString = "24"+"6";
var myNum = 24+6;
alert(myString); // Outputs "246"
alert(myNum); // Outputs 30
```

When strings are added together they are joined together, using a process known as concatenation. This is the same even when the strings are numbers, because JavaScript sees anything within quotation marks as a string, not a number.

Primitive data types

These are the building blocks of data, they are primitive because they cannot be broken down into other types of data. They include the following:

- **Numbers**: Integers (whole numbers), and floating point numbers (e.g., 2.04).
- **Booleans**: Truth values, can be either *true* or *false*.
- **Strings**: A number of characters enclosed within quotations marks (e.g., "Rob Hawkes").

Composite data types

These data types are slightly more advanced and contain values that are primitive, or composite data types. An example of a recursive composite data type is an array that contains more arrays, or an array that contains objects.

- **Arrays**: Commonly used for storing a list of related values.
- **Objects**: The base for all objects in JavaScript.

These data types are a little more confusing. I'll be covering both arrays and objects in much more detail later on in this chapter.

Other data types

As well as your standard data types, there are a couple of others that refer to non-existent and empty values.

- **Null**: Means nothing, or no value.
- **Undefined**: Given to a variable after it has been declared, but before a value has been assigned to it.

You'll often see these data types when something has gone wrong with a variable declaration, or a value has not been properly assigned to a variable, but they do have legitimate uses as well. One use would be to assign the value of null to a variable when you want to clear its original value, or you can use them in conditional statements to check whether a variable has been declared or has had a value assigned to it.

Conditional statements

Would you like a cup of tea: yes, or no? What I've done there is given you a choice. I've asked you a question and you have the option of saying, "Yes, a tea would be lovely Rob," or, "No, what are you on, you fool? I hate tea!" If *yes*, you get a tea; if *no*, you don't. It's as simple as that. Conditional statements in JavaScript are very much the same, as they deal with choices – they are basically just questions written in code.

Conditional statements are an incredibly useful part of your JavaScript toolkit because they allow you to deal with situations that aren't always going to have the same outcome. They also allow you to make decisions, like working out what a variable is, or if something is right (*true*) or wrong (*false*).

If statements

The most basic conditional statement is the if statement. It allows you to make a true or false decision about something; if *true*, then the code within the if statement runs, if *false*, then nothing happens.

Here is a really basic example:

```
var age = 24;
if (age == 24) {
        alert("You're 24 years old"); // Will output only if age equals 24
};
```

We set a variable called *age* and then create an if statement to perform a true or false decision on that variable. In our case, we're checking to see if *age* is equal to 24, which it is, so the alert will be displayed. If we changed the *age* variable to something that isn't 24, like 30, the alert won't be displayed because *age* (now 30) does not equal 24. Our code has become intelligent, sort of.

It's important to note that we're using a double equals symbol, which is referred to as a comparison operator. This double equals symbol is nothing like the single equals (the assignment operator) that you use to assign values to a variable. Getting the two confused can lead to all sorts of problems. For example, using a single equals symbol in the if statement in the previous example would lead to the statement always running:

```
var age = 24;
if (age = 24) {
        alert("You're 24 years old"); // Will output all the time
};
```

You could even change the age to something that you know is wrong, but the statement will still run because the condition is always going to be true because the age variable is being set inside the if statement. We'll cover this in more detail shortly.

Another common use of an if statement is to explicitly check a variable for truth by using the boolean data type, which can only ever contain the values *true* or *false*. Here is an example using boolean values:

```
var wouldLikeATea = true;
if (wouldLikeATea == true) {
        alert("Milk, 1 sugar. Thank you!"); // Will output if the user wants tea
};
```

In this example we have a variable that tells us if the user wants a cup of tea or not; *true* for yes, *false* for no – boolean values. We then construct an if statement that uses boolean values to see if the user would like a cup of tea and, if so, output an alert. We could actually take a shortcut and rewrite the example like this:

```
var wouldLikeATea = true;
```

```
if (wouldLikeATea) {
        alert("Milk, 1 sugar. Thank you!"); // Will output if the user wants tea
};
```

Notice we've dropped the double equals symbol and the word *true* in the if statement. We can do this because if statements check for truth by default. If the variable being checked is *true* then the code inside the statement will run. It's important to note that if you used this method to check a variable that isn't a boolean value, like a string or number, it would always return true, unless it's the number zero. This is because values that aren't boolean will return true if they contain any data at all. For example, the following code shows how a number can return true if it's non-zero, and false if it is zero:

```
var myInteger = 7;
if (myInteger) {
        alert("This code executes.");
};

myInteger = 0;
if (myInteger) {
        alert("This code does not execute.")
};
```

Comparison operators

You aren't just limited to checking for one thing to be equal to another thing, there are a whole range of other checks that can be performed. In JavaScript, you change the way a conditional statement checks something by changing the comparison operator that it uses. Table 2-1 shows a list of the most common operators available:

Table 2-1. List of comparison operators in JavaScript

Operator	Name	Notes
a == b	Equal	True if a is equal to b.
a === b	Identical	True if a is equal to b, and are of the same data type.
a != b	Not equal	True if a is not equal to b
a !== b	Not identical	True if a is not equal to b, or they are not of the same data type.
a < b	Less than	True if a is less than b.
a > b	Greater than	True if a is greater than b.
a <= b	Less than or equal to	True if a is less than or equal to b.
a >= b	Greater than or equal to	True if a is greater than or equal to b.

> Note: Notice that in conditional statements two equals symbols (==), known as a comparison operator, are used to check if something is equal to another. An assignment operator (one equals symbol, =) is only ever used to assign a value to a variable. Getting the two mixed up is a really common error in code, so keep an eye out for it if things don't seem to be working the way they should.

Multiple truth checks within an if statement

As well as comparison operators, you also have logic operators. These operators allow you to check more than one thing in a single conditional statement. If we wanted to see if two checks were true, we'd use the *and* (&&) operator:

```
var age = "24";
var userName = "Rob Hawkes";
if (age == 24 && userName == "Rob Hawkes") {
        alert("You're definitely Rob Hawkes"); // Will output if both checks are
true
};
```

The if statement will now only work if both checks return true, that the *age* variable is 24, and that the *userName* variable is "Rob Hawkes." If either of those checks return false then the if statement won't run. To run the if statement if only one of the checks is true, you would use the *or* operator (||):

```
var age = "30";
var userName = "Rob Hawkes";
if (age == 24 || userName == "Rob Hawkes") {
        alert("You're either 24 or Rob Hawkes"); // Will output if either check is
true
};
```

Using these logic operators allows you to combine checks and build some pretty powerful conditional statements.

Else and else if statements

Now, if statements are great if you only care about the true outcome, but what if you want to do something else when the outcome is false? This is where the else and else if statements come in.

If you just want to do something else when the if statement is false, then you'd use the else statement:

```
var age = 30;
if (age == 24) {
        alert("You're 24 years old"); // Will output only if age equals 24
} else {
        alert("You're not 24 years old"); // Will output if age doesn't equal 24
};
```

You can take things further by performing a further check if the original if statement is false. For this, you'd use the else if statement:

```
var age = 30;
if (age == 24) {
        alert("You're 24 years old"); // Will output only if age equals 24
} else if (age == 30) {
        alert("You're 30 years old"); // Will output only if age equals 30
} else {
        alert("You're not 24 or 30 years old"); // Will output if age doesn't equal
24 or 30
};
```

The else if statement is another way of asking question after question: *Is it this?* No. *Well what about this?* No. *Well what about this?* And so on.

Functions

One problem you'll inevitably encounter when programming is code duplication. Sometimes it's because of the sheer quantity of code; other times it's the result of a lazy programmer. Either way, code duplication can cause a whole world of pain if not dealt with; from simply wasting your time creating it all, to completely ruining your day because you've got to edit 50 different lines of the same code.

Now, anyone with their head screwed on is probably wondering why you would ever duplicate code. What's the point? The simple answer is that some pieces of code will be used over and over again because you want to perform a similar action multiple times. For example, a piece of code that lets you output a full name by combining a first name and last name:

```
var firstName = "Rob";
var lastName = "Hawkes";
var fullName = firstName+" "+lastName;
alert(fullName);

var anotherFirstName = "John";
var anotherLastName = "Smith";
var anotherFullName = anotherFirstName+" "+anotherLastName;
alert(anotherFullName);
```

Notice how the code to combine the first name and last name is practically identical in both cases. The only difference is that they use different variables. It doesn't look like much in just two different places, but imagine if you needed to combine people's names in tens of places in your code. Now imagine if you needed to change the way those names were formatted so the last name came first, it would be mayhem. What if you missed one out? It's not worth thinking about! Wouldn't it be awesome if we had some special code that meant we only had to change the name formatting once and have it automatically updated in every place that it's used? This is what a function does.

Creating functions

Using functions is quite straightforward. You just need to understand how they work. The basic premise of functions is that they're like a little machines that perform the same actions over and over again, exactly the same way each time. You can also feed information into them, and get information back out of them. The easiest way to explain this is by showing you how a function works.

If you rewrote the name formatter we used earlier as a function, it would look like this:

```javascript
function formatName(firstName, lastName) {
        return firstName+" "+lastName;
};
```

The `function` keyword declares our function and lets JavaScript know that the following word is the name of our function, in this case it's *formatName*. The words inside the parentheses are called arguments (or parameters) – they are variables that declare values that are being inputted into the function. If your function has no arguments, you still need to include the parentheses; but in such a case you just leave them empty. All the code that you want to run in the function is placed within the curly brackets.

It's quite common to require a function to output, or return some kind of value. To do this you use the `return` keyword, which returns whatever value comes after it. The `return` keyword also quits the function, so any code after the `return` will not run.

Calling functions

A function is pointless unless you can actually use it, or call it, in developer-speak. Calling a function allows you to run the code that has been packaged up inside of it, and allows you to access any values that are returned from the function. When calling a function you can also include values (arguments) that will be used as input. By putting this all together we can call our new *formatName* function like this:

```javascript
formatName(firstName, lastName);
```

Or, together with the rest of the code:

```javascript
var fullName = formatName("Rob", "Hawkes");
alert(fullName);

var anotherFullName = formatName("John", "Smith");
alert(anotherFullName);
```

Calling a function is a little like accessing a variable, you just use the name that you used when creating it in the first place. The difference is that when calling a function you need to include a pair of parentheses after the function name. Inside of the parentheses you place the input values for the function, in our case we use the first and last name variables. If we take a look at the function again we can see what's going on:

```javascript
function formatName(firstName, lastName) {
        return firstName+" "+lastName;
};
```

In the first example we call the *formatName* function and send it the *first name* (Rob) and *last name* (Hawkes). The function takes these strings as input arguments, called *firstName* and *lastName*, which we can refer to as normal variables. Our function is really simple and returns the formatted name right back, no messing around. The returned value is then stored in the *fullName* variable, just like it was when we weren't using functions. To do the same for the second name we call the function in the same way, just replacing the input variables with a different *first name* and a different *last name*.

The benefits to using this method are huge. Firstly, we saving time by not rewriting the same code over and over again, which I'm sure you'll appreciate. Secondly, if we want to edit the way a name is formatted we now only have to change the code in one place, rather than multiple places. This is a really, *really* good thing. For example, you could easily reverse the function to output the last name, followed by the first name:

```
function formatName(firstName, lastName) {
        return lastName+" "+firstName;
};
```

Objects

Some people would argue that objects are a fairly advanced topic for a foundation book, but I tend to disagree. Objects will make things easier for us in the long run, so why should I teach you a bad habit when you can learn the right way from the start? We're going to use them extensively in the games and, in all honesty, they really aren't as complicated as people make out. You'll understand how to use them in no time.

What are objects?

Before we dive into how to create and use objects, it would be a good idea to make sure we know what they are and why they're awesome. A technical reference would describe objects as a collection of properties (variables) and methods (functions) that deal with related values and tasks. They're also a data type, which means we can assign them to variables, but we'll get on to that later.

The best way to think of objects in JavaScript is to imagine them like real-world objects, like a car, or a rocket – I like rockets. An object in JavaScript has properties and methods, as does our real-world rocket object. If we take this example further, the properties of a rocket would be things like the number of engines it has, the amount of thrust it has, the number of astronauts on board, or even something as simple as its color. A property is essentially a value that describes something about the object. On the other hand, the methods of a rocket would be things like turning the engines on and off, opening the door for the astronauts, or sending a message to ground control. A method is an action of some sort that is performed either on or by the object at hand.

So what is an object in a nutshell? And why are nutshells so great for explaining things? Well, I can't help with the nutshells, but I can certainly try and describe an object in one line. JavaScript objects are templates, they describe the features of something, and they define the actions that it can perform.

From personal experience, I've found that the best way to really understand objects is to start playing with them, so let's do just that.

Creating and using objects

There are a few ways to create an object in JavaScript, the simplest being:

```
var rocket = new Object();
```

What you've done here is create a new instance (version) of an `Object`, a blank object template, and assigned it to a variable. Technically we're using the `Object` object here, but I'm going to refer to it as plain old object so we don't get confused. Unless you're already confused? I do hope not.

Right now there's nothing in our rocket object apart from some built-in JavaScript methods. This isn't good enough, we want engines, thrust, and astronauts! Declaring these descriptive elements of an object (its properties) is no more complicated that creating variables:

```
var rocket = new Object();
rocket.engineCount = 2;
rocket.thrust = 5000;
rocket.astronautCount = 4;
rocket.colour = "red";
```

The pattern here is quite straightforward, you refer to the object variable, then use a dot, then type in the property name we'd like (just like a variable), then assign a value. Objects aren't scary, they just look a bit odd.

Unfortunately, there is a big problem with this method, being that our object is unique. We've created it from a blank object template and had to declare all the properties manually, it's a one off. If we wanted more than one rocket we'd have to duplicate this code over and over again, and code duplication is bad! It also means we can't trust each rocket object to have the same properties and methods, like you can see here:

```
var rocket = new Object();
rocket.engineCount = 2;

var anotherRocket = new Object();
anotherRocket.engineCount = 1;
anotherRocket.wings = 2;
```

Both rocket objects are seemingly identical, apart from the second rocket has a new property called *wings*. Because the first rocket doesn't have this, we encounter a pretty killer problem. For example, if we outputted the number of wings on the second rocket, we'd be returned "2", but if we did the same to the first rocket, we'd be returned "undefined". The first rocket has no wings, they were never created for it.

So how do we overcome this issue of objects being unique and unpredictable? By creating our own rocket object template with all the properties and methods of a rocket already declared inside, of course. It's easier to show why this is better with an example:

```
function Rocket(engineCount, thrust, wings) {
        this.engineCount = engineCount;
        this.thrust = thrust;
```

```
        this.wings = wings;
};
```

You'll probably recognize that as a function, and that's for a very good reason – functions are objects. This allows you to create a function as you'd normally do so, then use it in a way that treats it as an object. It's important to point out that the major difference between a regular function and our object template function is the way variables are declared. We want to declare properties, not variables, so we use the this keyword instead of var. The this keyword just means that the property is assigned to *this* instance of the object, allowing different instances to have different property values. It's a bit confusing, but bear with me.

Using the new rocket object template is really easy:

```
var rocket = new Rocket(2, 5000, 4);
var anotherRocket = new Rocket(1, 2000, 2);
```

Not only is this so much neater, but we've completely dropped the code duplication. The other benefit is that we can trust that our rocket objects have the same properties:

```
alert(rocket.wings); // Outputs 4
alert(anotherRocket.wings); // Outputs 2
```

Hooray! But properties are pretty static, how do we make our rocket object actually do something? For this we're going to need methods, which are surprisingly simple to implement. The following will add a method to turn the rocket's engines on:

```
function Rocket(engineCount, thrust, wings) {
        this.engineCount = engineCount;
        this.enginesOn = false;
        this.thrust = thrust;
        this.wings = wings;

        this.turnEnginesOn = function() {
                this.enginesOn = true;
                alert("Engines are now on");
        };
};
```

An object method is basically a function assigned to an object property. Remember, functions are objects so they're a data type, which means they can be assigned to variables (and properties). The name of the method will take the name of the property the method is assigned to, this will make sense when we come to calling the method later on.

For our purposes we have declared a new rocket property called *enginesOn* that tells us whether the engines are on (true), or off (false). By using this in the *turnEnginesOn* method we effectively turn the rocket's engines on, and to clarify matters we also pop up an alert box for good measure (remember, we're only using alert boxes for testing purposes).

Now we've set up the rocket *turnEnginesOn* method, it's a trivial task to actually use it:

```
var rocket = new Rocket(2, 5000, 4);
rocket.turnEnginesOn();
```

Object methods are functions, so they are called exactly as you would a function. That's really as complicated as methods get. They may take a while to get your head around, but they aren't scary at all.

I completely understand if you still don't quite get objects, they took me a little while to grasp as well. My hope is that this brief overview of them will at least give you the necessary knowledge to not get scared by our use of objects in the games. You'll have to trust me on this one, but objects will make much more sense when you start to use them in proper programming projects.

Arrays

At some point you're going to get the urge to be rebellious and store more than one value in a variable. I mean, those variables are just too damn restrictive, right? Fortunately, there is a perfect feature in JavaScript that allows you to continue your disruptive streak. That feature is the Array object.

Arrays (created using the Array object) are essentially containers that allow you to store multiple values. The great thing is that they're a data type, which means they can be assigned to variables, just like we've seen variables used with numbers and strings so far. So one variable with an Array object assigned to it can effectively hold countless values (known as elements) – pretty cool stuff!

The purpose of an array is to stop you having to write out a huge amount of variables when you want to store lots of related data, like a list of planets in the solar system. An array acts like a list, keeping a number of related values happily contained inside a single variable.

Creating arrays

There are a few methods available for creating an Array object, the most verbose of which looks like this:

```
var planets = new Array();
planets[0] = "Mercury";
```

The first line creates an empty Array object and assigns it to the variable *planets*. The second line assigns a planet name, as a string, to the first element of the array. It's important to note that the first element in an Array object has an index value of 0, not 1.

To add further elements to the same array you would do the following:

```
planets[1] = "Venus";
planets[2] = "Earth";
planets[3] = "Mars";
```

You can also create the Array object and assign some values in one go, like so:

```
var planets = new Array("Mercury", "Venus", "Earth", "Mars");
```

Or, if you really want to impress people you can use something called literal notation – a shortcut that uses square brackets:

```
var planets = ["Mercury", "Venus", "Earth", "Mars"];
```

Each method produces the same result, so feel free to use the method that you understand best when creating an Array object.

Accessing and modifying arrays

It's all well and good creating an Array object and packing all your values in a neat list, but how do you get those values back out again? It's easy. In fact, we've already seen the code that lets us do it.

This is how you can access the second element in the array of planets:

```
var planets = ["Mercury", "Venus", "Earth", "Mars"];
alert(planets[1]); // Outputs Venus
```

Notice again how the index number for elements in an array starts at 0, so the second value would be 1, not 2. And to access the fourth element in the array? Simple:

```
alert(planets[3]); // Outputs Mars
```

And that is really as complex as arrays need to get right now. There are many more things that you can do with them, but we'll cover those as we require them further on in the book.

Loops

We've already learnt that functions are great for automating chunks of code. However, there's one downside to functions, and that is that you have to call them every single time you want to use them. For example, want to run a function 5 times? Then call it 5 times. Want to run it 100 times? Call it 100 times. As you can see, writing 100 lines of code to call the same function is a little pointless. It would seem a bit odd for JavaScript to let us down now after being so awesome with functions and arrays. If you're doing the same thing 100 times, surely there's an easier way to do it? The good news is that JavaScript has not let us down (it's too good for that), it has a perfect set of features to deal with this – loops.

As a really simple example, imagine if we had a list of names in an array and wanted to run our good friend the *formatName* function 5 times, once for each name. Without loops it would look something like this:

```
var names = [["Rob", "Hawkes"], ["John", "Smith"], ["Jane", "Doe"], ["Queen",
"Elizabeth"],➥
 ["Steve", "Jobs"]];

var first = formatName(names[0][0], names[0][1]); // "Rob Hawkes"
var second = formatName(names[1][0], names[1][1]); // "John Smith"
var third = formatName(names[2][0], names[2][1]); // "Jane Doe"
var forth = formatName(names[3][0], names[3][1]); // "Queen Elizabeth"
var fifth = formatName(names[4][0], names[4][1]); // "Steve Jobs"
```

You're probably wondering what on earth is going on with that array. Fear not, it's just a multi-dimensional array, which basically means an array inside an array. The main array being a list of 5 other arrays, those 5 other arrays being the first and last name of a group of people. Don't fret about it too much if you don't get it; the focus is on loops so just go with the flow.

Now for only 5 iterations this isn't necessarily a bad thing, but it's certainly not pretty or efficient. So let's try it again, this time with a loop:

```
var names = [["Rob", "Hawkes"], ["John", "Smith"], ["Jane", "Doe"], ["Queen",
"Elizabeth"],↵
 ["Steve", "Jobs"]];

for (var i = 0; i < names.length; i++) {
        var fullName = formatName(names[i][0], names[i][1]);
};
```

There's no denying that this already looks much more efficient, let alone neater. The loop we're using here is a `for` loop, which is commonly used for running a block of code a specific number of times. Inside the parentheses we have three main areas of importance, each separated by a semi-colon. Let's look at each area in turn.

```
var i = 0;
```

In the first area we declare a variable (`i`) to be used as the counter for the loop, which we assign a value of 0 (remember: the first element of an array is 0).

```
i < names.length;
```

The second area is a check that is performed on our counter before each loop, in this case we're checking to see if our counter is less then the number of elements in the names array – its length, which is a property of every `Array` object. If this check returns true we move on to the third and final area, if not, we exit the loop.

```
i++
```

The final area is run at the end of each loop and, in our case, increases the counter by one by using the increment operator. This is the same as using `i = i+1`.

The result of all this is a counter variable that loops from 0 to 4, allowing us to access the 5 elements of the *names* array with just a single line:

```
var fullName = formatName(names[i][0], names[i][1]);
```

Notice how we place the *i* variable where we had the numbers 0 to 4 in the example without a loop. This is a much simpler way of doing things!

> *Note: There are other kinds of loops out there, like the* while *loop, but we won't be using them in this book. They aren't any more complex than* for *loops, so don't let me stop you learning them in your own time.*

Timers

As the name implies, timers are methods that allow you to run blocks of code once after a certain amount of time has passed (like a cooking timer), or many times after a repeating interval (like the indicator in your car). Both methods are incredibly useful, and will actually form an integral part of the games later in the book.

Setting one-off timers

The setTimeout method allows us to run a block of code after a specific delay in milliseconds. It's dead easy to set up, and it uses nothing that we haven't already seen before:

```
function onTimeout() {
        alert("Ding dong!");
};
var timer = setTimeout(onTimeout, 3000);
```

There are two arguments in a setTimeout method; the code or function you want to call when the timer runs, and the delay in milliseconds before running the timer. In our case we're calling a function in the timer, but notice how we left out the parentheses. This is because if we left the parentheses in, the function would be called immediately when setting up the timer – not what we want to happen. It's a bit counterintuitive, but bear with it. The second argument is the delay in milliseconds, which in our case is 3000, or 3 seconds. Remember that there are 1000 milliseconds in a second, forgetting that has caught me out a few times.

If all went well, then after three seconds you'll get an alert with the message "Ding dong!".

Unsetting one-off timers

Sometimes you'll want to stop a setTimeout method from running, usually when something has happened after setting it that means you don't need it any more. To unset a timer created using setTimeout you need to use the clearTimeout method. By placing the variable you assigned the timer to as an argument in the clearTimeout method, you'll stop it from running:

```
clearTimeout(timer);
```

Obviously, if you're too late clearing the timer then it will run as normal.

Setting repeating timers

A lot of the time a single-use timer isn't enough, you want something that repeats over and over again. For these situations you want to use the setInterval method, which is set in an identical way to setTimout:

```
function onInterval() {
        alert("Ding dong!");
};

var interval = setInterval(onInterval, 3000);
```

The only difference between this and the setTimeout method is that the function we pass to the setInterval method will be run every 3000 milliseconds, forever. So be warned, running this in your browser will cause an alert box to pop up every 3 seconds! I'd hope in a real-world situation that you'd be doing something other than annoying users with alert boxes.

Unsetting repeating timers

Just like the clearTimeout method, we have a similar way of clearing intervals, the clearInterval method. It's used in exactly the same way, except this time we pass the variable we assigned the setInterval method to as an argument:

```
clearInterval(interval);
```

To avoid things like infinite loops (when something never ends), you'll probably want to call the clearInterval method once your timer has achieved what you wanted from it. Leaving it running would just be a waste of resources, and would also be really annoying.

> Note: It's important to note that both setTimeout and setInterval are methods of the DOM window object. They aren't truly JavaScript, although we do access and manipulate them through JavaScript. This will make more sense to you as we learn more about JavaScript and the DOM.

The DOM

We encountered the DOM earlier in this chapter, its purpose is to represent the raw structure of our content and HTML elements in our web page. In other words, the DOM is where you'll be going if you want to access or manipulate your content with JavaScript. For the purposes of this book we won't be covering absolutely everything you can do with the DOM, but we'll certainly cover everything needed for games. Anything else can be found easily online or in other books, some dedicated entirely to teaching the DOM.

An example HTML web page

We'll be accessing HTML elements a lot in this section, so let's set up a cut down version of the HTML5 blog page we used in the first chapter. It's not a particularly useful web page, but it will serve the purpose for the coming examples:

```
<!DOCTYPE html>

<html>
        <head>
                <title>The DOM</title>
                <meta charset="utf-8">

                <script type="text/javascript" src="http://ajax.googleapis.com↪
/ajax/libs/jquery/1/jquery.min.js"></script>
```

```
            <script type="text/javascript">
                $(document).ready(function() {
                    // JavaScript will go in here
                });
            </script>
        </head>

        <body>
            <section id="blogArticles">
                <article>
                    <header>
                        <hgroup>
                            <h1><a href="/blog/first-post-
link/">Main➥
 heading of the first blog post</a></h1>
                            <h2>Sub-heading of the first blog
post</h2>
                        </hgroup>
                        <p>Posted on the <time pubdate datetime=➥
"2010-10-30T13:08">30 October 2010 at 1:08 PM</time></p>
                    </header>

                    <p>Summary of the first blog post.</p>
                </article>
            </section>
        </body>
</html>
```

Accessing the DOM using pure JavaScript

Before I show you the easier jQuery way, it's important to highlight how to access the DOM using pure JavaScript. The way we do this is by using the document object, which is the root of your web page that contains all of the HTML elements. As well as containing elements, the document object also provides a few methods that allow you to access specific elements, based on their attributes or tag name. For example, the following would give you access to the first HTML element with the id blogArticles:

```
document.getElementById("blogArticles");
```

The method we're using is very much self-explanatory, as are the rest of them. It's quite obvious that the method will get a HTML element by its id attribute. You can see why it's so important to name things well, it makes it crystal clear about what they do.

Another document object method allows you to access all the elements with a specific tag name. In our example, we can access the p elements like this:

```
document.getElementsByTagName("p");
```

The getElementsByTagName method returns an array containing all the matching HTML elements. In our case it returns an array containing one p element from the header element, and another from the article element.

Now, simply calling getElementById and getElementsByTagName doesn't achieve much. The really interesting stuff happens when you dig a little deeper into the HTML elements they both return. Once you have accessed a HTML element using the DOM, a whole range of properties becomes available to you. Some let you access the value of the elements' attributes, while one in particular lets you access the content contained within the element. This property is quite an interesting one, so let's take a quick look at how to access the content of a HTML element by using the innerHTML property:

```
var secondaryHeadings = document.getElementsByTagName("h2");
alert(secondaryHeadings[0].innerHTML);
```

The first thing we do here is search for all HTML h2 elements and assign the resulting array to the *secondaryHeadings* variable. Now, remembering that arrays start at 0, we're able to access the innerHTML property of the first (in our case, the only) h2 element on the page. The result is an alert box that outputs the text inside of the h2 element. This is the point at which I started to get excited when I first learnt about the DOM, but maybe that's just me.

Accessing the DOM using jQuery

Using pure JavaScript to access the DOM isn't particularly scary, although it's a bit long-winded if anything. Still, jQuery allows us to access the DOM in a simple, yet ridiculously powerful way. For example, the jQuery equivalent of the getElementById method is:

```
$("#blogArticles");
```

Check out how short it is! But seriously, it's 21 characters shorter – that's really, *really* short. It's worth noticing the hash symbol (#) before the id name, this is because jQuery uses the same prefixes for matching elements as CSS – a hash for an id name, a dot for a class name, and nothing to match a tag name. It's also worth noting the dollar symbol ($) at the beginning of the code; this is a shortcut for accessing jQuery, and is the equivalent of calling jQuery("#blogArticles").

So, by now you'd probably find it trivial to rewrite the getElementsByTagName example in jQuery, but I'll show you just in case. It's really easy:

```
$("p");
```

That is genuinely all there is to it. It goes beyond belief that so few characters can do so much, but do much those 7 characters can.

And what about the innerHTML property, is that easy in jQuery as well? You betcha!

```
var secondaryHeadings = $("h2");
alert(secondaryHeadings.html());
```

All you need to do is use the jQuery html method, it's does exactly the same as the innerHTML property really. The main difference with the html method is that is always returns the first HTML element, so you don't need to refer to the array index, like you do with innerHTML.

Manipulating the DOM

Being able to access content in the DOM is cool, but being able to edit that content is even cooler. The best part is that we already know the code to do it, it's all to do with the `html` method in jQuery, or the `innerHTML` property in pure JavaScript.

Let's jump in and change the h2 element content in our cut-down HTML5 blog page:

```
var secondaryHeadings = $("h2");
secondaryHeadings.html("Now we've changed the content");
```

If you did everything right you should get something a little like Figure 2-4 (notice the heading has changed):

Figure 2-4. Manipulating the DOM using jQuery.

It's important to realize that we haven't edited the actual HTML file, we have merely changed the way it is being outputted in the browser. I really can't stress this enough. If you don't believe me, try disabling

JavaScript in your browser and looking at the page again – the heading will be back to what it was originally.

As I mentioned at the beginning of this section, we have only scratched the surface with what the DOM can really do. The scope of this book means I can't teach you everything, instead I must focus on the functionality we are actually going to use. This is the same for everything I'm teaching you about JavaScript, there is much that has been left out. If you want to learn more about the DOM or JavaScript then I definitely recommend picking up a book that focuses on them, or checking out the W3Schools website at www.w3schools.com.

Summary

We've covered an absolutely massive amount in this chapter, I commend you for making it this far. In just one chapter I've tried to explain everything I possibly can about JavaScript, something that really deserves a whole book dedicated to it! Still, we've learnt things like where JavaScript has come from, why libraries like jQuery make things easier for us, and how to add JavaScript to a HTML web page. We've also covered the fundamental features of JavaScript, like variables, data types, conditional statements, functions, arrays, loops, timers, the DOM, and objects. It sounds like quite a lot when you list it like that, doesn't it?

Perhaps you should take a little break now. Have a cup of tea, let your brain take in what we've covered, and then pick the book back up again. Next up, we're going to learn how to use HTML5 canvas (my not-so-secret favorite part of HTML5).

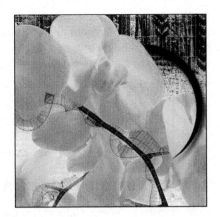

Chapter 3

Learning the Basics of Canvas

By now you should already have a good idea about what canvas is and why it's a fantastic part of HTML5. In this chapter, we will take a proper look at the features of canvas, from learning how to actually get it into a HTML document to drawing shapes and other kinds of objects on it. We will also look at how to change how shapes and objects are drawn on canvas, as well as finding out how to erase it. Finally, we'll end with an example showing you how to make canvas the same size as the browser window, an integral skill to have for developing immersive games. I hope by the end of this chapter that you feel even more excited about HTML5 canvas and the possibilities that it opens up in front of you.

Getting friendly with the canvas element

Just like video and audio, the canvas element uses absolutely no external plug-ins or voodoo to do its thing. All you need is some HTML and a sprinkling of JavaScript courtesy of the 2d rendering context API. Don't worry if you don't have a clue what the 2d rendering context API is right now— you'll be an expert in it soon enough.

Using the canvas element is simple—and I mean really, *really* simple. The following code is all you need to get started with it:

```
<canvas width="500" height="500">
        <!-- Insert fallback content here -->
</canvas>
```

I suppose I should be honest and tell you that this doesn't actually do anything spectacular. All it does is create a new blank canvas element, but you won't be able to see anything yet because you haven't done anything with the 2d rendering context. We'll get on to drawing things on to the canvas shortly, which is simple as well.

For now, it's important to note the width and height attributes used when creating the canvas element. These attributes obviously define the size of the canvas element, which in turn define the size of the 2d rendering context. Without defining a size like this the canvas element and the 2d rendering context would be set to the default width and height of 300 by 150, respectively. Later on in this chapter we'll look at the ways to create a canvas element that changes size dynamically and fills the whole browser window.

> Note: The position of the canvas element is defined by its location within your HTML document. It can be moved around with CSS as required, just like other HTML elements.

Browser support for canvas

Most modern browsers support the canvas element and the majority of its features, but it comes as no surprise that Internet Explorer doesn't, at least not in any version earlier than Internet Explorer 9. If you're happy with this fact of life, then you can put a suitable message in the fallback content for the canvas element that lets those poor IE users know that they should upgrade. The other option is to use the fantastic ExplorerCanvas script, which has been developed by some boffins at Google. The beauty of this method is that you only need to include one script into your Web page and the canvas element will work in Internet Explorer browsers prior to version 9.

If this is something you're interested in then you should download the script from the ExplorerCanvas website[1] and follow the instructions for installation.

The 2d rendering context

The canvas element isn't the cool part of canvas at all; that acclaim falls to the 2d rendering context, the piece of awesome that you draw absolutely everything on to. The purpose of the canvas element is to act as a wrapper around the 2d rendering context, providing you with all the necessary methods and juicy functionality to draw on and manipulate it. It's really important to understand this, so let me make it clear: you draw on to the 2d rendering context, not the canvas element. You access and display the 2d rendering context through the canvas element. I don't expect this to make complete sense yet, my hope is that things will clear up a bit when you get stuck in with using the canvas for yourself.

The coordinate system

The 2d rendering context is a standard screen-based drawing platform. Like other 2d platforms, it uses a flat Cartesian coordinate system with the origin (0, 0) at the top left. Moving to the right will increase the x value, and moving downwards will increase the y value (see Figure 3-1). Understanding how the coordinate system works is integral if you want to have things draw in the right place.

---

[1] http://code.google.com/p/explorercanvas/

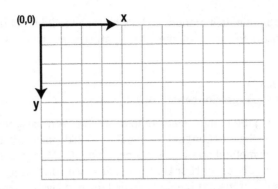

Figure 3-1. 2d rendering context Cartesian coordinate system

A single unit in the coordinate system is usually equivalent to 1 pixel on the screen, so the position (24, 30) would be 24 pixels right and 30 pixels down. There are some occasions where a unit in the coordinate system might equal 2 pixels, like with high definition displays, but the general rule of thumb is that 1 coordinate unit equals 1 screen pixel.

Accessing the 2d rendering context

There's no point faffing around trying to explain this all in words when we could just start using it. So let's do just that by creating a basic HTML web page with an empty canvas element:

```
<!DOCTYPE html>

<html>
        <head>
                <title>Learning the basics of canvas</title>
                <meta charset="utf-8">

                <script type="text/javascript" src="http://ajax.googleapis.com↪
/ajax/libs/jquery/1/jquery.min.js"></script>

                <script type="text/javascript">
                        $(document).ready(function() {

                        });
                </script>
        </head>

        <body>
                <canvas id="myCanvas" width="500" height="500">
                        <!-- Insert fallback content here -->
                </canvas>
        </body>
</html>
```

You won't see anything if you run it as it stands, so let's access the 2d rendering context so we can start to draw stuff. Place the following inside of the jQuery statement, just like we did with the previous JavaScript examples:

```
var canvas = $("#myCanvas");
var context = canvas.get(0).getContext("2d");
```

All we're doing here is assigning the canvas element to a variable then assigning the 2d rendering context to another variable by calling the getContext method. I should point out that, because we're using jQuery, we need to call the get method so we gain access to the DOM for the canvas element, from there we then have access to the canvas getContext method. I wouldn't worry too much about trying to understand why: just be aware that the get method has nothing to do with canvas itself.

Now we have a variable that contains the 2d rendering context we can start to draw stuff. Exciting times! Add the following line after declaring the context variable:

```
context.fillRect(40, 40, 100, 100);
```

If you refresh the page you'll see something amazing has happened; a black square has appeared (see Figure 3-2)!

Figure 3-2. Drawing an object using canvas

You've just drawn your first element using canvas. Feels good, doesn't it? The square is black because that is the default color of elements drawn with canvas; we'll look at how to use something other than the default color later in this chapter.

Drawing basic shapes and lines

As you can see, drawing a square is pretty straightforward; it's just one line of code, the `fillRect` method:

```
context.fillRect(40, 40, 100, 100);
```

The obvious thing you'll notice is that the method is called `fillRect` and not `fillSquare`. I'm sure most of you already know that a square is actually a rectangle with sides of the same length, but for those who don't, a square is actually a rectangle with sides of the same length!

There are four arguments needed to create a rectangle. The first two are the (*x*, *y*) coordinate values for the origin of the square (its top left corner), and the final two are the width and height of the rectangle. The width of a rectangle is drawn to the right of the (x, y) position, and the height of the rectangle is drawn downwards from the (x, y) position. You can see why it's important to know how the coordinate system works, otherwise you may have assumed the height would draw upwards from the (x, y) position. The `fillRect` method could be rewritten like this to visualise the arguments:

```
context.fillRect(x, y, width, height);
```

For the sake of clarity, change the width value of our square to 200, save the file, and refresh the page (see Figure 3-3).

Figure 3-3. Drawing a rectangle

What a surprise, it's a rectangle. And to draw the rectangle in a different position? Yup, just change the (x, y) position values. For example, an *x* position of 200 and a *y* position of 300 (see Figure 3-4).

Figure 3-4. Drawing a rectangle in a different position

This is the beauty of canvas; it's ridiculously easy to manipulate the objects you've drawn, you just change the values of a couple of arguments.

> Note: It may not seem obvious, but if you draw something with an origin point beyond the dimensions of the canvas element, it won't appear on the screen. Only shapes drawn with an origin point, or some part of the shape inside of the canvas element will be visible to you.

Alongside fillRect is the strokeRect method, the evil twin. Whereas fillRect draws a rectangle and fills it with a color (in our case black), the strokeRect method draws a rectangle and strokes it. That's not to say that strokeRect gives it a soothing pat with its hand (it wouldn't be an evil twin if it was that nice); it means that the outline of the rectangle has a line drawn around it. If you change the fillRect example to use strokeRect instead you'll see what I mean (see Figure 3-5).

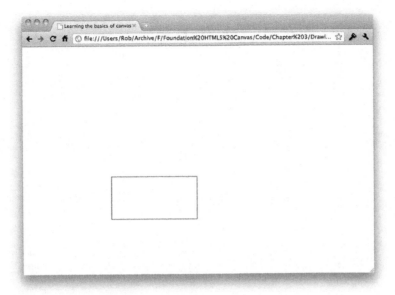

Figure 3-5. Drawing a stroked rectangle

The rectangle now has an outline; it's effectively hollow. Now this is fun and all, but how about we try something a little more adventurous, like a full-blown line? Why not.

Lines

Lines are created a little differently to shapes. They're actually known as paths. To create a simple path, you have to first call the beginPath method on the 2d rendering context, which effectively says, "get ready, we're about to start drawing a path." The next method to call is moveTo, which sets the (x, y) origin of the path we're about to draw. Following this is a call to lineTo with the (x, y) of the destination of our line, with a call to closePath to finish drawing the path. Finally, a call to stroke will make the line visible by drawing its outline. By putting this all together you come with something like this:

```
context.beginPath(); // Start the path
context.moveTo(40, 40); // Set the path origin
context.lineTo(340, 40); // Set the path destination
context.closePath(); // Close the path
context.stroke(); // Outline the path
```

Which should look like this, a nice and boring straight line (see Figure 3-6)

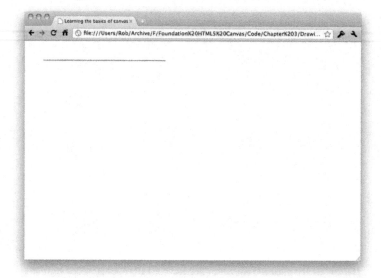

Figure 3-6. Drawing a line

Lines don't have to be horizontal or vertical though, by changing the (*x*, *y*) arguments of the lineTo method you can make it diagonal:

```
context.lineTo(340, 340);
```

Which would look like Figure 3-7.

Figure 3-7. Drawing a diagonal line

Straight lines aren't mighty exciting on their own, but they can be combined to produce complex shapes that *are* exciting. I'll go through the advanced features of paths in the next chapter. For now, let's try something else. How about drawing circles? They're definitely a bit more exciting.

Circles

It doesn't take a genius to realize circles are very different to rectangles. However, knowing this goes some way to explaining why creating a circle in canvas is very different to creating a rectangle. A circle is a fairly complex shape, and because of this there isn't actually a special method in canvas to create a circle. What there *is* is a method for drawing arcs, which is all a circle really is—an arc joined at both ends. It's a bit confusing, so how about we jump in and create a circle in canvas:

```
context.beginPath(); // Start the path
context.arc(230, 90, 50, 0, Math.PI*2, false); // Draw a circle
context.closePath(); // Close the path
context.fill(); // Fill the path
```

You should already recognize the first and last two lines, they just start and close the path (the arc) and then fill it when we're done (`fill` is the companion method to `stroke`). The juicy part is the second line, which does everything necessary to draw a circle. It may look a bit complicated, so let me break it down for you.

There are six arguments used in the creation of an arc; the (*x*, *y*) coordinate values for the origin of the arc (the centre of the circle in our case), the radius of the arc, the start angle, the end angle, and finally a boolean value that draws the arc anti-clockwise if true, or clockwise if false. The `arc` method could be rewritten in a more readable way like so:

```
context.arc(x, y, radius, startAngle, endAngle, anticlockwise);
```

The first three arguments are self-explanatory so I'll skip past those. The start angle and end angle arguments are seemingly simple, but they deserve some explaining to properly understand how they work. In short, an arc in canvas is defined as a curved path that starts at a distance from the (*x*, *y*) origin equal to the radius, and is at the angle defined by the start angle. The path ends at the end angle one radius away from the (*x*, *y*) origin (see Figure 3-8).

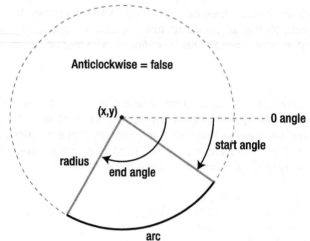

Figure 3-8. Drawing an arc

It's important to note that angles in canvas are in radians and not degrees and, without going into too much detail, it's safe to assume that 360 degrees (a complete circle) is 2π (pi multiplied by 2) radians. People much cleverer than me have worked out how to convert from degrees to radians and they have come up with the following formula (written in JavaScript for our purposes):

```
var degrees = 1; // 1 degree
var radians = degrees * (Math.PI / 180); // 0.0175 radians
```

We're going to be using radians throughout the book, as it saves us from performing unnecessary conversions from degrees, so to make things easier you can use Figure 3-9 as a quick guide for the angle along a circle in radians.

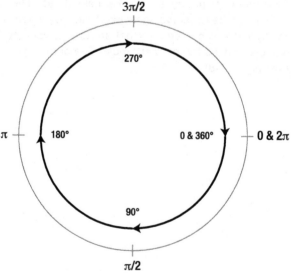

Figure 3-9. Converting between degrees and radians

For anything more complicated you should use the formula described previously.

So now you know how angles work in canvas. Let's bring the focus back to the circle example. You can see now that the start angle is 0, the beginning of our arc, and the end angle is Math.PI*2 (pi multiplied by 2); these angles are the start and end of a circle. If you don't believe me then check out Figure 3-9.

> Note: To get access to the value of pi in JavaScript you use the Math object, which is a special object that allows you to do all sorts of cool math-based stuff. We'll be using it in the future for tasks like generating random numbers.

If you run the example you should get a display in your browser like Figure 3-10.

Figure 3-10. Drawing a circle

A circle, hooray! Now, what would the end angle be if you wanted to draw half a circle instead? Check Figure 3-10 if you want. That's right, it would be plain and simple π, which looks like this in JavaScript:

```
context.arc(230, 90, 50, 0, Math.PI, false); // Draw a semi-circle
```

If all went well should have a lovely semi-circle in your browser (see Figure 3-11).

> Although the sixth argument in the arc method is meant to be optional, Firefox will throw an error if it is left out. Because of this, it's worth keeping it in and explicitly defining a direction to draw the arc.

Figure 3-11. Drawing a semi-circle

You could fiddle with the angles all day to create quarter circles, pizza slices—all sorts really. However, I'll leave it up to you if you want to play around with that. We've got more important things to be getting on with, like changing the color of stuff!

Style

Black is so last season. If only there was a way to change the color of our shapes and lines. Wait, there is? And it's really easy? Like one line of code easy? Awesome! I'm not lying about it being easy by the way. Let's jump straight in and change the color of the square we made at the beginning of the chapter.

```
context.fillStyle = "rgb(255, 0, 0)";
context.fillRect(40, 40, 100, 100);
```

By setting the fillStyle property of the 2d rendering context you're able to change the color that shapes and paths are filled in as. In the previous example, an rgb (red, green, and blue) color value is assigned, although you could also use any valid CSS color value, like a hex code (eg. #FF0000 or the word "red"). In the example, the color is set to red (full red, no green, no blue) and your square should look something like Figure 3-12.

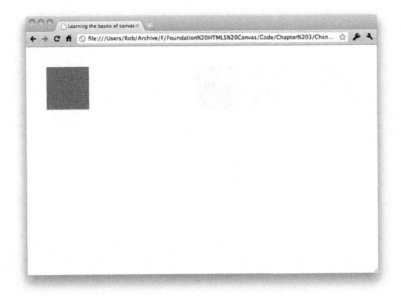

Figure 3-12. Changing the fill color to red

I told you it was easy, but don't get too excited, as there is a downside. The issue is that setting the fillStyle property means that everything you draw after setting it will be in that color. This isn't a problem if that's what you want to happen, but it's important to be aware of in case you only wanted to change the color of one object. One way to get around this is to set the fillStyle property back to black (or another color) once you've drawn your objects to canvas, like so:

```
context.fillStyle = "rgb(255, 0, 0)";
context.fillRect(40, 40, 100, 100); // Red square
context.fillRect(180, 40, 100, 100); // Red square

context.fillStyle = "rgb(0, 0, 0)";
context.fillRect(320, 40, 100, 100); // Black square
```

Which will look like Figure 3-13 in the browser

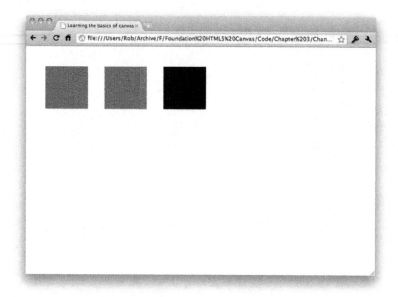

Figure 3-13. Changing the fill color back to black

You can also do the same thing with stroked shapes and paths by using the strokeStyle property. For example, the following is the same as previous example except it's using stroked outlines instead of fills:

```
context.strokeStyle = "rgb(255, 0, 0)";
context.strokeRect(40, 40, 100, 100); // Red square
context.strokeRect(180, 40, 100, 100); // Red square

context.strokeStyle = "rgb(0, 0, 0)";
context.strokeRect(320, 40, 100, 100); // Black square
```

Which looks like Figure 3-14.

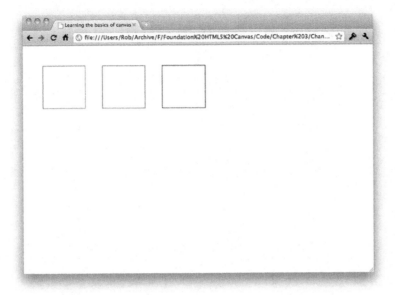

Figure 3-14. Changing the stroke color

> *Note: There's nothing stopping you from combining both* fillStyle *and* strokeStyle *to give a shape a fill and stroke that are completely different colors.*

Nothing complicated here, it's all very basic stuff. It's just as easy to change the color of lines as well:

```
context.strokeStyle = "rgb(255, 0, 0)";
context.beginPath();
context.moveTo(40, 180);
context.lineTo(420, 180); // Red line
context.closePath();
context.stroke();

context.strokeStyle = "rgb(0, 0, 0)";
context.beginPath();
context.moveTo(40, 220);
context.lineTo(420, 220); // Black line
context.closePath();
context.stroke();
```

Which should look like Figure 3-15.

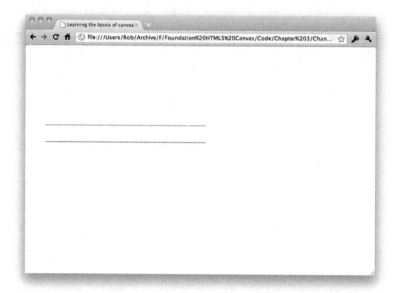

Figure 3-15. Changing the color of lines

And that really is all there is to changing color in canvas.

Changing line width

Changing color is good fun, but our line examples have been a bit on the thin side. Fortunately in canvas, there is a method of fattening them up a bit, and that is the `lineWidth` property of the 2d rendering context. By default the `lineWidth` property is set to 1, but you can set it to anything you want. For example, let's change the width of our red and black lines:

```
context.lineWidth = 5; // Make lines thick

context.strokeStyle = "rgb(255, 0, 0)";
context.beginPath();
context.moveTo(40, 180);
context.lineTo(420, 180); // Red line
context.closePath();
context.stroke();

context.lineWidth = 20; // Make lines even thicker

context.strokeStyle = "rgb(0, 0, 0)";
context.beginPath();
context.moveTo(40, 220);
context.lineTo(420, 220); // Black line
context.closePath();
context.stroke();
```

The result of this is a slightly thicker red line and an overly thick black line (see Figure 3-16).

Figure 3-16. Changing the width of lines

And lineWidth works just as well on shapes:

```
context.lineWidth = 5; // Make lines thick

context.strokeStyle = "rgb(255, 0, 0)";
context.strokeRect(40, 40, 100, 100); // Red square
context.strokeRect(180, 40, 100, 100); // Red square

context.lineWidth = 20; // Make lines even thicker

context.strokeStyle = "rgb(0, 0, 0)";
context.strokeRect(320, 40, 100, 100); // Black square
```

Which as you've probably guessed, makes two slightly thicker red squares with an overly thick black square (see Figure 3-17).

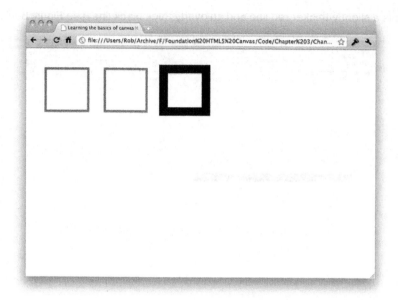

Figure 3-17. Changing the line width of shapes

You've practically mastered the basics now, but there are still a couple of things left to cover before we move on to the *really* cool stuff.

Drawing text

Canvas is not just for graphics and images, you can also use it to display text. Although if I'm to be truthful, there aren't many occasions where drawing text using canvas is a better option compared to creating text using a more traditional HTML element approach (like with a p element). Let me explain.

Text in canvas is drawn as an image, which means that it isn't selectable with a mouse cursor like normal text in a HTML document—it isn't actually text, it just looks like it. If you've used Microsoft Paint before, then you'll understand what I mean; once text has been drawn it can't be edited unless you erase it and redraw it again. The benefit to drawing text in canvas is that you can use all the wonderful transformations and other functionality that comes with drawing in canvas. However, I must stress that you shouldn't create text in canvas unless you have a legitimate reason not to create it using normal, selectable HTML elements. Instead, you should use normal HTML elements to create text, and then layer them over the top of the canvas with CSS positioning. The point here is that HTML was built to deal with text (content), whereas canvas has been built to deal with pixels and graphics.

Now that's out the way I can show you how to draw text in canvas, it's really easy:

```
var text = "Hello, World!";
context.fillText(text, 40, 40);
```

That is all you need to draw a string of text. The fillText method of the 2d rendering context takes four arguments (one is optional, so we've left it out for now); the first is the string of text you want to draw, and the second and third are the (*x*, *y*) coordinate values for the origin of the text (the bottom left). I told you it was easy.

I won't show you the output just yet as it's going to be too small to see, that is because the default font settings for text in canvas are 10px sans-serif (absolutely tiny). So let's change the size now, and while we're at it I might as well show you how to change the font. To do this you need to set the font property of the 2d rendering context, like so:

```
var text = "Hello, World!";
context.font = "30px serif"; // Change the size and font
context.fillText(text, 40, 40);
```

The font property takes a string value in exactly the same way as the font property in CSS. In the previous example, you give the pixel size to want the font to be, followed by the name of the font family you want to use. You've set it to serif which means the default font on the computer that is a serif font (something like Times New Roman). When put together it should look something like Figure 3-18.

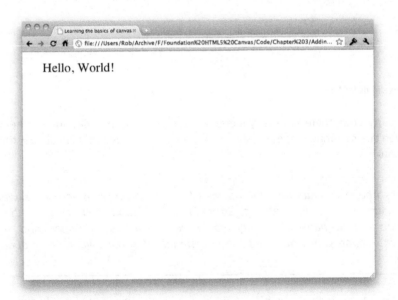

Figure 3-18. Drawing text and changing the font size

That's a bit better, you can actually read it now. You could even make the text italic if you really wanted by doing this:

```
var text = "Hello, World!";
context.font = "italic 30px serif";
context.fillText(text, 40, 40);
```

All that's changed here is the word italic has been added to the font string, which produces something like Figure 3-19.

Figure 3-19. Drawing italic text

As the font property goes there are many more settings you can use, like the line height, and fallback font families. I won't be covering these, but if you're interested in using text in canvas, then I suggest that you check them out.

> Note: As I hope you can see, the basics of canvas are very much self-explanatory. The reason for this is that the 2d rendering context API uses methods and properties that are named in a way that makes them easy to understand. It should now make sense why I stressed the importance of naming variables properly back in Chapter 2.

Before we move on, let me show you how to create stroked text—this is useful to know:

```
var text = "Hello, World!";
context.font = "italic 60px serif";
context.strokeText(text, 40, 100);
```

This time you're using the strokeText method, which takes exactly the same parameters as fillText. It looks a bit weird at a small font size so in this example the size is larger and the origin has been moved down slightly so the text doesn't go off the top of the screen. It should look a little something like Figure 3-20.

Figure 3-20. Drawing stroked text

Generally I don't see much excitement to stroked text, but you might have an amazing project that just wouldn't be complete without it. If that's the case then I suggest you knock yourself out and go crazy with it.

Erasing the canvas

Drawing on to the canvas is really fun, but what do you do when you make a mistake or want to wipe the slate clean and draw something else? Fortunately there are two options at your disposal: the clearRect method, or the width/height trick. Let's take a look at the clearRect method of the 2d rendering context first.

Say you've just drawn a square and a circle on to the canvas:

```
context.fillRect(40, 40, 100, 100);

context.beginPath();
context.arc(230, 90, 50, 0, Math.PI*2, false);
context.closePath();
context.fill();
```

And you've now decided, for whatever reason, that you want to wipe the canvas clean. To do this all you need to do is call clearRect with the (x, y) origin of our canvas, its width, and its height. If the canvas was 500 pixels wide and 500 pixels tall then the call to clearRect would look like this:

```
context.clearRect(0, 0, 500, 500);
```

Which, when run, would display nothing in the browser, because you've just wiped the entire canvas clean. You can also even call `clearRect` when you don't know the size of the canvas by using the jQuery `width` and `height` methods, like so:

```
context.clearRect(0, 0, canvas.width(), canvas.height());
```

Which would look like this in its entirety:

```
var canvas = $("#myCanvas");
var context = canvas.get(0).getContext("2d");

context.fillRect(40, 40, 100, 100);

context.beginPath();
context.arc(230, 90, 50, 0, Math.PI*2, false);
context.closePath();
context.fill();

context.clearRect(0, 0, canvas.width(), canvas.height());
```

I've included the original canvas variable in this example just to remind you where we're calling it from in the `clearRect` method.

> Note: The canvas element actually provides you with width and height properties, so it's up to you whether you want to use the jQuery way, or the pure JavaScript way of accessing the dimensions of the canvas.

You don't have to clear the entire canvas though; you can just as easily clear a particular area of it. For example, if we wanted to remove only the square in the example then you would call `clearRect` like so:

```
context.clearRect(40, 40, 100, 100);
```

Which leaves you with a lonely circle (see Figure 3-21).

Figure 3-21. Erasing a particular area of the canvas

The way this works is that the arguments in clearRect can be changed so a very specific area is cleared. In our case we've moved the origin of the area we want to erase (the top left) to be the top left of the square (40, 40), and the width and height of the area we want to erase has been set to the width and height of square (100). The result is that only a specific area around the square is set to be cleared. You could quite easily remove the circle instead by changing the arguments of clearRect to the following:

```
context.clearRect(180, 40, 100, 100);
```

Which, if our calculations are correct, should leave us with just a square (see Figure 3-22).

Figure 3-22. Erasing a particular area of the canvas

Remember that the origin of an arc is its centre, so to get the correct origin for the clearRect method we need to take the origin of the arc and subtract its radius for both the *x* and *y*.

Not that you would ever need to do this, but there's nothing to stop you erasing only part of an object in canvas:

```
context.fillRect(40, 40, 100, 100);

context.beginPath();
context.arc(230, 90, 50, 0, Math.PI*2, false);
context.closePath();
context.fill();

context.clearRect(230, 90, 50, 50);
```

This example should take a big slice out of your circle (see Figure 3-23).

Figure 3-23. Erasing part of a shape

This technique is sometimes used to draw complex shapes quickly and easily by drawing a basic shape and chopping bits off of it.

The width/height trick

If you only want to erase everything on the canvas and start again from scratch then you might want to consider the width/height trick. If I'm honest this isn't really a trick, but rather a potent and little-documented method to reset a canvas back to its default, fresh state. The idea is that when the width and height attributes of a canvas element are set, at any point, the canvas should be cleared back to its original state. This method does have some drawbacks, so let me give you an example:

```
context.fillStyle = "rgb(255, 0, 0)";

context.fillRect(40, 40, 100, 100);

context.beginPath();
context.arc(230, 90, 50, 0, Math.PI*2, false);
context.closePath();
context.fill();
```

This will draw a red square and circle onto the canvas, nothing crazy yet. Now let's add in the canvas reset:

```
canvas.attr("width", canvas.width());
canvas.attr("height", canvas.height());
```

What's happening here is a bit of jQuery magic. You need to change the width and height attributes of the canvas element, so to do this you use the attr method in jQuery. My hope is that by now you should be comfortable enough to guess what is going on. If not, we're passing the name of the attribute we want to edit (width and height) followed by the value we want to set it to (the same width and height as it was previously). If all went well you should see a blank canvas.

Now add the following line after clearing the canvas with the width/height trick:

```
context.fillRect(40, 40, 100, 100);
```

Surely this should draw a red square, right? (Remember: we set the fillStyle property previously.) So why on earth is it drawing a black square (see Figure 3-24)?

Figure 3-24. Resetting the canvas using the width/height trick

The downside with the width/height trick is that absolutely everything in the canvas is reset, including styles and colors. This is why you should only use this trick if you're prepared to completely reset the canvas, not just wipe the display clean.

Making canvas fill the browser window

Up until now the canvas element has been at a fixed width and height of 500 pixels, which is great, but what if we wanted to make it fill the entire browser window. How do you do it? Well with a normal HTML element you can normally set the width and height attributes to 100% and you're all sorted. However, the canvas element doesn't work this way and ignores the percentage, interpreting 100% as 100 pixels, 200% as 200 pixels, and so on. A different method is required.

The easiest way to do it is to set the width and height of the canvas element precisely to the pixel width and height of the browser window. We can get access to the width and height of the window by using the window browser object and a bit of jQuery magic:

```
var canvas = $("#myCanvas");
var context = canvas.get(0).getContext("2d");

canvas.attr("width", $(window).get(0).innerWidth);
canvas.attr("height", $(window).get(0).innerHeight);

context.fillRect(0, 0, canvas.width(), canvas.height());
```

The reason I've used $(window).get(0).innerHeight instead of $(window).height() is that the latter doesn't seem to return the full height in all browsers. You'll notice that this method hasn't actually worked properly as there is still a white gap around the canvas element and scrollbars in the browser window (see Figure 3-25).

Figure 3-25. White padding around the canvas

To fix this we need to use some CSS, so open up a new file in your favourite text editor and save it as canvas.css in the same directory as your HTML document. Put this inside of the CSS file and save it:

```
* { margin: 0; padding: 0; }
html, body { height: 100%; width: 100%; }
canvas { display: block; }
```

The first line resets the margin and padding of every HTML element to 0, removing the white border you can see in the screenshot above. This is commonly known as a CSS reset; there are much better ways of doing it, but this will serve our purposes right now. The second line isn't entirely necessary, but makes sure that the html and body elements are the full width and height of the browser window. The final line changes the canvas element from inline to block, which allows the width the height to be set properly, in turn allowing it to take the full width and height of the browser window without causing scrollbars.

To use this CSS in the HTML document you need to add the following line before the jQuery script element, inside of the head element:

```
<link href="canvas.css" rel="stylesheet" type="text/css">
```

This links to the CSS file you just created and runs the styles within it. The result is a canvas element that perfectly fills the browser window (see Figure 3-26).

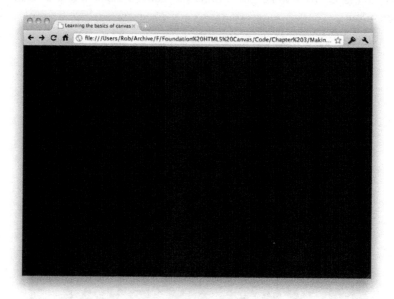

Figure 3-26. Making the canvas fill the browser window

Unfortunately we're not done yet. If you resize the browser window the canvas element will stay at the size it was before, causing scrollbars if you shrink it too much (see Figure 3-27).

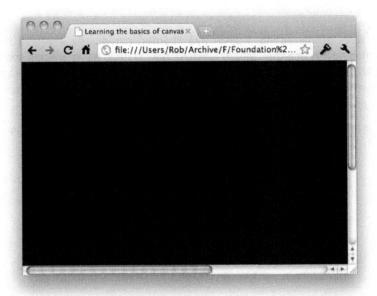

Figure 3-27. Issues when resizing the browser window

To get around this you need to resize the canvas element at the same moment that the browser window is resized. If only jQuery had a resize method that was fired at the moment a browser window was resized, a little like how the ready method is fired when the DOM is ready. Well luckily for us, it does have have a resize method, and it does exactly that!

```
$(window).resize(resizeCanvas);

function resizeCanvas() {
        canvas.attr("width", $(window).get(0).innerWidth);
        canvas.attr("height", $(window).get(0).innerHeight);
        context.fillRect(0, 0, canvas.width(), canvas.height());
};

resizeCanvas();
```

There isn't much new here, most of the code has just been moved around a little. The main addition is the jQuery resize method which has been set to call the resizeCanvas function when the browser window is resized. All the functionality you had previously to set the width and height of the canvas element has been moved into that function, including the drawing of the rectangle the size of the canvas (remember: changing the width and height will reset the canvas, so everything has to be redrawn). The final addition is a call to the resizeCanvas function to kick things off when the page is loaded for the first time.

If you try that now you'll notice the canvas element resizes beautifully and no scrollbars appear. It works, well done!

Summary

We've covered all sorts of interesting stuff in this chapter, particularly if you've never used canvas before. You've learned how to use the canvas element, how to draw basic shapes and paths, and how to change the color of those shapes and paths. You've also learned how to draw text, erase the canvas, and how to make canvas fill the browser window. It's a huge amount really, so I think you should pat yourself on the back and go make yourself another cup of tea to let things soak in.

The next chapter is going to get interesting, as you're going to learn all about the advanced drawing features in canvas!

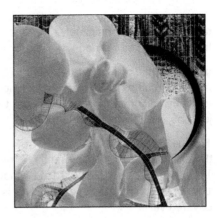

Chapter 4

Pushing Canvas Further

In this chapter you're going to explore some of the more advanced functionality that canvas provides. You'll be looking at ways to save time if you want to use lots of different drawing styles, as well as how to transform and manipulate your drawings so they look more exciting. Toward the middle of the chapter you'll learn how to create shadows and gradients to make your shapes more realistic and interesting. The chapter ends with a look at creating exotic shapes using advanced paths, followed by finding out how to export the canvas as an image so you can store it or use it at a later date.

This is an exciting chapter that I hope will really open your eyes to some of the cooler things that canvas can do.

Saving and restoring the drawing state

In Chapter 3 we switched between styles a lot, sometimes even going from one color to another, then back to the first color again. This repetition can get pretty tedious, and it means that you have to duplicate a lot of code if you want to revert back to a set of styles that you've already used before. The good news is that canvas has functionality baked in that allows you to remember styles and other attributes so you can use them again in the future (yay). This is known as saving and restoring the drawing state of the canvas. However, the bad news is that it can be a little confusing if you want to remember more than one state, so you'll have to have your head screwed on to keep track of what's happening (boo). But have no fear; once I'm done explaining it you'll wonder what all the fuss was about.

What is the canvas drawing state?

If I walked up to you and said, "Look at the state of you!", not only would I have potentially offended you, but I'd have also directly referred to the way that you look (although, I'm confident you look lovely). The term "state," in both the offline world and the canvas world, is used to describe the condition of something at a *particular point in time*. It's important to grasp that the state of an object is directly connected to the time that it was described. For example, if I described the state of you yesterday and again today, I'd be talking about two completely different states – you might look worse today (although, I'm sure you don't). In short, state can change.

In canvas, the drawing state refers to a whole range of properties that describe the look and feel of the 2d rendering context at that point in time, from simple color values all the way to complex transformation matrices and other fun stuff. We'll get to transformation matrices later on in this chapter, so don't worry if I just spewed a load of gobbledygook.

The full list of properties that are referred to as the canvas drawing state are: the transformation matrix, the clipping region, globalAlpha, globalCompositeOperation, strokeStyle, fillStyle, lineWidth, lineCap, lineJoin, miterLimit, shadowOffsetX, shadowOffsetY, shadowBlur, shadowColor, font, textAlign, and textBaseline. In this chapter, you'll learn about most of the properties that we haven't covered yet.

It's important to be aware that the current path and the current bitmap of the canvas (what's being displayed) aren't part of the state. It might help to look at the state as a description of the 2d rendering context properties, rather than a copy of everything that you can see on the canvas.

Saving the drawing state

Before we begin, make sure you've got a fresh HTML web page set up as described at the start of Chapter 3. Don't let me stop you if you want to use your own HTML, or you just want to look at the examples and not type them out just yet.

Now, the great thing about saving the state of the canvas is that it's dead easy to perform. All you need to call is the save method of the 2d rendering context. That's it. There are no arguments or anything else, just plain and simple save:

```
var canvas = $("#myCanvas");
var context = canvas.get(0).getContext("2d");

context.fillStyle = "rgb(255, 0, 0)";
context.save(); // Save the canvas state
context.fillRect(50, 50, 100, 100); // Red square
```

So what actually happens when you save the drawing state? Surely it must be stored somewhere, right? Correct. The 2d rendering context holds a stack of drawing states, basically a list of previously saved states with the most recently saved state at the top – just like a stack of paper. The default stack of drawing states is empty, and a new state is only pushed (added) to the stack if you call the save method. This means that there is absolutely nothing stopping you from calling the save method multiple times and pushing multiple drawing states onto the stack one after another, with the oldest state on the bottom. However, this is where things can get a little confusing as you can't pull any drawing state back out of the stack, there is a strict order to the process. But don't worry about that just now – we'll cover multiple states shortly. In the meantime, let's have a look at how to access the state that you've just saved.

Restoring the drawing state

Getting access to an existing drawing state is just as easy as saving it; the only difference being that this time you call the `restore` method. Now, if you draw another square, this time using blue as the `fillStyle`, you'll soon see the benefit behind canvas drawing states:

```
context.fillStyle = "rgb(0, 0, 255)";
context.fillRect(200, 50, 100, 100); // Blue square
```

This doesn't do anything special just yet; you've only changed the fill color (see Figure 4-1).

Figure 4-1. Changing the fill color before restoring the drawing state

But what if you want to revert back to the red fill color we used earlier? I hope you aren't thinking about rewriting the `fillStyle` property again and setting it to red! Oh, you're not? Phew. No, fortunately you saved the drawing state after setting the color to red, so it's happily sitting in the stack waiting for you to grab it back out again by adding a call to `restore` after the existing code:

```
context.restore(); // Restore the canvas state
context.fillRect(350, 50, 100, 100); // Red square
```

By calling the `restore` method you automatically pull out the last drawing state that was added to the stack and apply it to the 2d rendering context, overwriting all existing styles with those from the saved state. This means that, although you don't change it directly in the code, the `fillStyle` property will take the value of the saved drawing state – it will turn red (see Figure 4-2). This might not look much when just changing color, but the same concept works for all the canvas properties that are saved into the drawing state.

Figure 4-2. Restoring the drawing state

Saving and restoring multiple drawing states

At the beginning of this section I told you that dealing with more than one state at a time is a little confusing. My hope is that by now, after your sterling work up to this point, you're ready to handle it. Really, in all honestly, it's not that confusing if you understand the concept of the stack and how new items are added on top, with items being removed from the stack from the top as well. The stack is basically a last in, first out system; the most recent drawing state that was saved to the stack will be the first state that is restored later on.

If you update the previous example to save the state after setting the blue fillStyle then you'll see what I mean:

```
context.fillStyle = "rgb(255, 0, 0)";
context.save();
context.fillRect(50, 50, 100, 100); // Red square

context.fillStyle = "rgb(0, 0, 255)";
context.save();
context.fillRect(200, 50, 100, 100); // Blue square

context.restore();
context.fillRect(350, 50, 100, 100); // Blue square
```

The third square is now blue instead of red. This is because the last drawing state that was saved to the stack was the blue fillStyle, so it's the first to be restored (see Figure 4-3).

Figure 4-3. Saving multiple drawing states

The other state with the red `fillStyle` is still waiting in the stack; you just need to call `restore` again to access it:

```
context.restore();
context.fillRect(50, 200, 100, 100); // Red square
```

This will return and remove the final state from the stack, leaving it empty (see Figure 4-4).

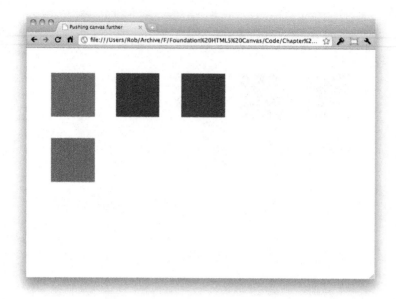

Figure 4-4. Restoring multiple drawing states

Now, there's much more to saving and restoring drawing states, but the purpose of this section is to give you the basics. From now on you'll be able to understand the use of the drawing state in future sections to save time and do some pretty cool things.

Transformations

So far, all the elements you've drawn on to the canvas have been left as they were intended to be drawn. For example, a rectangle is drawn at the position and in the dimensions that you define in the `fillRect` method, and it is drawn with horizontal and vertical lines; nothing out of the ordinary there. But what if you wanted to draw something unique? What if you wanted to rotate a rectangle? What if you wanted to scale it? What's great is that the transformation functionalities of the 2d rendering context allow you to do all of these tasks and more. The stuff they allow you to do is pretty amazing.

Translation

At the most basic level you have translation, which is the act of moving the origin of the 2d rendering context from one location to another. In the case of canvas you use the `translate` method, which actually moves the coordinate origin of the 2d rendering context, rather than moving the objects that you're trying to draw (see Figure 4-5).

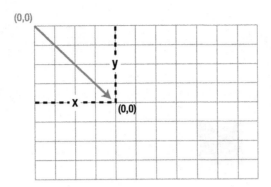

Figure 4-5. The translate method moved the origin of the 2d rendering context.

This is how to call the `translate` method:

```
context.translate(150, 150);
```

The two arguments are the (*x*, *y*) coordinate values that dictate how far to move the origin of the 2d rendering context. It's important to understand that the (*x*, *y*) coordinate values that you provide are added on to the existing translation of the origin, which is (0, 0) by default. For example, if you performed two translations exactly like above, you'd actually have moved the origin 300 units (0+150+150) in the *x* direction, and 300 units (0+150+150) in the *y* direction.

By moving the origin of the 2d rendering context, all objects drawn to the canvas will now appear to be moved by the same amount:

```
context.fillRect(150, 150, 100, 100);

context.translate(150, 150);

context.fillStyle = "rgb(255, 0, 0)";
context.fillRect(150, 150, 100, 100);
```

Normally the second call to `fillRect` would draw a square with an origin point at the coordinate (150, 150), but by performing a translation the square will now appear to have an origin of (300, 300) (see Figure 4-6).

Figure 4-6. Translation affects the origin of shapes.

It's important to understand exactly what has gone on here. The red square still has an origin of (150, 150), it just appears to have shifted over another 150 pixels because the origin of the 2d rendering context has moved 150 pixels as well since drawing the black square. If you wanted the red square to appear where the point (150, 150) used to be (where the black square is), you'd simply set its origin as (0, 0):

```
context.translate(150, 150);
context.fillStyle = "rgb(255, 0, 0)";
context.fillRect(0, 0, 100, 100);
```

This works because you've already translated the 2d rendering context to the position (150, 150), so anything drawn from now on at the point (0, 0) will actually appear to be at the point (150, 150) (see Figure 4-7).

Figure 4-7. Keeping the origin while translating

> *Note: Every transformation method, including* translate, *affects all elements drawn after it has been called. This is because they all act directly on the 2d rendering context, not on the shape you're drawing. Think of it like what happens when you change something like the* fillStyle *property; the new color affects every element drawn from there on.*

Scaling

Another transformation method is scale which, as the as the name suggests, scales the 2d rendering context in size. It works in a slightly different way to translate in that the (*x*, *y*) arguments are multipliers rather than pixel values.

```
context.scale(2, 2);
context.fillRect(150, 150, 100, 100);
```

This example is set to scale the 2d rendering context by a multiple of two in both the *x* and *y* directions. In layman's terms, the 2d rendering context and all objects drawn onto it are now twice as big (see Figure 4-8).

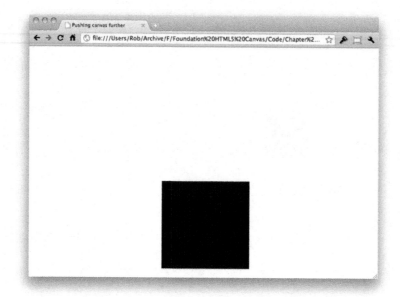

Figure 4-8. Scaling the 2d rendering context

Using scale on its own is going to result in absolutely everything being made bigger, and it will also cause objects to be drawn in positions you wouldn't expect. For example, a scale of 2 will effectively mean that 1 pixel now equals 2 pixels; so if you draw something at an *x* of 150, it will now end up looking like it's at an *x* of 300. If this is not what you want, or if you want to only scale a single shape, you can combine the scale method with translate.

```
context.save();
context.translate(150, 150);
context.scale(2, 2);
context.fillRect(0, 0, 100, 100);
```

In this example you're first saving the state of the canvas, before translating the origin point to (150, 150). You then scale the canvas by two and draw a square at the position (0, 0). Because you've translated the origin of the 2d rendering context to (150, 150), the square will be drawn in the correct position whilst still being scaled. Job done! (See Figure 4-9.)

Figure 4-9. Keeping the origin while scaling

The problem is that anything else you draw from now on will be translated by 150 pixels and scaled by 2 in both directions. Fortunately you've already implemented the first half of the solution; saving the drawing state before performing the transformations. The second half of the solution is to restore the drawing state as it was previously.

```
context.restore();
context.fillRect(0, 0, 100, 100);
```

By restoring the drawing state, anything you draw from then on will appear as if the transformations never happened (see Figure 4-10). Cool, eh? I told you that saving and restoring the drawing state allowed you to do some pretty nifty stuff.

Figure 4-10. Restoring the drawing state after performing a transformation

Rotation

If I had to choose a favorite transformation, the rotate method would definitely be the one. It always seems amazing when you can break the concept of square pixels by twisting something at an angle, but perhaps that's just me. Simple pleasures!

The common theme with all the transformations thus far is that they're easy to call. The rotate method is no different, you just pass in the angle in radians that you want to rotate the 2d rendering context by:

```
context.rotate(0.7854); // Rotate 45 degrees (Math.PI/4)
context.fillRect(150, 150, 100, 100);
```

However, the result of this rotation might not be what you expected. Why is the square trying to escape out the side of the browser? (See Figure 4-11).

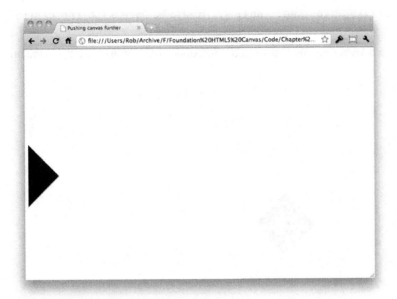

Figure 4-11. Rotating the canvas can cause shapes to draw in odd positions.

The reason for this odd behavior is that the `rotate` method rotates the 2d rendering context around its (0, 0) point of origin, which in this above is at the top left hand corner of the screen. Because of this the square you've drawn is not being rotated itself; it's actually being drawn onto a canvas that is now at a 45-degree angle. Figure 4-12 should help shed some light on the matter.

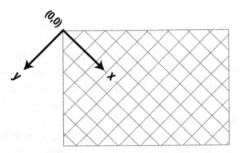

Figure 4-12. The 2d drawing context after rotation

Of course, this isn't ideal if you want to only rotate the shape that you're drawing. This is where your friend `translate` comes in to save the day, again. To get this effect you need to translate the origin of the 2d rendering context to the centre of the shape that you're drawing. From here you can perform a rotation on the canvas and then draw your shape at the current position. It's a little overwhelming in text, so let me show you in an example in code:

```
context.translate(200, 200); // Translate to centre of square
context.rotate(0.7854); // Rotate 45 degrees
```

```
context.fillRect(-50, -50, 100, 100); // Draw a square with the centre at the point↦
of rotation
```

Which will give you a lovely square drawn at a 45-degree angle, in exactly the position you're after (see Figure 4-13).

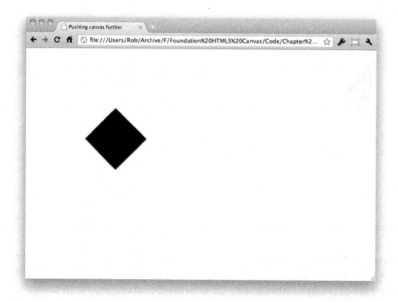

Figure 4-13. Rotating a shape around its origin

> *Note: The order that you perform transformations is incredibly important. For example, if you rotated the canvas 45 degrees before performing a translation then you'd be translating at an angle of 45 degrees. An example from the WHATWG specification points out that a scale transformation that doubles the width of anything drawn, followed by a rotation of 90 degrees, and then drawing a rectangle that is twice as wide as it is tall, will result in a square. It makes sense when you think about it, but it highlights the need to think about the order of your transformations. If something doesn't look right, check the order!*

The transformation matrix

All of the transformation methods you've used up to this point affect something called the transformation matrix. Without going into unnecessary detail (they aren't the most exciting things in the world), a transformation matrix is an array of numbers, each of which describes a particular kind of transformation that I'll explain shortly. A matrix is split into a number of columns and rows; in the case of canvas you're using a 3x3 matrix – three columns and three rows (see Figure 4-14).

$$\begin{bmatrix} a & c & e \\ b & d & f \\ 0 & 0 & 1 \end{bmatrix} = \begin{bmatrix} x\ scale & x\ skew & x\ trans \\ y\ skew & y\ scale & y\ trans \\ 0 & 0 & 1 \end{bmatrix}$$

Figure 4-14. The 2d rendering context transformation matrix

For our purposes you can ignore the bottom row as you'll never have to or be able to change its values. The rows that are important are the first and second, which contain number values that you'll later refer to in canvas as *a* to *f*. You can see in the illustration that each number value corresponds to a particular transformation. For example, *a* refers to the scale multiplier in the *x* direction, while *f* refers to the translation in the *y* direction.

Now, before we learn how to manipulate the transformation matrix manually, I should highlight what the matrix looks like by default. A new 2d rendering context will contain a fresh transformation matrix, called an identity matrix (see Figure 4-15).

$$\begin{bmatrix} 1 & 0 & 0 \\ 0 & 1 & 0 \\ 0 & 0 & 1 \end{bmatrix}$$

Figure 4-15. The identity matrix

This special matrix has every value set to 0, apart from the ones on the main diagonal, the line from top left to bottom right. The full reasoning behind this is better suited to a book on mathematics, but it's safe to say that an identity matrix means that absolutely no transformation is performed. Fully understanding an identity matrix isn't important; what is important is knowing what the default values are in a transformation matrix.

Manipulating the transformation matrix

The final two methods that we're going to look at in this section are transform and setTransform. These both help us manipulate the transformation matrix of the 2d rendering context. I've done enough explaining for the time being, so let's jump in and perform a translation and scale using transform, then draw a square to show it all working:

```
context.transform(2, 0, 0, 2, 150, 150);
context.fillRect(0, 0, 100, 100);
```

The transform method takes six arguments, one for each value of the transformation matrix; the first representing *a*, through to the last representing *f*. In this example you want to scale the canvas so it's double the size; so to do that you set the first and fourth arguments to 2, which are *a* and *d* – the *x* scale and the *y* scale. Makes sense. And to translate the canvas origin? That's right: you set the fifth and sixth arguments, which are *e* and *f* – the *x* translation and the *y* translation (see Figure 4-16).

Figure 4-16. Scaling a translating using the transformation matrix

As I hope you can see by now, it's really not that scary to manipulate the transformation matrix manually. So long as you are aware of what each value does, you'll be fine. On that note, let's do something a little more advanced with the transformation matrix – let's rotate it!

Performing a rotation transformation without using the rotate method may look tricky from the outside, but if you bear with me it'll all make sense soon enough:

```
context.setTransform(1, 0, 0, 1, 0, 0); // Identity matrix
var xScale = Math.cos(0.7854);
var ySkew = -Math.sin(0.7854);
var xSkew = Math.sin(0.7854);
var yScale = Math.cos(0.7854);
var xTrans = 200;
var yTrans = 200;

context.transform(xScale, ySkew, xSkew, yScale, xTrans, yTrans);
context.fillRect(-50, -50, 100, 100);
```

The first thing you're doing here is calling the setTransform method. This is the second method that manipulates the transformation matrix. Its job is to reset the matrix to the identity matrix and then apply the transformation as described in the six arguments. In this example you're using it to reset the transformation matrix so you can be sure you're working with a clean slate. The second thing you're doing is assigning values to the variables that you're going to use as arguments in the call to transform. By creating variables to use in the arguments you can keep things looking cleaner and making a little more sense.

It's important to point out that transform actually multiplies the existing transformation matrix by the values that you supply; it's not simply setting the values of the transformation matrix. What this means is that there is a cumulative effect. If you called transform multiple times, you'd be applying each transformation to the transformation matrix that results from the last transformation. I appreciate that it's a little confusing, but I hope that it helps shed some light on the way that transformations work.

You'll have noticed that the Math object has shown its face again. You're using it in this example to return the necessary values for the scale and skew transformations to produce the effect of rotation. I'll repeat that because it's important to grasp; rotation using the transformation matrix is the result of a combination of skewing and scaling. To do this you pass in the angle in radians to the cos (cosine) and sin (sine) trigonometric functions.

> Note: We'll be using trigonometric functions like cosine and sine later on in this book. I strongly advise you to read up on them elsewhere if you want to learn more about how they work and why we're using them. Unfortunately I don't have the luxury of explaining absolutely everything we use in minute detail. The Wikipedia page on transformation matrices is a great resource for finding out more: http://en.wikipedia.org/wiki/Transformation_matrix.

If you put this all together and cross your fingers you should come up with the following; a lovely rotated square (see Figure 4-17).

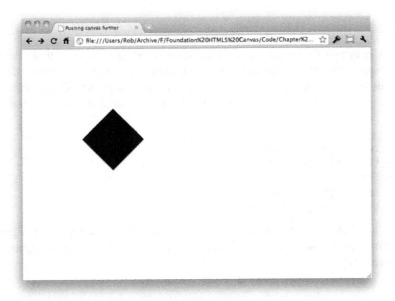

Figure 4-17. Rotating using the transformation matrix

Looks nice, doesn't it? And to think that you rotated that with your own bare hands; none of that cheating `rotate` malarkey! In all seriousness, most times the three core transformation methods will do you just fine, but for those times that they don't, an understanding of transformation matrices will get you far.

Compositing

The last section was definitely a lot of hard work, so well done for getting through it. I'm going to give you a breather this section as we'll be taking a look at something a little less mental and a little more fun; compositing! In short, compositing is the act of combining multiple visual elements together into a single visual element. It's used in all walks of life, from graphic design all the way to Hollywood film production (scenes shot with a green screen are composited – combined with another image – at a later date).

Everything you draw in canvas is already being composited; meaning everything you draw is combined with the existing elements that have been drawn already. This is really basic compositing, simply adding something on top of another thing. I'll touch on these aspects of compositing shortly, but for now let's look at the easiest compositing method in canvas, the `globalAlpha` property.

> Note: Both of the global compositing properties that we're covering in this section affect everything that is drawn to the 2d rendering context. It's important to be aware that changing a global compositing property will affect everything that is drawn from that point onwards.

Global alpha

Before any object is drawn to the canvas, an alpha value is applied to it that matches that of the `globalAlpha` property. The value assigned to `globalAlpha` must range between 0.0 (transparent) and 1.0 (opaque); the default value is 1.0. If it isn't already obvious, the `globalAlpha` property will affect how transparent the objects that you're drawing will be. For example, you could draw a half transparent square like so:

```
context.fillStyle = "rgb(63, 169, 245)";
context.fillRect(50, 50, 100, 100);
context.globalAlpha = 0.5;
context.fillStyle = "rgb(255, 123, 172)";
context.fillRect(100, 100, 100, 100);
```

Because you set the `globalAlpha` property after drawing the blue square, only the pink square will be affected by the alpha value. The result will be a pink square with the blue square slightly showing through behind it (see Figure 4-18).

Figure 4-18. Setting the globalAlpha property

Now, you could also produce the same effect by setting the `fillStyle` to an rgba value that includes an alpha value less than 1. The difference with `globalAlpha` is that it sets the global alpha value that is then referenced when applying an alpha using something like an rgba color. For example, if the `globalAlpha` is 0.5 and you then apply a `fillStyle` with an rgba of alpha 0.5, the resulting alpha will actually be 0.25. The global alpha value of the 2d rendering context (0.5) acts as the baseline for calculating other alpha values (0.5 * 0.5 = 0.25).

Composite operations

As I mentioned at the beginning of this section, even a brand-new 2d rendering context uses compositing from the get go. You probably wouldn't notice it because it uses a type of compositing that results in shapes being drawn exactly as you'd expect; one on top of the other. This type of compositing is called source over destination; the source being the new shape that you're drawing, and the destination being the 2d rendering context that may have already been drawn on to. We know this because the `globalCompositeOperation` property of the 2d rendering context has a default value of "source-over," and this property defines the type of compositing that is performed on everything drawn to the 2d rendering context (out of 11 possible choices). I should probably point out that all the values for the `globalCompositeOperation` that depend on order will mention either the source or destination, never both. For example, "source-over" is short for "source over destination;" the destination is implied because it is not named in the value (the source has to be drawn over *something*).

Let's take a look at each of the 11 possible options available for the `globalCompositeOperation`. You'll be using the following code as a template to study each of the composite operations; the blue square being the destination and the pink square being the source. The only reason we're using blue and pink instead of other colors is that they will better show the effect of the composite operations:

```
context.fillStyle = "rgb(63, 169, 245)";
context.fillRect(50, 50, 100, 100);
context.globalCompositeOperation = "source-over";
context.fillStyle = "rgb(255, 123, 172)";
context.fillRect(100, 100, 100, 100);
```

> Note: Some browsers don't support the full range of globalCompositeOperation values, so for the sake of clarity I'll be using illustrations instead of in-browser screenshots to show you how they should look. I'm using the WHATWG specification as the basis for how each operation should look.

source-over

This is the default value and it means that the shape that you're drawing (the source) will be drawn on top of the existing canvas (the destination):

```
context.globalCompositeOperation = "source-over";
```

Which looks exactly like everything you've drawn so far (see Figure 4-19).

Figure 4-19. The source-over composite operation

destination-over

This is the opposite of the previous value, so the destination is now drawn on top of the source:

```
context.globalCompositeOperation = "destination-over";
```

Which looks like the reverse of the first operation (see Figure 4-20).

Figure 4-20. The destination-over composite operation

source-atop

This draws the source on top of the destination, but only where both are opaque (not transparent). The destination is drawn everywhere else where it is opaque, but the source is transparent (see Figure 4-21).

Figure 4-21. The source-atop composite operation

destination-atop

This is the reverse of "source-atop;" the destination is drawn on top of the source where both are opaque, with the source drawn everywhere else where it is opaque and the destination is transparent (see Figure 4-22).

Figure 4-22. The destination-atop composite operation

source-in

The source is drawn where the both the source and destination overlap. Anything that doesn't overlap will be made transparent (see Figure 4-23).

Figure 4-23. The source-in composite operation

destination-in

This is the reverse of "source-in;" the destination is kept where both the source and destination overlap. Anything that doesn't overlap will be made transparent (see Figure 4-24).

Figure 4-24. The destination-in composite operation

source-out

The source will be drawn where there is no overlap with the destination. Everything else will be made transparent (see Figure 4-25).

Figure 4-25. The source-out composite operation

destination-out

The destination will be kept where there is no overlap with the source. Everything else will be made transparent (see Figure 4-26).

Figure 4-26. The destination-out composite operation

lighter

This value has no order and will add together the color values of the source and destination if they overlap. The resulting color values will be capped at 255, which is white (see Figure 4-27).

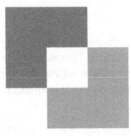

Figure 4-27. The lighter composite operation

copy

This value has no order and will draw the source instead of the destination (see Figure 4-28).

Figure 4-28. The copy composite operation

xor

This value has no order and will draw the source and destination where neither overlaps. Anything that does overlap will be made transparent (see Figure 4-29).

Figure 4-29. The xor composite operation

Together, these composite operations allow you to perform interesting effects without having to draw complicated shapes. Some operations, like "destination-out," can be useful for erasing areas of the canvas that aren't rectangular; for example, by using a circle as the source.

Shadows

Everybody loves a good shadow; they're probably the most over-used effect in Adobe Photoshop and can be seen all over the Web and in graphic design. This is for good reason though – if done well, they can really add a sense of realism to an image. Done wrong, however, they can completely ruin an image. However, I'm not here to dictate my opinion on graphic design; I'm here to teach you how to become a master at canvas.

Creating a shadow in canvas is relatively straightforward and can be manipulated using four possible global properties. These properties are shadowBlur, shadowOffsetX, shadowOffsetY, and shadowColor. We'll go over each shortly. By default, the 2d rendering context does not draw shadows because shadowBlur, shadowOffsetX, and shadowOffsetY are set to 0, and shadowColor is set to transparent black. The only way you can make a shadow appear is by changing the opacity of the shadowColor to something non-transparent, while also setting either shadowBlur, shadowOffsetX, or shadowOffsetY to a value that isn't 0:

```
context.shadowBlur = 20;
context.shadowColor = "rgb(0, 0, 0)";
context.fillRect(50, 50, 100, 100);
```

In this example you've given the shadow a 20 pixel blur and have set its color to a fully opaque black. The offset values for the shadow are kept at their default of 0 pixels in the x direction, and 0 pixels in the y direction. It's probably worth mentioning that, even though its opaque black, the shadow will appear slightly transparent at the edges because of the blur (see Figure 4-30).

Figure 4-30. A basic shadow

If you change the shadowBlur, shadowOffsetX, and shadowOffsetY properties you'll be able to create a different drop shadow effect:

```
context.shadowBlur = 0;
context.shadowOffsetX = 10;
context.shadowOffsetY = 10;
context.shadowColor = "rgba(100, 100, 100, 0.5)"; // Transparent grey
context.fillRect(200, 50, 100, 100);
```

By changing the blur to 0 you create a razor-sharp shadow, and by moving the offset just slightly to the right and downward you end up with a drop shadow variant. The icing on the cake is to set the shadowColor as a slightly transparent mid-gray, using the rgba color type that was mentioned in the section on compositing (see Figure 4-31).

Figure 4-31. Creating a drop shadow variant

Shadows in canvas work for any shape that you can draw, so there's nothing to stop you using them on circles or anything else that you want. You can even change the color to something a little more exotic, although I'd definitely question your motives before doing so:

```
context.shadowColor = "rgb(255, 0, 0)"; // Red
context.shadowBlur = 50;
context.shadowOffsetX = 0;
context.shadowOffsetY = 0;
context.beginPath();
context.arc(400, 100, 50, 0, Math.PI*2, false);
context.closePath();
context.fill();
```

This gives you a rather dashing circle with a horrific red shadow effect behind it (see Figure 4-32).

Figure 4-32. Drawing a shadow on a circle

By using a combination of various blur and color values, you can achieve some effects that are completely unrelated to shadows. For example, you could use a blurred yellow shadow to create the effect of a light flare around an object, like a sun or a glowing object perhaps.

Gradients

Sometimes a plain color just isn't exciting enough, or perhaps you just really need to add an extra element of realism to the color of a shape. Either way, gradient colors in canvas are definitely an option for you to consider; both `fillStyle` and `strokeStyle` accept gradient colors in the form of a `CanvasGradient` object.

There are two types of gradient available to you in canvas: linear and radial. Each type of gradient is created using its own method in the 2d rendering context; for a linear gradient, you use `createLinearGradient`, and for a radial gradient you use `createRadialGradient` (five points if you guessed that before you read it). Both of these methods return a `CanvasGradient` object for you to further manipulate using the `addColorStop` method of the `CanvasGradient` object itself. Let's create a basic linear gradient to see how this all fits together.

```
var gradient = context.createLinearGradient(0, 0, 0, canvas.height());
gradient.addColorStop(0, "rgb(0, 0, 0)");
gradient.addColorStop(1, "rgb(255, 255, 255)");

context.fillStyle = gradient;
context.fillRect(0, 0, canvas.width(), canvas.height());
```

The first thing you're doing here is creating a new CanvasGradient object using createLinearGradient, then assigning it to a variable so you can access it again. There are four arguments in the createLinearGradient method; the (x, y) coordinates for the start point of the gradient, and the (x,) coordinates for the end point of the gradient. The start and end points describe the length, position, and direction that the gradient is drawn. In the example you're drawing a gradient from the canvas origin in the top left, all the way to the bottom left. A linear gradient is drawn perpendicular to the line described by the start and end points, so in the example the gradient will be going from top to bottom.

Defining a CanvasGradient object is not enough; you need to apply some color to it. To do this you use two calls to the addColorStop method of the CanvasGradient object that you saved to a variable. There are two arguments in the addColorStop method; the offset of the color (between 0 for the start, and 1 for the end of the gradient), and a color value for that offset. The color value can be any CSS color value, just like fillStyle. In the example the gradient is going from black at the start (an offset of 0) to white at the end (an offset of 1).

Finally, the gradient is applied as a color value to the fillStyle property, which gives you a gradient from black to white that covers the entire canvas (see Figure 4-33).

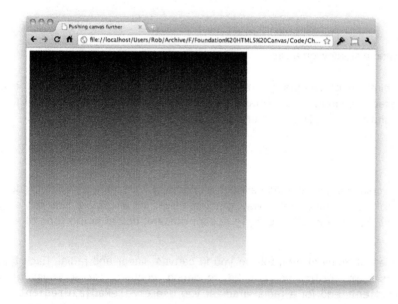

Figure 4-33. Drawing a linear gradient

Creating a radial gradient is a little different. In fact, creating a radial gradient can be damn confusing if you don't understand exactly how they work, especially because the results aren't the same across browsers (yet). Fortunately for you, my job is to break them down so they make sense to you, so let's give that a go now.

A radial gradient is created using the createRadialGradient method. This method requires six arguments; the first three describe one circle (the start circle), and the last three describe another (the last circle). These two circles themselves describe not only the direction and where the gradient starts and ends, but also the shape of the gradient. The three arguments that describe each circle are the (*x*, *y*) coordinate of the circle origin and the radius. The arguments described as strings are:

```
createRadialGradient(x0, y0, r0, x1, y1, r1);
```

The actual gradient is drawn as a cone that touches the edges of both circles, with the part of the cone before the start circle displaying in the color at offset 0, while the part of the cone beyond the end circle displaying in the color at offset 1. I appreciate that this is a difficult concept to grasp, so I've put together a diagram that will hopefully clear things up (see Figure 4-34).

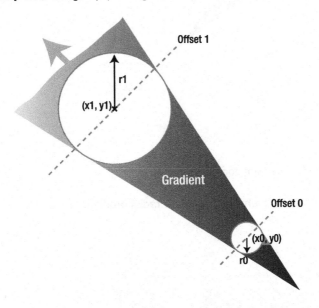

Figure 4-34. A graphical representation of how radial gradients work in canvas

Written in canvas code, this would look a little something like this:

```
var gradient = context.createRadialGradient(300, 300, 10, 100, 100, 50);
gradient.addColorStop(0, "rgb(0, 0, 0)");
gradient.addColorStop(1, "rgb(150, 150, 150)");

context.fillStyle = gradient;
context.fillRect(0, 0, canvas.width(), canvas.height());
```

The start circle is at the coordinate position (300, 300) and has a radius of 10, while the end circle has a coordinate position of (100, 100) and a radius of 50. The resulting cone should look roughly like that in Figure 4-34, and will be black from the start circle (offset 0), fading to gray at the end circle (offset 1) (see Figure 4-35).

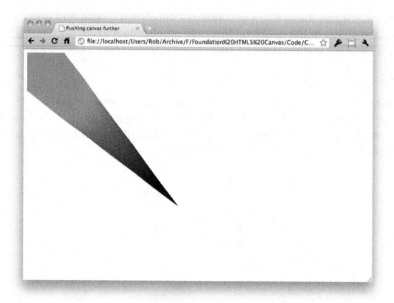

Figure 4-35. Drawing a radial gradient cone

Now if I'm to be honest, this isn't what I imagined a radial gradient to look like; I imagine one to look like Figure 4-36.

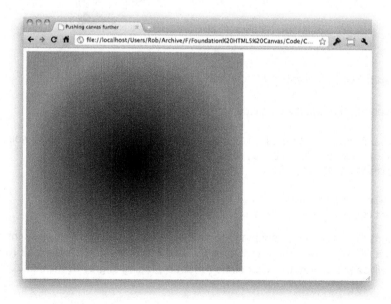

Figure 4-36. Drawing a more common radial gradient

This kind of radial gradient is actually surprisingly simple to achieve; you just place the start and end circles at the same origin. That's it!

```
var canvasCentreX = canvas.width()/2;
var canvasCentreY = canvas.height()/2;

var gradient = context.createRadialGradient(canvasCentreX, canvasCentreY, 0,
canvasCentreX, canvasCentreY, 250);
gradient.addColorStop(0, "rgb(0, 0, 0)");
gradient.addColorStop(1, "rgb(150, 150, 150)");

context.fillStyle = gradient;
context.fillRect(0, 0, canvas.width(), canvas.height());
```

By placing both circles on top of each other you cause the gradient cone to wrap around in 360 degrees and, so long as one of the circles is larger than the other, the gradient will run from the smaller circle all the way to the boundary of the larger circle.

> Note: Although gradients are pretty awesome, it isn't always best to create them using canvas, especially if you're using them for entire backgrounds. It would be worth considering other options, such as CSS3 gradient backgrounds that are designed specifically for this task.

Complex paths

We covered paths briefly in the last chapter by learning how to draw straight lines, and arcs (to create circles). What's great about paths in canvas is that they get much more exciting than lines and simple circles; you can actually create all sorts of weird and wonderful shapes with them.

A solitary straight path is great; it draws a lovely line. What we failed to cover in Chapter 3 was how to draw more than one line at a time and have them combine to make a single shape. In fact, we already know all the code to do this, so I'm going to jump right in and show you how to connect multiple paths together.

```
context.beginPath();
context.moveTo(100, 50);
context.lineTo(150, 150);
context.lineTo(50, 150);
context.closePath();
context.stroke();
context.fill();
```

You should recognize all the code; it begins a path, moves the origin of the current path, draws a line from the current path origin to a particular point, and wait... it draws another line to another point... and then it does it again! What's going on here then? What you've just done is uncover the secret behind connecting multiple paths together; you just keep drawing them. It's really as simple as that; any call to moveTo or lineTo will add the corresponding (x, y) coordinate value to something called a *sub path*. In fact, moveTo actually creates a whole new sub path, where as lineTo just adds on to an existing sub path. This sub path keeps track of the last coordinate value that was added to it, which is exactly how you can call multiple lineTo methods in a row. Each lineTo you call starts from the last coordinate value in the sub path (left by a moveTo call or a lineTo call), draws a line all the way to the coordinate value defined in the lineTo arguments, and then updates the sub path with that new coordinate value.

The triangle is finished off with a call to the closePath method, which will draw a line from the last point in the sub path to the first point – it closes the path. It also adds the start and end point, which is the same coordinate value now, to the sub path (see Figure 4-37).

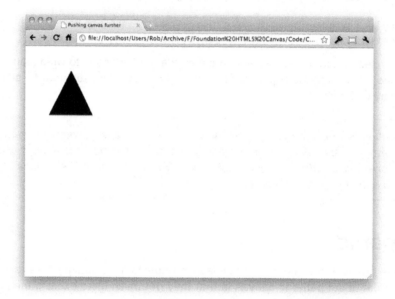

Figure 4-37. Connecting paths to draw a triangle

Bézier curves

To draw a curved line in canvas you could use the arc method or even the arcTo method (which draws an arc from one point to another), but these arcs have only one curved line that has the same radius. To create something a little more exciting you'll need to use one of the Bézier curve methods; either quadraticCurveTo, or bezierCurveTo.

> *Note: Don't be fooled by the names of the Bézier curve methods; they're both Bézier curves, even if one of them doesn't have Bézier in the name. The reality is that quadraticCurveTo is a quadratic Bézier curve, while bezierCurveTo is a cubic Bézier curve. Now, I dare you to go wow someone with this impressive fact.*

Both kinds of Bézier curve use control points to manipulate a straight line into a curve; a quadratic Bézier curve has just one control point, meaning you have only one curve along the line, and a cubic Bézier curve has two controls points, meaning you have two curves along a single line. Figure 4-38 should help you visualize how both of these curves actually work; the quadratic Bézier is on the left, with the cubic Bézier on the right.

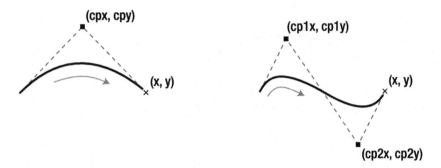

Figure 4-38. The construction of Bézier curves

Creating either of these curves in canvas is just a case of calling either quadraticCurveTo, or bezierCurveTo. Let's start with quadraticCurveTo and see what happens.

```
context.lineWidth = 5;
context.beginPath();
context.moveTo(50, 250);
context.quadraticCurveTo(250, 100, 450, 250);
context.stroke();
```

You know everything in this code apart from the quadraticCurveTo method. This method takes four arguments; the (x, y) coordinate value of the control point (cpx and cpy in Figure 4-38), and the (x, y) coordinate origin of the destination of the path. The control point has been placed at the horizontal (x) centre of the line and slightly above it in the vertical (y) direction (just like in Figure 4-38), which gives you a nice curved line like Figure 4-39.

Figure 4-39. Drawing a quadratic Bézier curve

And, creating cubic Bézier curves is just as easy:

```
context.lineWidth = 5;
context.beginPath();
context.moveTo(50, 250);
context.bezierCurveTo(150, 50, 350, 450, 450, 250);
context.stroke();
```

The bezierCurveTo function takes six arguments; the (x, y) coordinate value of the first control point (cp1x and cp1y in Figure 4-38), the (x, y) coordinate value of the second control point (cp2x and cp2y), and the (x, y) coordinate origin of the destination of the path. Both control points are placed in a similar position to those in Figure 4-38, which gives you a funky double curve across your screen (see Figure 4-40). Cool, isn't it?

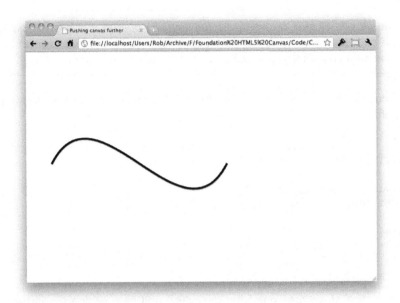

Figure 4-40. Drawing a cubic Bézier curve

Now Bézier curves look cool, but they aren't that practical all on their lonesome. The great thing about Bézier curves is that they can be combined and attached to other paths to create some pretty wild and complicated shapes. No longer are you limited by straight lines and boring arcs!

> Note: If you're freaking out right now wondering how on earth you're going to work out all the coordinate positions for your complicated shape, don't worry about it. There's a plug-in for Adobe Illustrator, called Ai->Canvas (http://visitmix.com/labs/ai2canvas/), that lets you convert your lovely vector drawings into canvas code; meaning that you don't have to calculate a single thing!

Exporting the canvas as an image

So far, everything you've drawn on to the canvas has remained stuck inside of the canvas, unable to be used anywhere else. This really sucks, especially if you want to export your beautiful canvas drawing and save it. But wait! Haven't I told you about canvas' amazing toDataURL method? I haven't? Darn. Well, this amazing little method turns your canvas drawing into something called a data URL, which you can use later to display it as a proper image in the browser. How cool is that?

Note: The Mozilla Firefox browser has functionality built in that allows you to right-click on a canvas element and save it as an image. The method it uses to do this is exactly the same as what you're doing with code using toDataURL.

There really isn't much to the method, so let's go straight for it and export a basic drawing. I'll explain how it all works afterward.

```
context.save();
context.fillRect(50, 50, 100, 100);

context.fillStyle = "rgb(255, 0, 0)";
context.fillRect(100, 100, 100, 100);

context.restore();
context.fillRect(150, 150, 100, 100);

var dataURL = canvas.get(0).toDataURL();
```

This will draw a selection of squares one after the other, and then assign the image data URL to the dataURL variable. You'll see the three squares in the browser (see Figure 4-41), but this is still the canvas image from earlier and not the exported image; I'll show you how to display that later.

Figure 4-41. Preparing the canvas to be exported

The interesting thing in this example is the dataURL variable, and this is a snippet from the value that you've just stored in it:

```
data:image/png;base64,iVBORwOKGgoAAAANSUhEUgAAAfQAAAHOCAYAAADL1t+KAAAXvElEQVR4Ae3XQQ
4dNxYDwPkD3//KPZMDRItAOovI8tINS81iG8T/fd/3H38IECBAgACBtwX++/bre3sCBAgQIEDgLwGGD7jsgQI
AAAQIBAgY9oEQRCBAgQICAQfcNECBAgACBAAGDHlCiCAQIECBAwKD7BggQIECAQICAQQ8oUQQCBAgQIGDQfQ
MECBAgQCBAwKAH1CgCAQIECBAw6L4BAgQIECAQIGDQAooUgQABAgQIGHTfAAECBAgQIGHTfAAECBAgQCBAw6AElikCAAAECBA
y6b4AAAQIECAQIGPSAEkUgQIAAAQIG3TdAgAABAgQCBAx6QIkiECBAgAABg+4bIECAAAECAQIGPaBEEQgQIE
CAgEH3DRAgQIAAgQABgx5QoggECBAgQMCg…
```

The actual output is much, *much* longer than that, but it's really only the first four words that you're interested in right now. Up first are the three words data:image/png; these describe that the text following is going to be a data URL in the format of a PNG image. The fourth word, base64, describes that the data is in the base64 encoding format. This format is common for the transmission of binary data (like images) over a system that uses text as data. All the crazy numbers, letters, and symbols after the base64 are actually the canvas image, as text.

> *Note: The canvas specification supports other types of images using the toDataURL method. However, PNG support is the default requirement and it's up to the individual browser manufacturers to implement support for anything else.*

It's a pretty weird concept, but if you copied the string in the dataURL variable and pasted it into the address bar of a modern browser (so long as it doesn't limit the length of the URL you enter), you'd see an image of what you drew on the canvas. From there you can right click on it and save it to your desktop if you really want. Or, you can replace the canvas element in the example with the generated image:

```
var dataURL = canvas.get(0).toDataURL();
var img = $("<img></img>");
img.attr("src", dataURL);

canvas.replaceWith(img);
```

All you're doing here is creating a brand new HTML img element using jQuery, and then assigning the image data to its src attribute. The last thing you do is use the replaceWith method of jQuery to replace the canvas element with the img element that you've just created. What you should get as a result is an image where the canvas was that looks identical to what you drew on the canvas. You'll be able to tell if it's an image by right-clicking on it and seeing if you get an option to "Save Image As...", or similar (see Figure 4-42).

> *Note: It's worth pointing out that base64 data is about 50 percent larger than the original binary image data that it represents. This might not be an issue if you're only dealing with a small number of low file size images, but it has ramifications if you are dealing with large images, and images in general in a large quantity.*

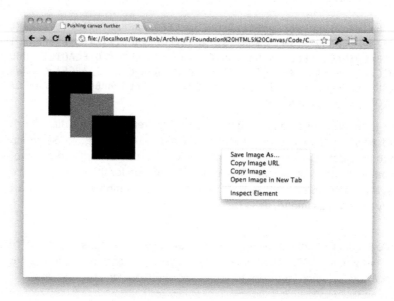

Figure 4-42. Displaying the saved canvas image data as a HTML image element

It's really up to you what you do with the image data, but knowing it's there and that you can actually export the canvas is pretty darn cool. You could even take things further and use canvas to draw a wild image and then export it and use it as a CSS background.

Summary

This has been a tough chapter, but I hope that you enjoyed it. You've learned about the drawing state and how it can be used to save you a lot of time. You've also learned about transformations and compositing, which allow you to create some pretty awesome shapes. On top of that you've seen how shadows and gradients can be used to help make your drawings slightly more realistic. From there you found out how to break away from simple shapes and create something a little more exotic with advanced paths. The chapter ended with a look at exporting the canvas as an image so you can save it to your computer or use it elsewhere within the browser.

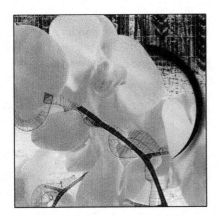

Chapter 5

Manipulating Images and Video

In this chapter, you're going to learn all about using images in canvas, from loading images to manipulating every single pixel within an image. This functionality of canvas is going to allow you to create some impressive effects, and will teach you a whole bunch about how image manipulation works in general.

The chapter ends with a special look at how to manipulate HTML5 video using canvas – applying amazing effects onto a video, on the fly. It's genuinely exciting stuff!

Loading an image into canvas

In the previous chapter you learned how to export canvas as an image, allowing you to save it locally and share it with others. You're now going to learn how to do the complete opposite; loading an image into canvas. The main reason you'd want to do this is that it allows you to perform all of the 2d rendering context methods and transformations on an image that wasn't originally created in canvas. You can also perform a few special pixel manipulation methods that let you do some pretty amazing things with images, which we'll go through after this section.

> Note: Pixel manipulation in canvas doesn't actually require you to load in a traditional image, like a photo. Instead, the canvas itself is treated as an image, which means that anything you draw can be manipulated using the methods you'll learn in this chapter.

Loading an image into canvas is effectively as simple as drawing shapes – it's just one method. You need to call the `drawImage` method with at least three parameters: the image that you're drawing, and the (x, y) coordinate position to draw the image. The method in full, written in notational format, looks like this:

```
context.drawImage(image, x, y);
```

The image argument can be a HTML img element, a HTML5 canvas element, or a HTML5 video element. The fact that you're not limited to basic images makes this feature of canvas very interesting. You'll learn how to use and manipulate the HTML5 video element in canvas at the end of this chapter.

> *Note: There are actually two other ways to call the drawImage method, and each requires a different number of arguments. We'll go through both of these in the next section.*

Let's start by drawing an HTML img element to the canvas using an image from the same directory as the HTML file (see Figure 5-1 for what the image looks like).

```
var image = new Image();
image.src = "example.jpg";
$(image).load(function() {
        context.drawImage(image, 0, 0);
});
```

Figure 5-1. The image used as an example within this chapter

The first thing that you're doing here is assigning a blank DOM object for a HTML img element by using the Image class. By then setting the src attribute to the path of a valid image file, you load that image into the image object just as if you set the src attribute of an actual HTML img element. This effectively creates a normal HTML img element, but without displaying it in the browser. You'd want to use this method if you want to pass an image to the canvas without actually putting it into the HTML code. If you still want to see the HTML image, there's nothing to stop you from skipping these steps completely and assigning the value of the image variable to the DOM object of an existing HTML img element.

> *Note: You're using a locally stored image file in this example, but you can quite easily load an image from another web site if you'd like. However, there are a few limitations to using external images, so I'd urge you to hold off until I explain those limitations in the section on accessing pixel values. For now, just know that canvas locks out certain functionality when external images are used.*

Regardless of which method you used, you should now have access to the DOM object of an image. The last thing left to do is to pass that image object into the drawImage method of the 2d rendering context, but before you can do that, you need to make sure that the image has fully loaded. To do this, use the load method in jQuery, which is called when the load event is triggered on an element after it has fully loaded. You might remember this event from Chapter 2 when we discussed the various ways to load JavaScript after the page has loaded. One of those ways involved the load event on the window DOM object, and it's exactly the same event that you're using here. The reason you want to use this now and didn't want to use it before is that the load event is only triggered after everything has finished loading, including images. By assigning the jQuery load method to the image object directly, you can be sure that you're only waiting for the image to load and nothing else.

Now you know when the image has fully loaded; you place the drawImage method inside of the callback event that's run when the load event is triggered. The arguments for the drawImage method are the image object that you've just created, and the (x, y) coordinate values for the origin point of where you want to draw the image.

If you cross your fingers, you should get the image drawn onto canvas, albeit a little cropped (see Figure 5-2). However, there's no need to fear, because the cropping is due to the canvas being smaller than the image that you're drawing onto it, as the image is drawn at full size. In this example, the canvas is 500 pixels in width and height, and the example image is 1024 pixels in width, and 683 pixels in height.

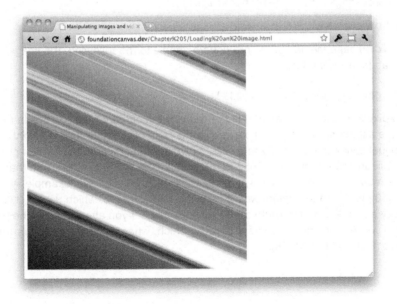

Figure 5-2. Drawing an image onto the canvas at full size

As you can see, loading an image into canvas isn't incredibly hard. However, not being able to see half of the image isn't much fun, so let's take a look at how to fit it correctly.

Resizing and cropping images

You already know about the first way of calling the drawImage method, which draws an image onto the canvas at its full size with the chance of being cropped at the edges. To overcome the cropping problem, you need to either resize the image or control the way that it is cropped. Perhaps unsurprisingly, there is a means to perform both of those tasks using the final two ways of calling the drawImage method; the first can resize the image, and the second can both resize and crop the image. The only difference between all of the ways to call drawImage is the amount and type of arguments used.

Resizing images

Just like drawing one at full size, resizing an image is really easy to understand; you literally just pass the width and height at which you want the image to be drawn. In notational form, the drawImage method with the arguments for resizing looks like this:

```
context.drawImage(image, x, y, width, height);
```

It's pretty straightforward really.

By changing the drawImage method in the previous example to the following, the image will be resized to fit within the canvas (see Figure 5-3).

```
context.drawImage(image, 0, 0, 500, 333);
```

You've used 500 pixels for the width, as that is the width of the canvas. The 333 pixels for the height were calculated from the aspect ratio of the original image (the ratio of the width to the height). To calculate the aspect ratio, you just divide the height by the width, which for the original image (1024 pixels wide and 683 pixels tall) results in an aspect ratio of 0.666992188 (683 ÷ 1024). You can then use that ratio to work out the height of the resized image by multiplying the width by the ratio. For example, you know that the resized width is 500 pixels, so the height would be 500 × 0.666992188, which equals 333. You could also work the other way and calculate the width of the resized image if you already know the height. To do that you just divide the resized height by the aspect ratio, which, when using the numbers from the example, would result in 500 (333 ÷ 0.666992188).

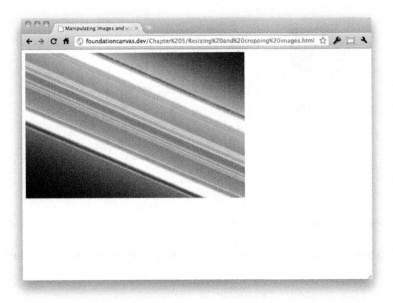

Figure 5-3. Resizing an image to fit within the canvas

Resizing is great if you want to draw the entire image, but it doesn't give you enough options for those times where you want a little more control over the part of the image to draw. This is where cropping comes in.

Cropping images

The purpose of cropping is to cut something to a smaller size, usually because you only care about a particular part of the object that you're cropping. It's a technique that is commonly used in photography to focus on a particular area of a photograph. Cropping in canvas works in exactly the same way as it does in popular photo-editing applications, like Adobe Photoshop: you define a rectangle that represents the area that you want to keep, and everything outside of the rectangle will be removed.

Cropping is the final way of using the drawImage method, and it uses a total of nine arguments: the source image, the (x, y) coordinate origin of the crop on the source image, the width and height of the crop on the source image, the (x, y) coordinate origin to draw the image on the canvas (the destination), and the width and height to draw the image on the canvas. In notational format, the arguments look like this (*w* stands for width, and *h* stands for height):

```
context.drawImage(image, sx, sy, sw, sh, dx, dy, dw, dh);
```

Trying to visualize exactly what all those arguments do can be quite hard, so Figure 5-4 should help clear things up.

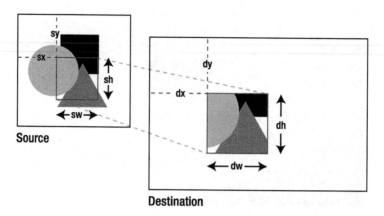

Figure 5-4. How image cropping works in canvas.

By putting this into practice you can crop out a small area of the image you used earlier and draw it onto the canvas:

```
context.drawImage(image, 0, 0, 250, 250, 0, 0, 250, 250);
```

In this example, you're cropping a 250 pixel square from the top left corner (0, 0) of the source image, then drawing it at the top left corner of the canvas with the same width and height (see Figure 5-5).

Figure 5-5. Cropping an image without changing its dimensions

You can also resize the cropped image as you draw in onto the canvas, like so:

```
context.drawImage(image, 0, 0, 250, 250, 0, 0, 500, 500);
```

This does exactly the same as the last example, but instead of drawing the image at the same size as the cropped section, you're drawing it twice as large (see Figure 5-6).

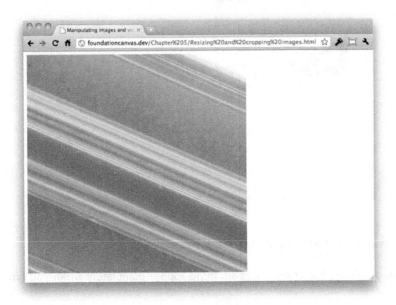

Figure 5-6. Cropping and resizing an image at the same time

Shadows

It's important to briefly highlight an issue with the way shadows work on images when you crop them. In short, shadows work fine when you resize an image (see Figure 5-7).

```
context.shadowBlur = 20;
context.shadowColor = "rgb(0, 0, 0)";

var image = new Image();
image.src = "example.jpg";
$(image).load(function() {
        context.drawImage(image, 50, 50, 300, 200);
});
```

Figure 5-7. Shadows work perfectly when you resize an image.

In some browsers, however, the shadows seem to disappear completely when you crop the image (see Figure 5-8).

```
context.shadowBlur = 20;
context.shadowColor = "rgb(0, 0, 0)";

var image = new Image();
image.src = "example.jpg";
$(image).load(function() {
        context.drawImage(image, 0, 0, 250, 250, 50, 50, 250, 250);
});
```

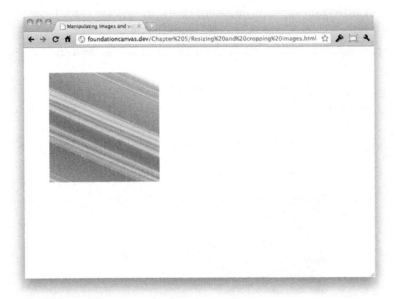

Figure 5-8. Shadows fail to work in some browsers when you crop an image.

This only happens in the current release of WebKit browsers, like Safari and Chrome. The official specification states that images should be affected by shadows when drawn onto the canvas; it just seems like some browsers are yet to fully take on this approach.

And that is really all there is to resizing and cropping images in canvas. If you want to do more you can always use the transformation functionality of the 2d rendering context, as you're about to see.

Transforming images

As I mentioned in the first section of this chapter, drawing an image into canvas allows you to perform all of the 2d rendering context methods on it. Transformations are a set of methods that allow you to do some pretty cool things with images, as you learned in Chapter 4. You already know how transformations work, so let's jump right in and look at how they can be used with images.

Translation

This is by far the easiest transformation to perform on images.

```
context.translate(100, 100);

var image = new Image();
image.src = "example.jpg";
$(image).load(function() {
```

```
        context.drawImage(image, 0, 0, 500, 500, 0, 0, 300, 300);
});
```

It will translate the canvas before drawing the image onto it; nothing that amazing (see Figure 5-9).

Figure 5-9. Translating an image

Rotation

Rotating an image has previously been hard to achieve within the browser, but with canvas it's simple (see Figure 5-10).

```
context.translate(250, 250);
context.rotate(0.7854); // Rotate 45 degrees

var image = new Image();
image.src = "example.jpg";
$(image).load(function() {
        context.drawImage(image, 0, 0, 500, 500, -150, -150, 300, 300);
});
```

Again, this is nothing new in terms of code. What's interesting is that these methods can be used on previously static and boring images.

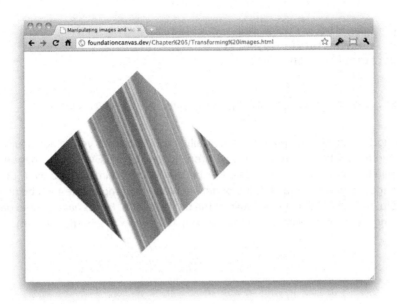

Figure 5-10. Rotating an image

Scaling and flipping

One of the most random uses of transformations is to completely flip the image. For example, you can create a kind of kaleidoscope effect by flipping the same image in various ways (see Figure 5-11).

```
var image = new Image();
image.src = "example.jpg";
$(image).load(function() {
        // Top left
        context.translate(50, 50);
        context.drawImage(image, 0, 0, 500, 500, 0, 0, 200, 200);

        // Bottom left
        context.setTransform(1, 0, 0, 1, 0, 0); // Reset the transformation matrix
        context.translate(50, 450);
        context.scale(1, -1);

        context.drawImage(image, 0, 0, 500, 500, 0, 0, 200, 200);

        // Bottom right
        context.setTransform(1, 0, 0, 1, 0, 0);
        context.translate(450, 450);
        context.scale(-1, -1);

        context.drawImage(image, 0, 0, 500, 500, 0, 0, 200, 200);
```

```
// Top right
context.setTransform(1, 0, 0, 1, 0, 0);
context.translate(450, 50);
context.scale(-1, 1);

context.drawImage(image, 0, 0, 500, 500, 0, 0, 200, 200);
});
```

This is quite a lot to take in, but the process is actually very simple. All you're doing is drawing the same image in four different locations, each with a different scale factor. By using a negative scale factor, you're able to cause the image to flip over. Bear in mind that when the image flips over, the origin will be on the right of the image, so you have to shift the origin over a bit to compensate for it being drawn from right to left. For example, the top right image is drawn at the position (450, 50) because it has been flipped in the *x* direction, meaning that it will now be drawn from an *x* of 450 to an *x* of 250 (right to left).

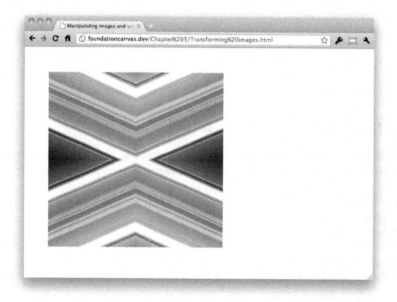

Figure 5-11. Flipping an image by using negative scale transformations

It's all a little bit counter-intuitive, but it's a really simple way to create some pretty interesting effects. For example, this is exactly how you could create faux reflections in canvas.

Accessing pixel values

While resizing, cropping, and transforming can be used to create interesting effects with images, there is yet another feature of canvas that lets you do even more: pixel manipulation. By accessing the individual pixels of the 2d rendering context, you're able to get information such as the color and alpha value of each pixel. You're also able to rewrite each pixel with a different color value so they look entirely different, but we'll get on to that in the following few sections.

The method that allows you to access pixels in canvas is `getImageData`. This method takes four arguments; the (*x, y*) coordinate origin of the pixel area you want to access, the width of the pixel area, and the height of the pixel area (see Figure 5-12). It looks like this in notational format:

```
context.getImageData(x, y, width, height);
```

Nothing visual will happen when you call `getImageData`, but you will get a 2d rendering context `ImageData` object returned. This `ImageData` object contains three attributes; `width`, the width of the pixel area you're accessing, `height`, the height of the pixel area, and `data`, a `CanvasPixelArray` that contains information about all the pixels in the area that you're accessing.

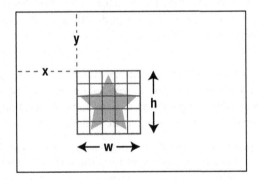

Figure 5-12. Visualizing a call to the getImageData method

My hope is that the `width` and `height` attributes are self-explanatory; what we're really interested in is the `data` attribute. Stored within the `data` attribute is a `CanvasPixelArray`, a one-dimensional JavaScript array; each pixel represented by four integer values ranging from 0 to 255 that refer to the red (r), green (g), blue (b), and alpha (a) values (see Figure 5-13). So, the first four entries in the array (0-3) are the color values for the first pixel; the next four entries (4-7) are the color values for the second pixel, and so on. The `CanvasPixelArray` is where all the fun stuff happens, so it's important to get an understanding about exactly how it works.

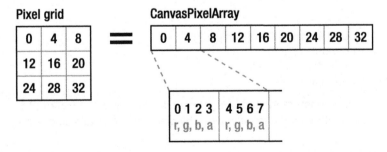

Figure 5-13. The CanvasPixelArray for a 3×3 region

As a brief example before I explain everything, this is how you would access the RGBA values for the first pixel in the CanvasPixelArray, using the index numbers defined in Figure 5-13.

```
var imageData = context.getImageData(0, 0, 3, 3); // 3x3 grid
var pixel = imageData.data; // CanvasPixelArray

var red = pixel[0];
var green = pixel[1];
var blue = pixel[2];
var alpha = pixel[3];
```

A CanvasPixelArray has absolutely no knowledge of the dimensions of the pixel area that you're accessing. Instead, the array that gets returned is effectively just one long set of RGBA color values, equal to the number of pixels in the area that you're accessing multiplied by four (four color values for each pixel). For example, if you accessed a pixel grid with a width and height of three pixels, the CanvasPixelArray would have a length of 36 ($3 \times 3 \times 4$); a width and height of 200 would mean a length of 160,000 ($200 \times 200 \times 4$), and so on.

The order of pixels within a CanvasPixelArray is straightforward: the top left pixel is at the start of the array (from positions 0, red, to 3, alpha), and the bottom right pixel is at the end of the array. This means that in the area that you're accessing, the pixels go in a left to right direction until they reach the end of a row, then return to the beginning of the next row and go from left to right again (see the grid in Figure 5-13).

So, if a CanvasPixelArray is just one long string of color values that has no knowledge of the dimensions of the pixel area, how do you access a specific pixel from the array? In the example in Figure 5-13, how would you access the central pixel in the grid at (x, y) position (2, 2)? By looking at the diagram you can obviously see that it starts at index 16 in the array, but how would you know that without drawing it out? I wouldn't worry if you have absolutely no idea, as this is where I became completely and utterly confused when I was learning canvas. It messes with your head! Fortunately, some people who are cleverer than I have come up with a formula that allows you to get exactly the right pixel that you want from a CanvasPixelArray, and it's surprisingly easy to understand:

```
var imageData = context.getImageData(0, 0, 3, 3); // 3x3 grid

var width = imageData.width;
var x = 2;
var y = 2;

var pixelRed = ((y-1)*(width*4))+((x-1)*4);
var pixelGreen = pixelRed+1;
var pixelBlue = pixelRed+2;
var pixelAlpha = pixelRed+3;
```

The part of this that you're most interested in right now is the formula to work out the index for the red value of the pixel. Let's run through the formula piece by piece to see what's going on:

```
(y-1)
```

Because you're using non-zero coordinate values to define the (x, y) coordinate position of the pixel, you need to subtract the coordinate by one. This just converts the coordinate system that you're used to from the canvas to a zero-starting coordinate system for referencing the array.

```
(width*4)
```

This gives you the number of color values per row in the image. By multiplying the result of (y-1) with this number, you get the array index number at the beginning of the row that you're accessing (the y position). In the case of this example the index returned is 12, which matches with the second row in Figure 5-13.

```
(x-1)*4
```

Here you're first repeating the same thing that you did with the y position – converting to a zero-starting coordinate system. You then multiply the column that you're after (the x position) by four to get the number of color values in a row that exist before the column that you're accessing.

By adding the column index number to the row index number, you get a final number that gives you the index of the first color (red) for the pixel that you're after; which should be 16 for this example (see Figure 5-14).

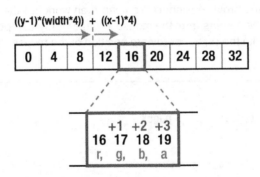

Figure 5-14. Accessing a pixel within the CanvasPixelArray

Once you have the index of the red pixel, the rest is trivial. To get the remaining three color values – green, blue, and alpha – you simply add one, two, or three to the red index, respectively.

I appreciate that this isn't an easy concept to grasp, but I hope that I've explained it enough for you to understand the how and why behind accessing pixel values in canvas.

Before you move on, let's have a bit of fun by creating a simple color picker.

```
var image = new Image();
image.src = "example.jpg";
$(image).load(function() {
        context.drawImage(image, 0, 0, 500, 333);
});

canvas.click(function(e) {
```

```
    var canvasOffset = canvas.offset();
    var canvasX = Math.floor(e.pageX-canvasOffset.left);
    var canvasY = Math.floor(e.pageY-canvasOffset.top);

    var imageData = context.getImageData(canvasX, canvasY, 1, 1);
    var pixel = imageData.data;
    var pixelColor = "rgba("+pixel[0]+", "+pixel[1]+", "+pixel[2]+",
"+pixel[3]+")";

    $("body").css("backgroundColor", pixelColor);
});
```

I'm going to skip over the first few lines, as you already know what they do. The part that is interesting to you is the jQuery click method, which is called when a mouse click event is fired on the attached element; in your case, the canvas. The callback function in the click method passes an argument to you that contains information about the event, which you've referred to as e. This argument contains the mouse (x, y) coordinates of the click in relation to the whole browser window, which you're going to use to work out where a click has happened on the actual canvas.

By using the jQuery offset method, you're able to find out how many pixels are between the canvas and the top and the left sides of the browser window. You can then work out the x position on the canvas by subtracting the left offset of the canvas from the mouse x (pageX). If you repeat the same for the mouse y and top offset, you'll end up with the (x, y) coordinate position of the mouse click in relation to the origin of the canvas (see Figure 5-15).

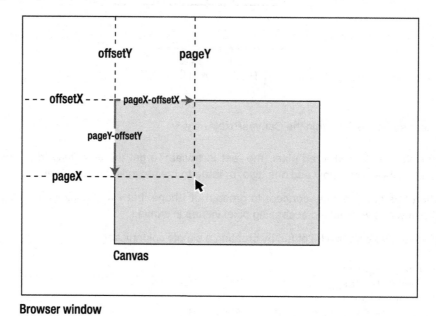

Figure 5-15. Finding the (x, y) coordinate of a mouse click on the canvas

Now you know the (*x, y*) position of the click on the canvas, the next step is retrieving the pixel color values at that point. To do that you pass the canvasX and canvasY values into a call to getImageData. You're only after the data for a single pixel, so that's why you've set the width and height of the call to getImageData to one; it just keeps the data as small as possible.

Once you have the ImageData object, it's just a case of storing it somewhere and accessing the CanvasPixelArray in the data attribute. As you only got the data of a single pixel, retrieving the color values is as simple as accessing the first four indexes in the CanvasPixelArray. You're going to change the CSS background of the whole Web page, so you use those values to construct a string representation of a CSS RGBA color value.

The final step is to pass that CSS color value to the jQuery css method, which allows you to change the background-color CSS property of the HTML body element. If all went well, this will set the background color of the Web page to the pixel that you clicked on the canvas (see Figure 5-16).

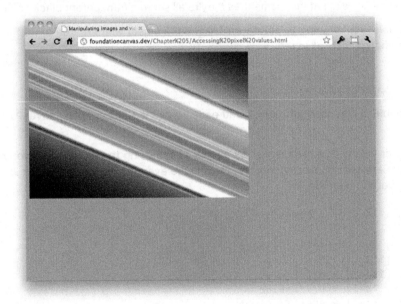

Figure 5-16. Changing the background color based on a canvas pixel color

Security issues

If you're working through these examples on your own computer, without uploading them to a web server, you might have noticed that either nothing happens or you get a security error. The reason for this is that canvas is pretty strict about accessing pixel-level data from images that aren't from the same place as the JavaScript that is controlling the canvas. The easy way to fix this problem is to run these examples on a web server, or a local development environment, like MAMP on the Mac, or WAMP on Windows. The important part of the solution is that both the JavaScript and image that you're accessing need to be accessed by the same domain name (such as rawkes.com). You might have noticed from the screenshots that I'm running the examples on a local development environment with the foundationcanvas.dev domain name.

As a rule of thumb, check that you're running everything off the same domain name if you run into issues with pixel manipulation.

Creating an image from scratch

The last section was pretty dense, but it will be worth it as you can now move onto the really cool stuff, like creating pixels from thin air to make your very own images.

To create pixels you need to call the createImageData method of the 2d rendering context. By passing the method a width and height, you'll get returned an ImageData object with all the usual attributes: width, height, and most important, data. The CanvasPixelArray contained in the data attribute holds your new pixels, which are invisible at the moment as they're all set to a transparent black color.

In the next example, you're going to create an ImageData object with an area of 200 × 200 transparent pixels, and then change them all to red.

```
var imageData = context.createImageData(200, 200);
var pixels = imageData.data;
```

The pixels variable is just used as a quick and easy way to the access the CanvasPixelArray for the pixels.

Changing the color values of a pixel is just as simple as retrieving the color value: you read or write the color value in the CanvasPixelArray. You want to change every pixel to red, so a for loop is needed that cycles through every single pixel.

```
var numPixels = imageData.width*imageData.height;

for (var i = 0; i < numPixels; i++) {
        pixels[i*4] = 255; // Red
        pixels[i*4+1] = 0; // Green
        pixels[i*4+2] = 0; // Blue
        pixels[i*4+3] = 255; // Alpha
};
```

The numPixels variable holds the number of pixels in the ImageData object, giving you the number of times needed to run the for loop. Within each loop you assign the color values for each pixel using a simple algorithm. You know each pixel has four color values, so by multiplying the pixel number by four you get the index of the red color value for that pixel in the CanvasPixelArray. You're then able to set the red color value to 255 (full color), green and blue to 0, and the alpha to 255 so it's opaque. Simple!

As it stands, all you've done is create an ImageData object and change the pixels to red. You won't be able to see anything on the canvas because you haven't drawn the new pixels onto it yet. To do this you need to call the putImageData method of the 2d rendering context. This method takes three or seven arguments: an ImageData object, the (x, y) coordinate origin to draw the pixel data, the (x, y) coordinate origin of something called a dirty rectangle, the width of the dirty rectangle, and its height. You can forget about the dirty rectangle for the purposes of this example; all it does is define which pixels to draw from the ImageData object.

```
context.putImageData(imageData, 0, 0);
```

This will draw your new red pixels at the canvas origin (see Figure 5-17).

Figure 5-17. Creating and drawing pixels from scratch

Randomizing pixels

A red set of pixels is great and all, but let's take things one step further and completely randomize the colors. It's really easy.

```
for (var i = 0; i < numPixels; i++) {
        pixels[i*4] = Math.floor(Math.random()*255); // Red
        pixels[i*4+1] = Math.floor(Math.random()*255); // Green
        pixels[i*4+2] = Math.floor(Math.random()*255); // Blue
        pixels[i*4+3] = 255; // Alpha
};
```

By changing the section of the previous example that deals with setting color values, you're able to insert a random number between 0 and 255. You want to keep the alpha value as 255, otherwise some of your pixels will be slightly transparent. Note how you're using Math.floor to round down the resulting random number (eg. 150.456 would become 150).

The result of this is a slightly sickening mess of pixels (see Figure 5-18).

Note: `Math.random` works by giving you a random decimal number between 0 and 1. You can then multiply that number by another number to get a random number between 0 and number that is being used for multiplication. For example, `Math.random()*255` will give you a random number between 0 and 255.

Figure 5-18. Randomizing the color of pixels drawn to the canvas

Creating a mosaic effect

So, a mess of pixels isn't the best use of canvas. How about creating a nice mosaic effect? That's definitely a little more interesting. You'll do this is by creating an area of new pixels, then splitting it up into a grid and setting each segment of the grid to a random color. The complicated part is trying to work out what segment each pixel falls into, so you can set the same color for the pixels that are in the same segment. If you look at Figure 5-19 you'll see how each segment would actually be made up of many pixels.

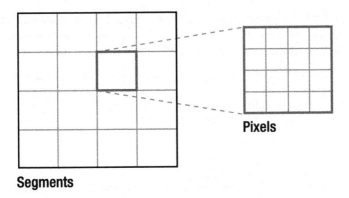

Pixels

Segments

Figure 5-19. Splitting the canvas into a grid of segments of pixels

I'll go through how to work out the pixels within each segment shortly. For now, let's set up the groundwork for the mosaic.

```
var imageData = context.createImageData(500, 500);
var pixels = imageData.data;

// Number of mosaic tiles
var numTileRows = 4;
var numTileCols = 4;

// Dimensions of each tile
var tileWidth = imageData.width/numTileCols;
var tileHeight = imageData.height/numTileRows;
```

The first two lines should be second nature to you by now; they set up an ImageData object of 500 × 500 pixels, and store the CanvasPixelArray in a variable. Following those lines are two variables that are being used to declare the number of segments that you want to break the area of pixels into; the amount per row, and the amount per column. From now on we'll refer to segments as tiles, as it's a better description of what they actually are. The last two lines calculate the width and height of each tile in pixels, based on the dimensions of the ImageData object, and the number of tiles per row and column.

You now have enough information to start looping through the tiles and changing the pixel color values.

```
for (var r = 0; r < numTileRows; r++) {
        for (var c = 0; c < numTileCols; c++) {
                // Set the pixel values for each tile
                var red = Math.floor(Math.random()*255);
                var green = Math.floor(Math.random()*255);
                var blue = Math.floor(Math.random()*255);


        };
};
```

This is a nested loop; the first looping through each row of tiles, the second looping through each column of tiles within the current row (see the left grid in Figure 5-20). Each tile has a new set of color values assigned, based on random numbers between 0 and 255. It's all pretty basic stuff so far.

Now, within the column loop and underneath the color values, you want to declare two more loops:

```
for (var tr = 0; tr < tileHeight; tr++) {
        for (var tc = 0; tc < tileWidth; tc++) {

        };
};
```

These loops cycle the same number of times as the pixels within each tile, based on the tile dimensions that you calculated previously. The tr and tc variables represent the pixel row (based on the tile height) and pixel column (based on the tile width) that you're accessing for the current tile (see the right grid in Figure 5-20). In this example, each tile is 125 pixels wide and 125 pixels tall, so tr will loop 125 times, and within each of those loops, tc will loop a further 125 times.

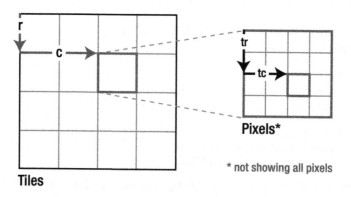

Figure 5-20. Looping through each tile, and each pixel within a tile

However, this still doesn't give you access to the actual pixels within each tile. All you know right now is the row and column of the tile that you're on (the r and c variables), and the row and column of the pixel that you're on within that tile (the tr and tc variables). On their own, these variables aren't enough to access a pixel from the CanvasPixelArray. To do that you need to convert them into a zero-starting (x, y) position of the pixel, as it would be if there were no tiles. It sounds a bit crazy, but bear with me.

Add the following within the second loop, and I'll explain what's going on; it's really simple:

```
var trueX = (c*tileWidth)+tc;
var trueY = (r*tileHeight)+tr;
```

These two variables calculate the true position of the pixel. For example, to calculate the x position you first multiply the current tile column (2) by the width of a single tile (125), which gives you the x position at the left hand edge of the tile that you're on (2 × 125 = 250). From there you add the column number of the pixel that you're accessing within that tile (e.g. 10), which will give you the exact x position as if there were no tiles (250 + 10 = 260). By repeating the same process for *y*, you get the (*x, y*) coordinates that you need to start changing pixels color values.

Add the following after assigning values to trueX and trueY:

```
var pos = (trueY*(imageData.width*4))+(trueX*4);

pixels[pos] = red;
pixels[pos+1] = green;
pixels[pos+2] = blue;
pixels[pos+3] = 255;
```

There is nothing new here; all you're doing is accessing the red color value for the pixel that you're after, and then assigning the color values that you set earlier. Because you're using zero-based counting here, you don't have to subtract trueX and trueY by 1, like you did when you originally saw this formula.

The final step is to draw your pixels onto the canvas, so add the following call to putImageData outside and underneath of the four loops:

```
context.putImageData(imageData, 0, 0);
```

If all went well, you should get a lovely mosaic effect on the canvas (see Figure 5-21).

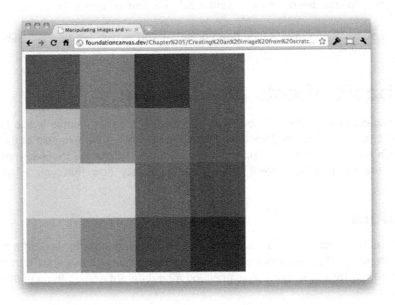

Figure 5-21. The finished mosaic effect

You can even change the number of tiles per row and column to create a much more interesting effect (see Figure 5-22).

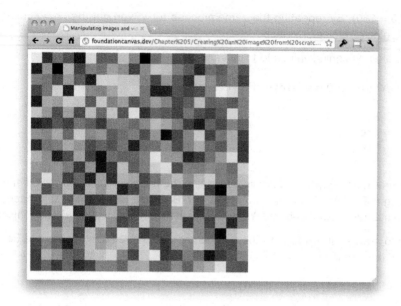

Figure 5-22. Changing the number of tiles to create a different mosaic effect

I think you should sit back and take a nice deep breath – you've achieved an incredible amount in this section!

Applying basic effects to an image

Changing color values of pixels doesn't mean that you have to create an entire image from scratch; you could always just change the look of something that already exists. One example of this would be basic photo manipulation – the modification of pixels within an image to change the way that it looks. These kinds of effects are trivial to implement in canvas, especially now that you're an expert in pixel manipulation.

Inverting colors

This effect reverses the color values of an image and causes it to look, for lack of a better word, a bit weird. The basic premise is that you subtract the existing color value of a pixel (150), from 255 to reverse, or invert, the color (255-150=105). Let's try something a bit different and go through the code in one go; there's nothing new.

```
var image = new Image();
image.src = "example.jpg";
$(image).load(function() {
        context.drawImage(image, 0, 0, 1024, 683, 0, 0, 500, 500);

        var imageData = context.getImageData(0, 0, canvas.width(), canvas.height());
```

```
        var pixels = imageData.data;
        var numPixels = pixels.length;

        context.clearRect(0, 0, canvas.width(), canvas.height());

        for (var i = 0; i < numPixels; i++) {
                pixels[i*4] = 255-pixels[i*4]; // Red
                pixels[i*4+1] = 255-pixels[i*4+1]; // Green
                pixels[i*4+2] = 255-pixels[i*4+2]; // Blue
        };

        context.putImageData(imageData, 0, 0);
});
```

The first few lines create a new `Image` object and load in the example image that you used in previous sections. After waiting for the image to load, you draw the image to the canvas and store the `ImageData` object containing all the pixels in a variable. Once you've got the pixels stored, you clear the canvas and start a loop that runs for as many times as there are pixels in the original image.

Within the loop you use the same approach as the first example in the previous section (the red square) to access the pixels and subtract the current values from 255. You don't need to do anything with the alpha value, as you want to keep the value that was used in the original image.

The last thing to do is draw the pixels back onto the canvas, which should leave you with an inverted image (see Figure 5-23). Weird!

Figure 5-23. Inverting the colors of an image

Grayscale

Another cool effect, and perhaps a slightly more useful one, is grayscale. This is the conversion of a color image into one that uses shades of gray; sometimes referred to as black and white, although that's not an accurate description. The code is identical to the inversion example, apart from the part that accesses and changes the color values.

```
for (var i = 0; i < numPixels; i++) {
        var average = (pixels[i*4]+pixels[i*4+1]+pixels[i*4+2])/3;
        pixels[i*4] = average; // Red
        pixels[i*4+1] = average; // Green
        pixels[i*4+2] = average; // Blue
};
```

Converting colors into grayscale requires you to find the average of the existing color values, by adding them all together and dividing by the number of colors. You use the averaged color as the value for all three colors; red, green, and blue. The result will be a shade of gray for each color (see Figure 5-24).

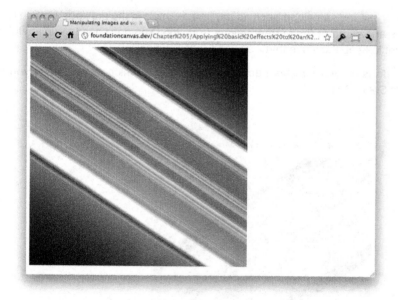

Figure 5-24. Converting an image to grayscale

Pixelation

Have you ever watched the news or a documentary and seen a person with a pixelated face? It's a great effect that allows you to make part of an image unrecognizable, without literally removing an entire section. It's actually relatively easy to recreate in canvas; you just split an image into a grid and either average the colors within each segment, or pick a color within each segment. The code that you're going to use is very similar to that of the mosaic example in the last section.

```
var image = new Image();
image.src = "example.jpg";
$(image).load(function() {
        context.drawImage(image, 0, 0, 1024, 683, 0, 0, 500, 500);

        var imageData = context.getImageData(0, 0, canvas.width(), canvas.height());
        var pixels = imageData.data;

        context.clearRect(0, 0, canvas.width(), canvas.height());

        var numTileRows = 20;
        var numTileCols = 20;

        var tileWidth = imageData.width/numTileCols;
        var tileHeight = imageData.height/numTileRows;

        for (var r = 0; r < numTileRows; r++) {
                for (var c = 0; c < numTileCols; c++) {

                };
        };
});
```

You already know everything up to the loops. You're accessing the image, waiting for it to load, drawing it to the canvas, storing the ImageData object, clearing the image from the canvas, and assigning values that define the quantity and dimensions of the tiles (segments) into which you're splitting the image.

The two loops work in the same way at the mosaic example: the first loops through each row of tiles, while the second loops through each tile within the current row. The juicy new stuff is within the loops; this is where you're accessing the color values and creating the pixelated effect.

You're going to use the second method to grab a color for the pixelated effect, picking a single color within each tile. The simplest way to do this is to use the pixel at the centre of the tile, which you can work out by adding the following code inside the second loop.

```
var x = (c*tileWidth)+(tileWidth/2);
var y = (r*tileHeight)+(tileHeight/2);

var pos = (Math.floor(y)*(imageData.width*4))+(Math.floor(x)*4);
```

The first two lines give you the zero-starting (x, y) coordinate of the central pixel within the current tile. The calculations work in a very similar way to the mosaic example, in that you find the (x, y) coordinate position at the edge of the tile, and then add half the width or height to find the centre. This (x, y) coordinate position is then plugged into the standard formula that gives you the index number of the pixel in the CanvasPixelArray. Although you'll notice that you're wrapping the (x, y) values in the floor method of the Math object. The reason for this is that the returned index will be wrong unless the (x, y) values are integers, so you use floor to round the value to the next lowest integer (e.g., 3.567 would become 3).

Finally, you now have everything you need to access the color values and draw the pixelated effect. Insert the following code after declaring the pos variable.

```
var red = pixels[pos];
var green = pixels[pos+1];
var blue = pixels[pos+2];

context.fillStyle = "rgb("+red+", "+green+", "+blue+")";
context.fillRect(x-(tileWidth/2), y-(tileHeight/2), tileWidth, tileHeight);
```

None of this should be new to you; all you're doing is accessing the red, green, and blue color values and using them to set the fillStyle. The final step is to draw a square in the place of the tile, which is filled using the color that you just accessed. The result is a pretty impressive looking pixelated version of the example image (see Figure 5-25).

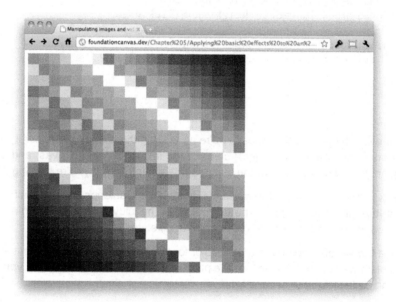

Figure 5-25. Pixelating an image using canvas

You could even take this a step further and change the squares to circles (see Figure 5-26).

```
context.beginPath();
context.arc(x, y, tileWidth/2, 0, Math.PI*2, false);
context.closePath();
context.fill();
```

Now that is very cool, if I do say so myself!

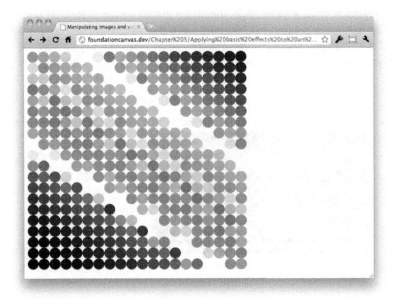

Figure 5-26. Pixelating an image in canvas using circles instead of squares

Manipulating video

Back in the first section of this chapter, I mentioned how the drawImage method can accept a HTML5 video element as input. It's now time to explore this interesting and exciting area of image manipulation in canvas, by pixelating a video. Now, if you're expecting video manipulation to be difficult, then I'm afraid you're going to be severely disappointed; it's hardly any different to manipulating images! However, it's definitely much cooler.

Creating the HTML5 video element

Before you can start doing the cool stuff, you need to set up the HTML5 video element. Insert the following inside of the body element of the HTML page.

```
<video id="myVideo" width="500" height="281" controls>
        <source src="example.mp4" type="video/mp4"></source>
        <source src="example.ogg" type="video/ogg"></source>
</video>
```

You're using an example video that has been provided with the code (thanks to James Watson), but feel free to use your own video if you'd like. If you do use your own video, then remember to change the width and height of the video element, and encode it in both MPEG-4 and OGG format if you want it accessible on the majority of browsers.

As it stands, the only code in your Web page should be the basic template that was provided when you learned about the 2d rendering context in Chapter 3, with the video element as the only code within the body element. If all went well you should have something that looks like Figure 5-27. You should be able to play the video, as you used the controls attribute when defining the video element.

Figure 5-27. Adding a HTML5 video to the web page

Accessing the HTML5 video API

Although this is undoubtedly cool (HTML5 video just *is*), it's nothing compared to what you're about to do. The next step is to create a couple of HTML button elements that you're going to use to control the video using JavaScript. Insert the following code below the video element.

```
<div>
        <button id="play">Play</button>
        <button id="stop">Stop</button>
</div>
```

Linking these buttons up with the video is a relatively straightforward task in JavaScript; you just access the HTML5 video element API. To do this you'll need to put the following code inside the document ready function in the script element.

```
var video = $("#myVideo");

$("#play").click(function() {
        video.get(0).play();
});
```

```
$("#stop").click(function() {
        video.get(0).pause();
});
```

The first line assigns the jQuery object for the `video` element to the `video` variable. Following that are two calls to the jQuery `click` method; each with a callback function. Within each callback function is a call to a HTML5 `video` element API method; one calling `play`, and the other calling `pause`. Both of these methods are part of the video DOM object; so you'll need to call the jQuery `get` method beforehand, just like you do when accessing the 2d rendering context with the `canvas` element. Calling `play` and `pause` is all you need to do to start and stop the video from JavaScript (see Figure 5-28); it really is that simple!

Figure 5-28. Controlling a HTML5 video through the JavaScript API

Setting up the canvas

Seeing as you're going to be using a near identical pixelation effect as in the previous section, you won't actually need to see the original video. So, let's kill two birds with one stone and put the `video` element inside of a canvas element that is the same dimensions as the original video.

```
<canvas id="myCanvas" width="500" height="281">
        <video id="myVideo" width="500" height="281" controls="true">
                <source src="example.mp4" type="video/mp4"></source>
                <source src="example.ogg" type="video/ogg"></source>
        </video>
</canvas>
```

It's also worth setting up the trusty JavaScript variables to store the canvas objects.

```
var canvas = $("#myCanvas");
var context = canvas.get(0).getContext("2d");
```

Anyone who uses a browser that supports HTML5 canvas will see nothing, while anyone using a browser that doesn't support HTML5 canvas, but that supports HTML5 video, will see the video. For now, you want to be able to see nothing; that's a good thing (see Figure 5-29).

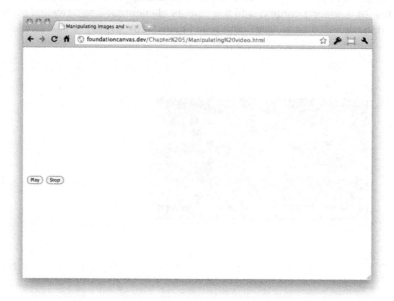

Figure 5-29. Putting the HTML5 video inside of a canvas element

There are a few things you need to do in preparation for manipulating the video. Insert the following code below the context variable:

```
video.bind("play", function() {
        drawCanvas();
});

function drawCanvas() {
        if (video.get(0).paused || video.get(0).ended)
                return false;

};
```

The first thing that you're doing is using the jQuery bind method to create a callback function that is run whenever the video starts playing; you do this by listening for the *play* event. Within the callback function, you're calling a custom function that you're about to create. This function will hold all the functionality that creates the pixelated effect and draws everything to the canvas.

Creating the drawCanvas function is the second thing that you're doing. By using a conditional statement, you're able to check whether the video is paused or stopped and, if so, stop the function from running by issuing a call to return. You can find out the status of the video by checking the values of the paused and ended attributes of the HTML5 video API. It's good practice to perform checks like this so you don't run things unnecessarily, like trying to pixelate the video if it's not actually playing any longer.

Now it's time to get creative and pixelate the video. This is the fun part! Insert the following code below the conditional statement.

```
context.drawImage(video.get(0), 0, 0, 500, 281);

var imageData = context.getImageData(0, 0, canvas.width(), canvas.height());
var pixels = imageData.data;

context.clearRect(0, 0, canvas.width(), canvas.height());

var numTileRows = 36;
var numTileCols = 64;

var tileWidth = imageData.width/numTileCols;
var tileHeight = imageData.height/numTileRows;

for (var r = 0; r < numTileRows; r++) {
        for (var c = 0; c < numTileCols; c++) {
                var x = (c*tileWidth)+(tileWidth/2);
                var y = (r*tileHeight)+(tileHeight/2);

                var pos = (Math.floor(y)*(imageData.width*4))+(Math.floor(x)*4);

                var red = pixels[pos];
                var green = pixels[pos+1];
                var blue = pixels[pos+2];

                context.fillStyle = "rgb("+red+", "+green+", "+blue+")";
                context.fillRect(x-(tileWidth/2), y-(tileHeight/2), tileWidth,
tileHeight);
        };
};
```

Everything in this code is the same as the pixelation code you used in the previous section, apart from the first line and the number of tiles per row and column. The first line, the call to drawImage, is different because it now takes the HTML5 video element as the first argument. This works because drawImage uses the current frame of a HTML5 video element to draw onto the canvas, which is useless if you only call it once (it would be a static image), but amazing if you call it at the same speed as the video. You'll see how to do that bit in a moment.

Calculating the number of tiles per row and column is done by first working out the ratio of the video (281÷500=0.562); then deciding on an arbitrary number of tiles per row (e.g., 64), and using the ratio to calculate the tiles per column (64×0.562=35.968=36). This will give you tiles that are, for all intents and purposes, square. Simple!

The final nail in the coffin for this effect is to add a timer to the end of the drawCanvas() method that calls the method again at roughly the same speed as the frame-rate of the video. You can do this by adding a setTimeout call after the two loops in the drawCanvas function.

```
setTimeout(drawCanvas, 30);
```

This timer will run very, very fast, but because of the check at the top of drawCanvas, it will only run if the video is actually playing.

If all went well, and I'm sure it did, you should get a pixelated video showing on the canvas when you click the play button (see Figure 5-30).

Figure 5-30. The finished pixelation effect on a HTML5 video

Clicking the stop button will pause the video and the pixelation effect, and clicking play again will continue from wherever you paused it. You could even change the rectangles for circles like in the pixelation example in the last section (see Figure 5-31)!

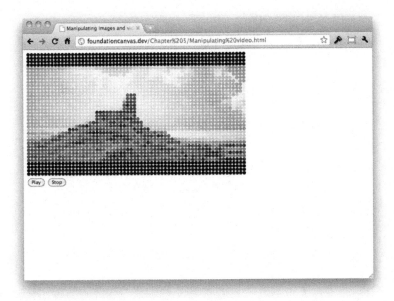

Figure 5-31. Using circles instead of square for the pixelation

Some congratulations are in order I reckon; you've achieved something pretty amazing in this section. You'd definitely find it incredibly difficult to find someone who doesn't drool at the awesomeness of this video manipulation.

Summary

On a scale of one to complex, this chapter was well up there on the old complexity. You should definitely be proud about what you've achieved in the space of a few pages. Actually, it was more than a few pages, but you get the idea.

You've learned how to load an image into the canvas, and you've learned about resizing and cropping of images to get them to display how you want. You even learned how to transform images to create some pretty wild effects. You've taken things to a higher level and discovered the world of pixel manipulation, something that is genuinely pretty hard to grasp on the first sitting. I'd definitely encourage you to go back and look at pixel manipulation again if you're still a little unsure about it.

The climax of the chapter was looking at how to use pixel manipulation to create your own images, as well as using it to perform modifications on existing images. The final project you created showed you how to modify HTML5 video; a feature of canvas that is pretty darn inspiring.

This has been a wild chapter, but the techniques that you've learn here will probably prove to be some of the most visually stunning out of everything that you'll learn in this book. From here on we're going to look at how to inject some motion into your static canvas drawings; learning everything that you'll need to create some amazing games.

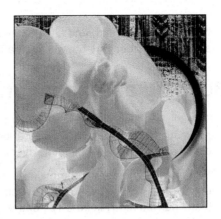

Chapter 6

Making Things Move

In this chapter, you're going to animate shapes using nothing but the power of JavaScript and your brain. You'll start by learning how animating in canvas actually works, which you'll then put into practice by creating your very first animation loop. From there, you'll discover a method that allows you to remember everything that you want to animate, and then you'll explore a variety of ways to actually animate your shapes. The chapter ends by showing you how to give your shapes a small amount of intelligence, which enables them to bounce off the edges of the canvas instead of disappearing off, never to be seen again.

Overview of animating in canvas

Animating in canvas is really no different from animating in general, at least in theory. If you cut it down to the basics, animation is just a bunch of images, each slightly different, that are displayed in succession at incredible speed. The trick is to show enough images per second to trick the human eye into thinking that what it sees is a moving object, not a bunch of static images being shown one after another. It's exactly how those paper flip-books work that you made back in school; if you flip the pages fast enough it looks like the little drawings are moving.

You can't flip pages in canvas, so a different approach is required. If you think about it, you only have one sheet of paper when animating using code; that sheet being the computer screen. This means that you can't physically flip through loads of pages of drawings, so instead you attack the problem from a different angle. Flipping through loads of pages of drawings is effectively the same as drawing something on the screen (the first page), clearing everything from the screen (the transition between the first and second page), and then quickly drawing something else on the screen—updating the drawing (the second page). It's the same concept as the flip-book, but it's executed in a slightly different way.

The great thing is that you already know everything that you need to know to create dynamic animations in canvas; you know how to draw something on the screen, and you know how to clear everything from the screen. That part is easy. The harder part is automating the whole process of animation so that it occurs many times a second, and also remembers exactly what you're drawing and where you want to draw it. I say it's the harder part, but what I meant to say was that it's really not that hard at all!

Building an animation loop

The animation loop is where the juicy fun stuff happens, and it's really easy to set up. I should probably point out that, although it's called a loop, it has nothing to do with for loops, or anything like that. It's called a loop because it happens over and over, which you'll see shortly.

You already know the three main elements of an animation loop: updating everything that needs to be drawn (e.g., moving the position of something), clearing the canvas, and then drawing everything back on to the canvas (see Figure 6-1). For the types of animations that you'll be creating in this chapter, it doesn't really matter which order you perform the tasks in; just make sure that you don't draw before clear, because otherwise you won't see anything!

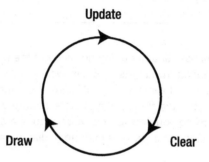

Figure 6-1. A typical animation loop in canvas

The loop

Let's jump right in and create the animation loop.

```
var canvas = $("#myCanvas");
var context = canvas.get(0).getContext("2d");

var canvasWidth = canvas.width();
var canvasHeight = canvas.height();

function animate() {
        setTimeout(animate, 33);
};

animate();
```

You're really only interested in the animate function, which you can see is very basic. As it stands, the animate function sets a timer using setTimeout that will call the animate function again in 33 milliseconds, which basically creates an endless loop. To start the loop, you just need to call the animate function outside of the loop. You probably don't want to leave the loop running forever, as it'll suck unnecessary computer resources, so it's best to stick in a kill switch.

Add the following buttons after your canvas element:

```
<div>
        <button id="startAnimation">Start</button>
        <button id="stopAnimation">Stop</button>
</div>
```

And then add the logic to deal with the buttons above the animate function:

```
var playAnimation = true;

var startButton = $("#startAnimation");
var stopButton = $("#stopAnimation");

startButton.hide();
startButton.click(function() {
        $(this).hide();
        stopButton.show();

        playAnimation = true;
        animate();
});

stopButton.click(function() {
        $(this).hide();
        startButton.show();

        playAnimation = false;
});
```

The logic here is quite simple: the playAnimation variable holds a boolean value that is used to stop or play the animation loop. The jQuery code hooks into the click event for each button, which then hides the button that you just clicked, shows the other one, and then sets the playAnimation variable to the right value. The start button is slightly different because once the animation is stopped, you need to manually start the loop again to bring it back to life. To do this you just add in an extra call to the animate function.

None of this will actually affect the animation loop yet; to do that, you need to add a single conditional statement around the setTimeout.

```
if (playAnimation) {
        setTimeout(animate, 33);
};
```

This will cause the animation loop to cease running if the playAnimation variable holds a false value. Try it out; you won't see anything animating, but the buttons should toggle between start and stop.

> *Note: Why are you using 33 milliseconds in the animation loop? Well, it's fairly common for animations to be between 25 and 30 frames per second. There are 1,000 milliseconds in a second, so when you divide that by 30 you get 33 milliseconds. You're more than welcome to put in a different number to speed up or slow down the animation. Anything between 30 and 40 will produce an adequate animation effect for your purposes in this chapter.*

Update. Clear. Draw.

Now that the basic animation loop has been set up, you can start to add in the functionality for the update, clear, and draw processes that were mentioned earlier (refer to Figure 6-1). Let's put together a simple animation that moves a square 1 pixel to the right on every frame. The first thing you need to do is set up a variable outside of the `animate` function that holds the current *x* position of the square:

```
var x = 0;
```

Now you have a way of remembering where the square is between each loop of the animation, you can add in all three processes (update, clear, draw) in one go. Place the following inside the `animate` function, above the `setTimeout`:

```
x++;
context.clearRect(0, 0, canvasWidth, canvasHeight);
context.fillRect(x, 250, 10, 10);
```

The first line updates the *x* position of the square by increasing it by 1 on each loop; double plus after a variable just means add 1 to the existing value. The same line could be rewritten as the following:

```
x = x + 1;
```

The second line is the clear process, and effectively just wipes the canvas clean, ready to draw the square on line 3, which is the third and final process. Plugging the *x* variable into the `fillRect` method call means that it will always draw the square at the current *x* position, which is always increasing (see Figure 6-2).

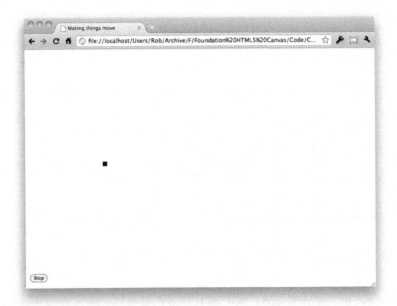

Figure 6-2. Moving a square using basic animation

If all went well, then you should have a little black square moving across the canvas. Clicking stop will cause the square to stop moving, and clicking start will set the square moving again. You've just created your first proper animation in canvas. Awesome!

Remembering shapes to be drawn

One of the main challenges to overcome once you've got an animation loop up and running is remembering exactly what you want to draw, and exactly where you want to draw it. We touched on this briefly in the last section by placing a variable outside of the loop, which held a value that described the position of the object to be drawn. Coupled with the `fillRect` call, within the loop that used the position variable, you have enough information to know what you're drawing, and where to draw it. But what if you want to animate multiple shapes? What if you don't even know how many shapes you're going to be animating when you create the loop? A slightly more robust approach is needed.

The wrong way

You might be tempted to store the position values for each shape as a separate variable outside of the animation loop. Why not? It worked for one shape, so why wouldn't it work for multiple shapes? And you'd be right – it would work, it would just be ugly, it would duplicate code, and it would be complicated to modify shapes in the future.

Here is an example of how you'd change the code in the previous section to animate multiple shapes:

```
var firstX = 0;
var secondX = 50;
```

```
var thirdX = 100;

function animate() {
        firstX++;
        secondX++;
        thirdX++;

        context.clearRect(0, 0, canvasWidth, canvasHeight);

        context.fillRect(firstX, 50, 10, 10);
        context.fillRect(secondX, 100, 10, 10);
        context.fillRect(thirdX, 150, 10, 10);

        if (playAnimation) {
                setTimeout(animate, 33);
        };
};

animate();
```

I've deliberately left out all the other code, like the button events, as we're only really interested in this part here for now.

The only difference between this example and the previous one is that you're effectively writing out three times as many position variables and calls to fillRect. However, there is absolutely no reason why it wouldn't work, as you can see in Figure 6-3.

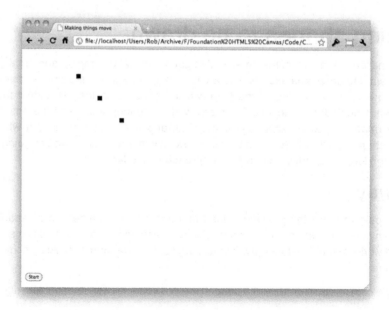

Figure 6-3. Remembering multiple shapes, the wrong way

This may work fine for you, but what if you have hundreds of shapes to draw? Are you seriously telling me that you'd be alright with writing out hundreds of position variables and hundreds of calls to fillRect? Of course not! This is why you're using code to animate, because it allows you to automate things and make them easier.

The right way

So if creating multiple variables is a long and complicated way, what can you use to make things easier? In short, objects and arrays. There are essentially two issues that need to be solved; the first is how to go about storing position values for each of the shapes, regardless of how many there are, and the second is how to go about drawing each of those shapes without duplicating your code.

The solution to the first issue is simple, and it will lead you directly to the solution for the second issue. You already know the position data needed for each shape – its x value. However, you're going to take this a step further and chuck in the y value as well. So if you know that each shape has the same two types of position value, you can create a JavaScript class that creates shape objects:

```
var Shape = function(x, y) {
        this.x = x;
        this.y = y;
};
```

If you don't remember how objects work, head back to Chapter 2 and run through them again. It's an important concept to grasp, as you'll be using it a lot in the games at the end of the book. In a nutshell, objects allow you to define a template for some *thing*, by giving it properties (like the number of wings on a rocket) and methods (like turning a rocket's engines on).

However, defining an object isn't enough; you still need a way to store them so you don't have to manually refer to hundreds of different shapes. To do this you can store your shape objects in an array, which keeps them all neatly tucked away in a single place:

```
var shapes = new Array();

shapes.push(new Shape(50, 50));
shapes.push(new Shape(100, 100));
shapes.push(new Shape(150, 150));
```

To add the shape objects to the array, you're using the push method of the Array object. It might sound complicated, but all it does is add something to the end of an array; which, in your case, is a shape object. It is exactly the same as doing something like this:

```
var shapes = new Array();

shapes[0] = new Shape(50, 50);
shapes[1] = new Shape(100, 100);
shapes[2] = new Shape(150, 150);
```

The benefit to using push is that you don't need to know the number of the last element in the array; it automatically adds it on to the end for you. It's pretty nifty!

What you have now is a set of shapes, each with a different *x* and *y* position, which are stored away inside an array that has been assigned to the shapes variable. The next step is working out how to get all these shapes back out of the array, update their positions (to animate them), and then draw them. To do that you need to put a for loop inside of the animation loop:

```
function animate() {
        context.clearRect(0, 0, canvasWidth, canvasHeight);

        var shapesLength = shapes.length;
        for (var i = 0; i < shapesLength; i++) {
                var tmpShape = shapes[i];
                tmpShape.x++;
                context.fillRect(tmpShape.x, tmpShape.y, 10, 10);
        };

        if (playAnimation) {
                setTimeout(animate, 33);
        };
};
```

The for loop cycles through every shape in the array and assigns it to the shape variable so you can access it easily. From there you now have a reference to the current shape in the array, so all you need to do is update its *x* property, and then use the *x* and *y* properties to draw it in the correct position.

Here is the full code, which should give you an animation identical to the previous example (see Figure 6-4):

```
var canvasWidth = canvas.width();
var canvasHeight = canvas.height();

var playAnimation = true;

var startButton = $("#startAnimation");
var stopButton = $("#stopAnimation");

startButton.hide();
startButton.click(function() {
        $(this).hide();
        stopButton.show();

        playAnimation = true;
        animate();
});

stopButton.click(function() {
        $(this).hide();
        startButton.show();

        playAnimation = false;
```

```
});

var Shape = function(x, y) {
        this.x = x;
        this.y = y;
};

var shapes = new Array();

shapes.push(new Shape(50, 50, 10, 10));
shapes.push(new Shape(100, 100, 10, 10));
shapes.push(new Shape(150, 150, 10, 10));

function animate() {
        context.clearRect(0, 0, canvasWidth, canvasHeight);

        var shapesLength = shapes.length;
        for (var i = 0; i < shapesLength; i++) {
                var tmpShape = shapes[i];
                tmpShape.x++;
                context.fillRect(tmpShape.x, tmpShape.y, 10, 10);
        };

        if (playAnimation) {
                setTimeout(animate, 33);
        };
};

animate();
```

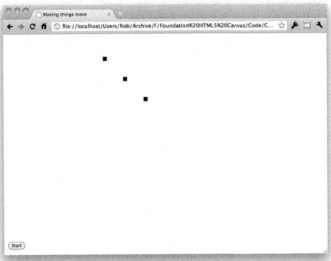

Figure 6-4. Remembering multiple shapes, the right way

Randomizing shapes

Now that you have a quick and easy way to create shapes, there's nothing to stop you randomizing their creation. The cool thing is that because you're using objects, it's dead simple. First off, you need to change the Shape class to define a width and height:

```
var Shape = function(x, y, width, height) {
        this.x = x;
        this.y = y;
        this.width = width;
        this.height = height;
};
```

Then, to randomize the starting position and size of each shape, replace the three shapes.push statements with the following:

```
for (var i = 0; i < 10; i++) {
        var x = Math.random()*250;
        var y = Math.random()*250;
        var width = height = Math.random()*50;
        shapes.push(new Shape(x, y, width, height));
};
```

The weird double assignment for the width and height variables gives them each the same value. You'll also need to change the call to fillRect to take the new width and height into consideration:

```
context.fillRect(tmpShape.x, tmpShape.y, tmpShape.width, tmpShape.height);
```

And that is all there is to it. The beauty of using classes and objects means that you really don't have to edit much to add or remove new features to your code. If you check out the new example, you should have a selection of ten shapes moving across the browser, all a different size and in a different position (see Figure 6-5).

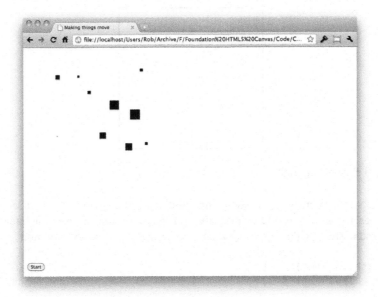

Figure 6-5. Randomizing the size and position of shapes

Changing direction

So far we've covered how to animate, but we haven't really focused on how to control the way a shape animates. I'm not sure about you, but I'd get pretty bored of animating shapes in a straight line all the time.

You already know about animating a shape to the right (by increasing the *x* value), but what about if you want to change the speed, or change the direction of the animation? It's easy; you just change the amount that you increase (or decrease) the *x* and *y* values by. If you use the same code from the previous example, you can easily cause the shapes to animate diagonally down to the right by swapping tmpShape.x++ for the following:

```
tmpShape.x += 2;
tmpShape.y++;
```

The difference here is that you're now increasing the *x* value by 2, instead of 1, and you're increasing the *y* value by 1. This has the effect of moving each shape two pixels to the right, and one pixel down on each loop of the animation; a diagonal line (see Figure 6-6).

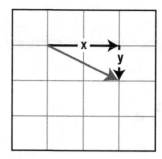

Figure 6-6. Moving a shape diagonally

Or, you could do something quite interesting and randomize the *x* and *y* values on each loop of the animation. This gives the effect of unpredictability and mayhem; the shapes will basically appear to be freaking out. It sounds silly, but it's a great way to make something look less scripted:

```
tmpShape.x += Math.random()*4-2;
tmpShape.y += Math.random()*4-2;
```

What you're doing here is creating a random number between 0 and 4 (`Math.random` gives you a number between 0 and 1, which you're then multiplying by 4), and then subtracting 2 to get a random number between –2 and 2. This will allow the shapes to move right (positive *x*), left (negative *x*), up (negative *y*), and down (positive *y*).

If you try this in the browser, the shapes will move randomly forward and backward, appearing to wiggle on the spot. Funky!

Animating along a circle

There is absolutely no reason why you should be limited to moving shapes in straight lines. What if you want to animate something to move around a circle, like an orbit (see Figure 6-7)? The good news is that it's completely possible, and it doesn't use much code; the bad news is that it uses trigonometry, which might take a little while to get your head around.

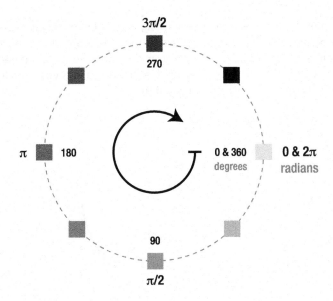

Figure 6-7. Animating a shape in a circular orbit

The concept is simple; you take a shape, and place it on the very edge of a circle (its perimeter). You can start at any position on the perimeter, but for the sake of simplicity you're going to place the shape at the angle of 0 radians on the perimeter; the right hand side (see Figure 6-7). From here you simply increase the angle that the shape is placed on the perimeter every loop of the animation, causing it to move around in a circular motion. It all sounds so easy when you write it out, so let's find out exactly how to do it.

Trigonometry

The issue that you are trying to solve, is how to calculate the (x, y) coordinate value of your shape at a position along a circle's circumference (see Figure 6-8). It sounds pretty tricky, but it's actually quite a simple problem that you're trying to solve; but you'll only notice that if you look at it in the right way.

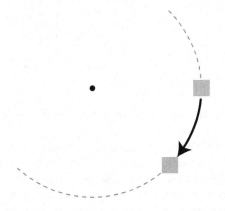

Figure 6-8. Finding the coordinate value at a position along a circumference

Before you can solve anything, you need to know how big the circle actually is. You can choose any size you want; after all, it's your example! The actual size doesn't matter; what's important is that you can describe the size of a circle by its radius (the length from the center to the circumference). If you plot the radius on the circle that you're trying to animate around, at the angle that you want to move your shape to, you'll start to notice something interesting (see Figure 6-9).

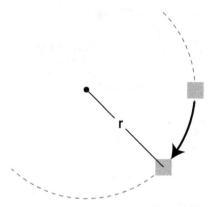

Figure 6-9. Plotting the radius highlights an interesting pattern

See it yet? If you squint extra hard, and perhaps even tilt your head a bit, you may just, if you're lucky, see the side of a triangle. I wouldn't worry if you don't; it's quite a stretch of the imagination if this is all new to you. The triangle I'm talking about is shown in Figure 6-10.

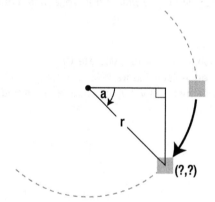

Figure 6-10. The radius is one side of a right-angle triangle within the circle

So, there's a triangle in your circle. Awesome. But why is it useful to you? Well, this triangle gives you absolutely everything you need to know to solve the (x, y) coordinate position of the shape in its new position along the circle. The long answer is that now you have a triangle and two angles (the position around the circle, and the 90 degree corner of the triangle), you can plug in some basic trigonometry to get the values that you're after. This is why mathematics is actually pretty darn useful. However, before you jump in and solve the problem, let me briefly explain how we're going to put trigonometry to work here.

The basic gist of trigonometry is that if you know one angle of a triangle is 90 degrees, and you know one of the other angles, you can then work out the ratio of the lengths of the triangle. This ratio can then be used to calculate the lengths of the sides in whatever unit you wish, which in your case is pixels. To do this, you need to know for which sides of the triangle you need to work out the lengths, as there is a different trigonometric rule that you use for each of them. The three sides are the hypotenuse (the longest side), the adjacent (the side that is adjacent to the angle you already know that isn't 90 degrees), and the opposite (the side opposite the angle you already know). Check out Figure 6-11 for a full rundown.

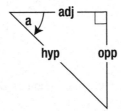

Figure 6-11. Describing the three sides of a right-angle triangle

To work out the ratio of each side, you use one of the three trigonometric functions: sine (sin), cosine (cos), or tangent (tan). Sine is the ratio of the opposite leg to the hypotenuse, cosine is the ratio of the adjacent to the hypotenuse, and tangent is the ratio of the opposite to the adjacent (see Figure 6-12). You may have heard of these functions referred to as SOH-CAH-TOA, which translates to sine-opposite-hypotenuse, cosine-adjacent-hypotenuse, and tangent-opposite-adjacent. By plugging in the angle that you know to the correct function, you'll get the ratio required to work this whole thing out

$$\sin(a) = \frac{opp}{hyp} \quad \cos(a) = \frac{adj}{hyp} \quad \tan(a) = \frac{opp}{adj}$$

Figure 6-12. SOH-CAH-TOA formula

For your example, you want to know the length of the adjacent and the opposite sides of the triangle, which translate to the *x* and *y* positions respectively (see Figure 6-13). To work out the lengths, you first need to work out the ratios by plugging the known angle into the respective trigonometric functions. In JavaScript, you can work out these ratios by using the Math object:

```
var angle = 45;
var adjRatio = Math.cos(angle*(Math.PI/180)); // CAH
var oppRatio = Math.sin(angle*(Math.PI/180)); // SOH
```

You'll notice a little calculation being performed in the cos and sin methods of the Math object. The calculation is converting the angle from degrees to an angle in radians, which is the unit used by JavaScript (as discussed in Chapter 3). It's worth noting that if you deal in radians from the start, you won't have to do any converting.

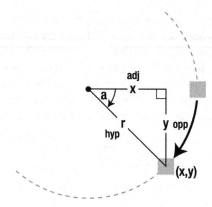

Figure 6-13. Using trigonometry to find the ratio of each side of the triangle

These ratios are only half of the story. The other half, and with it the final answer, is comparing those ratios to the length of the hypotenuse – the length of which you already know because it's the radius (see Figure 6-14). This is achieved by multiplying the radius by the ratios, like so:

```
var radius = 50;
var x = radius * adjRatio;
var y = radius * oppRatio;
```

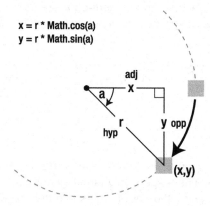

Figure 6-14. Calculating the coordinate values using the ratios of each side

Putting everything together

Now that you're able to calculate the (x, y) coordinate origin of a shape at an angle along a circle, you should have no problem putting it all together into a working example. The first step is to update the Shape class and give it a couple of new properties:

```
var Shape = function(x, y, width, height) {
    this.x = x;
```

```
        this.y = y;
        this.width = width;
        this.height = height;

        this.radius = Math.random()*30;
        this.angle = 0;
};
```

These two properties set the starting angle and calculate a random radius for the circle between zero and thirty. The penultimate step is to replace the existing code in the animation loop that updates the shapes, with the following:

```
var x = tmpShape.x+(tmpShape.radius*Math.cos(tmpShape.angle*(Math.PI/180)));
var y = tmpShape.y+(tmpShape.radius*Math.sin(tmpShape.angle*(Math.PI/180)));

tmpShape.angle += 5;
if (tmpShape.angle > 360) {
        tmpShape.angle = 0;
};
```

The first two lines are nothing new; they each calculate the *x* and *y* positions of the shape at its current angle along the circle, defined by the radius. This gives you a position value that assumes that the center of the circle is at (0, 0), so you move it into the correct position by adding it onto the (*x*, *y*) position you defined in the shape. Take note that the (*x*, *y*) position defined in the shape object now refers to the center of the circle, not the origin of the shape – the position that the shape will rotate around. The last few lines increase the angle in degrees on every loop of the animation, and reset the angle to 0 if it goes above 360 (a full circle).

Finally, plug in the new x and y variables into the fillRect method:

```
context.fillRect(x, y, tmpShape.width, tmpShape.height);
```

If everything went well, you should have a selection of shapes all moving around their own separate circles (see Figure 6-15). You'd never have guessed such a simple effect would have been so complicated to achieve!

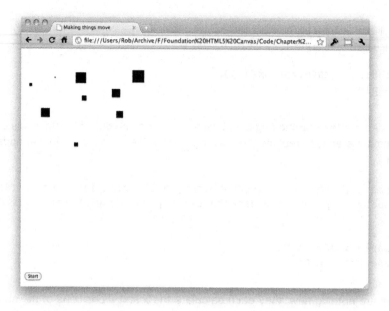

Figure 6-15. A selection of shapes moving in circular orbits

It's been a bit of a tough section, so here is the full code for you to get your head around:

```
var canvas = $("#myCanvas");
var context = canvas.get(0).getContext("2d");

var canvasWidth = canvas.width();
var canvasHeight = canvas.height();

var playAnimation = true;

var startButton = $("#startAnimation");
var stopButton = $("#stopAnimation");

startButton.hide();
startButton.click(function() {
        $(this).hide();
        stopButton.show();

        playAnimation = true;
        animate();
});

stopButton.click(function() {
        $(this).hide();
        startButton.show();
```

```
            playAnimation = false;
});

var Shape = function(x, y, width, height) {
        this.x = x;
        this.y = y;
        this.width = width;
        this.height = height;

        this.radius = Math.random()*30;
        this.angle = 0;
};

var shapes = new Array();

for (var i = 0; i < 10; i++) {
        var x = Math.random()*250;
        var y = Math.random()*250;
        var width = height = Math.random()*30;
        shapes.push(new Shape(x, y, width, height));
};

function animate() {
        context.clearRect(0, 0, canvasWidth, canvasHeight);

        var shapesLength = shapes.length;
        for (var i = 0; i < shapesLength; i++) {
                var tmpShape = shapes[i];

                var x =
tmpShape.x+(tmpShape.radius*Math.cos(tmpShape.angle*(Math.PI/180)));
                var y =
tmpShape.y+(tmpShape.radius*Math.sin(tmpShape.angle*(Math.PI/180)));

                tmpShape.angle += 5;
                if (tmpShape.angle > 360) {
                        tmpShape.angle = 0;
                };
                context.fillRect(x, y, tmpShape.width, tmpShape.height);
        };

        if (playAnimation) {
                setTimeout(animate, 33);
        };
};

animate();
```

Bouncing objects off a boundary

If you hadn't already noticed, there are effectively no boundaries to the examples used so far. What I mean by this is that nothing happens when a shape animates up to the edge of the canvas; it just disappears, never to be seen again. This may be the effect that you're after; for example, if you're only creating a short animation that stops long before you reach an edge, or if you want to animate a shape over the edge of the canvas. But, what if you don't want this behavior? What if you want shapes to be aware of their surroundings, by perhaps bouncing off the edges and reversing their direction? This is a behavior that changes an animation from something quite linear and scripted, to something more natural and unpredictable.

Before you start learning how to achieve this behavior, prepare the code using techniques learned from this chapter:

```
var canvasWidth = canvas.width();
var canvasHeight = canvas.height();

var playAnimation = true;

var startButton = $("#startAnimation");
var stopButton = $("#stopAnimation");

startButton.hide();
startButton.click(function() {
        $(this).hide();
        stopButton.show();

        playAnimation = true;
        animate();
});

stopButton.click(function() {
        $(this).hide();
        startButton.show();

        playAnimation = false;
});

var Shape = function(x, y, width, height) {
        this.x = x;
        this.y = y;
        this.width = width;
        this.height = height;
};

var shapes = new Array();

for (var i = 0; i < 10; i++) {
```

```
        var x = Math.random()*250;
        var y = Math.random()*250;
        var width = height = Math.random()*30;
        shapes.push(new Shape(x, y, width, height));
};

function animate() {
        context.clearRect(0, 0, canvasWidth, canvasHeight);

        var shapesLength = shapes.length;
        for (var i = 0; i < shapesLength; i++) {
                var tmpShape = shapes[i];
                context.fillRect(tmpShape.x, tmpShape.y, tmpShape.width,
tmpShape.height);
        };

        if (playAnimation) {
                setTimeout(animate, 33);
        };
};

animate();
```

All you're doing here is setting up a clean animation loop that is going through ten randomly generated shapes. As it stands, the code won't actually animate anything visually, as no modifications are made to the properties of a shape within the animation loop (like increasing the x position to move a shape to the right).

The process used to make your shapes aware of the canvas boundary is surprisingly simple. Let's assume that you have a shape that moves to the right one pixel every loop. Once that shape moves to the right edge of the canvas boundary (say 500 pixels), it will just continue on its journey, with the x value increasing, but will no longer be visible on the canvas. The behavior you actually want is for the shape to bounce off the right edge of the canvas, just like as if it were a solid wall. To do this you need to check to see if the shape is beyond the right edge of the canvas boundary and, if so, reverse its direction of travel so it appears to bounce off of it.

Figure 6-16 outlines the basic concept of this effect, with each loop of the animation being represented by the number within the moving ball. The left side shows how a shape would normally react, without a boundary, and the right side shows how a shape should react, if there was a boundary.

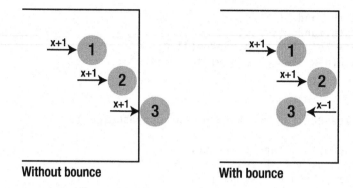

Without bounce **With bounce**

Figure 6-16. The concept of bouncing a shape off a boundary

Working out whether a shape is beyond the right edge of the canvas boundary is a case of checking its x position with the width of the canvas. If the shape's x position is larger than the width of the canvas, then the shape must be beyond the right edge. The same process is used to check whether the shape is beyond the left edge of the canvas, which you know has an x origin of 0. By checking to see whether the x position of the shape is lower than 0, you will know if the shape is to the left of the left edge of the canvas, and therefore to the left of the boundary. And again, the same process is used to check whether the shape is within the top and bottom edges of the canvas; by checking if the y position is below 0 for the top edge, and checking if the y position is above the height of the canvas for the bottom edge.

By putting this all together you can create a simple set of logic that bounces the shapes off all the edges of the canvas boundary. The first step is to add a couple of new properties to the Shape class, which will define whether the shape has hit a boundary and the direction of travel needs to be reversed:

```
this.reverseX = false;
this.reverseY = false;
```

These properties are set to false by default, which means that the shapes will travel to the right and downwards in this example. The next step is to add the logic that checks whether your shape is outside of the canvas boundary. Insert the following below the call to `fillRect` in the animation loop:

```
if (tmpShape.x < 0) {
        tmpShape.reverseX = false;
} else if (tmpShape.x + tmpShape.width > canvasWidth) {
        tmpShape.reverseX = true;
};

if (tmpShape.y < 0) {
        tmpShape.reverseY = false;
} else if (tmpShape.y + tmpShape.height > canvasHeight) {
        tmpShape.reverseY = true;
};
```

Each of these checks will reverse the direction of travel when a shape is seen to be outside of a boundary. However, setting the boolean values won't actually change the direction of travel, to do that you need to add some more checks, this time *above* the call to fillRect:

```
if (!tmpShape.reverseX) {
        tmpShape.x += 2;
} else {
        tmpShape.x -= 2;
};

if (!tmpShape.reverseY) {
        tmpShape.y += 2;
} else {
        tmpShape.y -= 2;
};
```

This is where the magic happens. These checks will either move the shape to the right (by adding to the *x* position) if there is no reversal on the *x* axis, or left (by subtracting from the *x* position) if the *x* axis is reversed. The same checks are performed on the *y* axis.

As a result of these relatively simple checks, you should get a set of shapes that appear to bounce off the edges of the canvas (see Figure 6-17). You could even change the default values of the Shape class properties for reversing direction to change the way the shapes move.

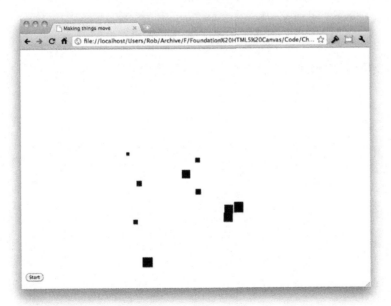

Figure 6-17. A set of shapes that bounce off of a boundary

This method of using a variety of simple checks is exactly how you'll be implementing some pretty awesome features in the side-scroller game in Chapter 9.

Summary

In this chapter, we've looked more at theory and animation techniques than at learning specifically about canvas. You've learned how animation works, with a loop and the remembering of shapes. You've also learned a variety of ways how to animate a shape, and how to change the direction of the animation, even animating the shapes around a circle. The chapter ended by showing you how to bounce shapes off the edges of the canvas, giving the appearance of basic intelligence and physical properties.

My hope is that this chapter has shown you that quite visually interesting and complicated effects can actually be produced using quite simple theories that require barely any code. The essence of animating, particularly in canvas, is often to take the simplest option, so long as it looks and feels like what you were trying to achieve. These are exactly the principles that you're going to explore in the next chapter, which is all about advanced animation with physics. Very cool stuff indeed!

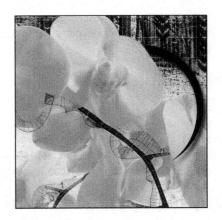

Chapter 7

Implementing Advanced Animation

In this chapter, you're going to take your animation to the next level by introducing physics. You're going to learn all there is to know about the concepts involved in realistic motion, and you'll find out exactly how to apply those concepts in JavaScript. Toward the end of the chapter, you'll explore the theory behind collision detection between objects, and how to cause objects to bounce off of each other.

This is the last chapter before you start making games. It's going to be a tough one, but I'm confident that you'll enjoy it; after all, the results will be incredibly impressive!

Introduction to physics

If you're anything like me, when you hear the word "physics" you instantly think of those tedious math and science lessons you had as a teenager. I think the problem with those lessons was that they just didn't make math and physics interesting enough. Why would I care how long it takes an apple to fall from a tree? What will calculating the trajectory of a ball thrown into the air tell me? And what use is knowing the physics involved in a car speeding up, slowing down, or moving in general? The problem I had back then was that, outside of the examples you got in class, there was absolutely nothing to apply these concepts to in real life. It felt like I was being taught math and science for the sake of being taught, rather than being taught with a particular purpose in mind.

Fast forward ten or so years and something strange has happened. Far from my younger self who found math and science interesting, but never got *why* I'd ever need it, I've now fallen in love with it all. More specifically, I've fallen in love with physics and the opportunities that it opens. I'm not going to lie to you; I'm no expert in physics, but I sure find it fun, and I'd love to try and make you feel the same way about it. The secret is to apply it to something practical; that is, learning it with a particular purpose in mind. In your case, that purpose is learning how to animate objects in a realistic way using JavaScript. See, it already sounds more fun than those old math lessons!

So let's crack on and explore some of the finer details of physics, starting with an overview of physics in general.

What is physics?

In short, physics is a natural science that explores matter and energy. Specifically, physics looks at the mechanics of the natural world and aims to understand how and why everything behaves as it does. The areas of physics that you're interested in right now are directly related to how objects move, and the things that affect the way objects move. There are many, many more branches of physics that could be explored, but for the sake of your sanity and mine, we'll stick with the basics for today.

Why is physics useful for animation?

If it isn't already obvious by now, by understanding physics you'll be able to produce much more realistic and dynamic animations. Whether you apply concepts like velocity and acceleration, or construct a fully fledged system with all sort of conflicting forces, learning physics will allow you to really open up the possibilities with animation. The concepts of physics aren't just things that I believe will make good animation; they are concepts that are tried and tested in all sorts of animation, from games and data visualizations all the way to cartoons and movies.

Some basics terms

One of the key aspects to understanding physics is being aware of the basic terms and units that are used in the more complex concepts. You won't actually be using them all, but just knowing about them is a good start. They'll make more sense once you start to use them in code.

Force

This is the push or pull that acts on an object. It is something that causes an object to change its speed, direction, or shape. A force has both a magnitude (size or length) and direction, which means it can be visualized as a vector. The unit of force is the newton (N).

Vector

This is an entity that has both a magnitude and direction, like a force. A vector is represented in a graphical sense by a straight line that travels from an origin point to a destination point. The length represents the magnitude of the vector, and an arrow is commonly used to indicate the direction of travel.

Mass

This is the resistance of an object to being accelerated by a force; it's also known as inertia. Mass directly affects the amount of acceleration that results when a force is applied to an object. For example, the same force applied to two objects with varying masses will result in the object with the larger mass accelerating slower than the object with the smaller mass. The unit of mass is the kilogram (kg).

Weight

This is the resulting force that occurs when an object's mass is affected by the gravitational force of another object; it is what makes an object feel heavy. Weight is calculated by multiplying an object's mass by the force of gravity, which is why an object on Earth is heavier than the same object in deep space – there is much less gravity in deep space. On Earth, weight is referred to in units of mass (kg), but it should actually be referred to in units of force: the newton (N).

Friction

This is the force that resists the movement of one object across the surface of another. It is friction that makes ice more slippery compared to something like a carpet.

Velocity

This is the direction and speed of an object. It is a vector, and is usually referred to in the unit meters per second with an attached direction (e.g., west). Average velocity is calculated by dividing the speed of an object by the period of time that has passed.

Speed

This is the magnitude of the velocity of an object, which represents the distance an object has traveled over time. It's a directionless quantity (scalar), and is usually referred to in the unit meters per second (m/s), kilometers per hour (km/h), or miles per hour (mph). Average speed is calculated by dividing the distance an object has traveled by the time it took to travel there.

Acceleration

This is the rate an object's velocity changes over time, in both magnitude and direction. Acceleration generally refers to an increase in speed, with deceleration referring to a decrease. An object can have a speed and no acceleration; this is because acceleration is relative to the previous velocity of an object. For example, if an object is traveling at a constant velocity, it is not accelerating (getting faster), but it does still have a speed. It is a vector, and is usually referred to in the unit meters per second per second (m/s^2). Acceleration is calculated via Newton's second law of motion, which is described in the next section.

Newton's laws of motion

Some genius, who went by the name of Sir Isaac Newton, decided it would be a fantastic idea to describe motion in three simple laws. These laws allow you to work out how forces affect the motion of an object, which is an incredibly useful thing to be able to do when you want natural and dynamic animation. Thanks, Isaac!

First law

If no force acts on an object, it will move in a straight line at a constant velocity. If the object is at rest, it will stay at rest. In short, an object will only move when an external force is applied to it.

Second law

A force applied to an object with mass will accelerate in the same direction as the force and at a magnitude that is proportional to the force (increases in size with), and inversely proportional to the mass (decreases in size with). It is represented by the famous equation $F = ma$, which means force equals mass multiplied by the acceleration. The same formula can also be used to calculate the mass, and acceleration of an object.

Third law

Every action has an equal and opposite reaction. Ring any bells? This is probably one of the most well known of Newton's three laws. In reality, it means that if an object (A) exerts a force on another object (B), then object B will exert an equal and opposite force on object (A). However, this doesn't mean that the two objects will accelerate at the same speed; as we already know from Newton's second law, that will only happen if they have the same mass.

There is plenty more to learn about physics, but I fear if I delve into anything more complex I will scare you away. It really is an area that holds immensely useful concepts and ideas that will aid in your quest for awesomely realistic animations and simulations. You'll be using a whole variety of the concepts discussed here when creating the games in the following two chapters, but first let's explore how to apply each of the main concepts to animation.

> *Note: If you want to learn more about physics, then definitely check out the various Wikipedia pages on the subject area.[1] Some of it takes a little while to understand, so my advice would be to try and make something practical in JavaScript that uses what you're trying to learn. I always find that I only truly learn by jumping in and putting concepts into practice.*

Animating with physics

It's important to get to grips with each of the core concepts of physics in JavaScript before you move on to creating amazing games with them. In this section, you're going to create a simple space scene, which has a dynamic asteroid field lurking in the deep. I'm not going to lie; it's going to be pretty darn cool.

Getting everything ready

If you haven't been doing so already, you're now going to split the JavaScript code away from the HTML page and store it in a separate JavaScript file. It was in Chapter 2 that I talked about how storing your JavaScript in a separate file can help keep things organized, and how it's generally good practice. The initial JavaScript for this section is nothing new; in fact, it's practically the same as what you used in the previous chapter. The main difference is that where you referred to shapes in the last chapter, you're now referring to asteroids.

---

[1] http://en.wikipedia.org/wiki/Index_of_physics_articles

Place the following code in an external JavaScript file and give it a useful name, like *asteroids.js*:

```javascript
$(document).ready(function() {
        var canvas = $("#myCanvas");
        var context = canvas.get(0).getContext("2d");

        var canvasWidth = canvas.width();
        var canvasHeight = canvas.height();

        $(window).resize(resizeCanvas);

        function resizeCanvas() {
                canvas.attr("width", $(window).get(0).innerWidth);
                canvas.attr("height", $(window).get(0).innerHeight);
                canvasWidth = canvas.width();
                canvasHeight = canvas.height();
        };

        resizeCanvas();

        var playAnimation = true;

        var startButton = $("#startAnimation");
        var stopButton = $("#stopAnimation");

        startButton.hide();
        startButton.click(function() {
                $(this).hide();
                stopButton.show();
                playAnimation = true;
                animate();
        });

        stopButton.click(function() {
                $(this).hide();
                startButton.show();
                playAnimation = false;
        });

        var Asteroid = function(x, y, radius) {
                this.x = x;
                this.y = y;
                this.radius = radius;
        };

        var asteroids = new Array();

        for (var i = 0; i < 10; i++) {
                var x = 20+(Math.random()*(canvasWidth-40));
```

```
                var y = 20+(Math.random()*(canvasHeight-40));
                var radius = 5+Math.random()*10;

                asteroids.push(new Asteroid(x, y, radius));
        };

        function animate() {
                context.clearRect(0, 0, canvasWidth, canvasHeight);
                context.fillStyle = "rgb(255, 255, 255)";

                var asteroidsLength = asteroids.length;
                for (var i = 0; i < asteroidsLength; i++) {
                        var tmpAsteroid = asteroids[i];

                        context.beginPath();
                        context.arc(tmpAsteroid.x, tmpAsteroid.y,
tmpAsteroid.radius, 0,↪
 Math.PI*2, false);
                        context.closePath();
                        context.fill();
                };

                if (playAnimation) {
                        setTimeout(animate, 33);
                };
        };

        animate();
});
```

The next step is the CSS file, which is going to prepare everything so you can make the canvas fit the full width of the browser window. You're also going to use the CSS to move the start and stop buttons, as they'll be pushed outside of the browser otherwise (as the canvas is filling the window).

Place the following code in an external CSS file in the same directory as the JavaScript file, and give it a useful name, like *canvas.css*:

```
* { margin: 0; padding: 0; }
html, body { height: 100%; width: 100%; }
canvas { display: block; }

#myCanvas {
        background: #001022;
}

#myButtons {
        bottom: 20px;
        left: 20px;
        position: absolute;
```

```
}

#myButtons button {
        padding: 5px;
}
```

Finally, you need to set up the HTML file that ties everything together. This is exactly the same as the HTML file in the previous chapters, but it's a lot smaller, because all the JavaScript is in an external file. Note the extra `script` element that is calling the JavaScript file; you'll need to change the name of the file if you chose something other than *asteroids.js*.

Place the following code in a HTML file in the same directory as the other files, and call it *index.html*:

```html
<!DOCTYPE html>

<html>
        <head>
                <title>Implementing advanced animation</title>
                <meta charset="utf-8">

                <link href="canvas.css" rel="stylesheet" type="text/css">

                <script type="text/javascript"
src="http://ajax.googleapis.com/ajax/libs/↵
jquery/1/jquery.min.js"></script>
                <script type="text/javascript" src="asteroids.js"></script>
        </head>

        <body>
                <canvas id="myCanvas" width="500" height="500">
                        <!-- Insert fallback content here -->
                </canvas>
                <div id="myButtons">
                        <button id="startAnimation">Start</button>
                        <button id="stopAnimation">Stop</button>
                </div>
        </body>
</html>
```

If you load up the HTML page in a modern browser, then you should see a blue spacey background (the canvas), with a stop button in the bottom left hand corner, and a splattering of asteroids (see Figure 7-1). You do? Excellent. Now you're ready to crack on and start becoming a master of physics. You should be able to feel your brain getting bigger as I speak!

Just a quick note: you may want to click the stop button to stop the canvas animation running unnecessarily in the background. It's up to you.

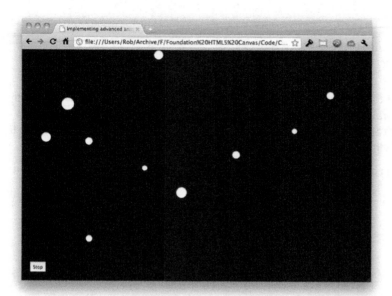

Figure 7-1. Setting up a basic space background

Velocity

In Chapter 6, you animated each shape by increasing or decreasing its *x* and *y* position. The cool thing is that, as simple as it was, you effectively gave each shape a velocity. Remember, velocity is the speed and direction of an object; the speed is the amount of pixels moved, and the direction is up and down (*x*), or left and right (*y*). So, you've already done some physics and you didn't even know it!

The problem with the velocity in the previous chapter is that it's either been completely random, or the same for each shape, so let's mix things up a little and give an individual velocity to each asteroid (remember: shapes have been renamed as asteroids in this chapter). To do this you need to define two new properties within the Asteroid class, like so:

```
var Asteroid = function(x, y, radius, vX, vY) {
        this.x = x;
        this.y = y;
        this.radius = radius;

        this.vX = vX;
        this.vY = vY;
};
```

By adding the vX and vY properties, each asteroid can now have an individual velocity. Notice how arguments for vX and vY have been included in the class function, so you can set the velocity when a new asteroid is created. The next step is to set a velocity for each asteroid as you create it, which defines how many pixels the asteroid will move on each animation loop.

Within the loop that creates all the asteroids, you want to place the following code below the radius variable:

```
var vX = Math.random()*4-2;
var vY = Math.random()*4-2;
```

And you'll also want to replace the line after that with the following code, so you actually pass the new velocity to the Asteroid class as an argument:

```
asteroids.push(new Asteroid(x, y, radius, vX, vY));
```

In this example, you're setting the velocity as a random number between –2 and 2, in both the x and y axis. You already know that Math.random on its own will give you a decimal fraction between 0 and 1, so to get a number between –2 and 2 you need to do two things. The first thing is to multiply the random number by four, which will give you a random number between 0 and 4. The next step is simple, you just subtract that number by two and you'll end up with a number between –2 (0 minus 2) and 2 (4 minus 2). You can use this process to calculate a random number between any range.

As it stands, nothing will happen. To change this you'll want to use the new velocity properties to update the x and y positions of each asteroid. Add the following below the declaration of the tmpAsteroid variable in the animation loop:

```
tmpAsteroid.x += tmpAsteroid.vX;
tmpAsteroid.y += tmpAsteroid.vY;
```

This is basically the same as what you were doing in the last chapter; it adds a defined number of pixels to the current position of the asteroid. The difference is that you're now using a separate velocity for each asteroid, which means that they're all going to move at a different speed (amount of pixels per loop) and in a different direction. Abstracting motion like this is the secret to getting animations to look random and natural.

If you refresh or load the HTML file, you should get a bunch of semi-asteroid looking objects moving around the canvas (see Figure 7-2). Keep refreshing the page to see the asteroids start in different positions and move with different velocities; it's pretty cool! Be aware that there isn't a boundary at the moment, so you might want to click the stop button before you lose all your asteroids off the edge of the screen.

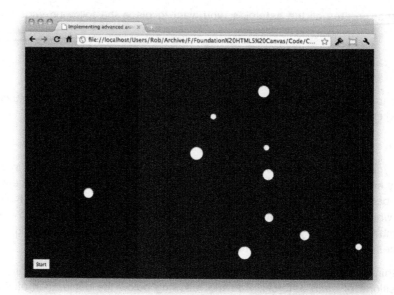

Figure 7-2. Setting up the asteroid field

Adding a boundary

Before we move on, let's put a boundary around the canvas to stop those pesky asteroids from escaping. The good news is that the code is very similar to what you used in the previous chapter; it just has a few tweaks to work with the new velocity logic. Add the following above the code in the animation loop that draws out each asteroid:

```
if (tmpAsteroid.x-tmpAsteroid.radius < 0) {
        tmpAsteroid.x = tmpAsteroid.radius;
        tmpAsteroid.vX *= -1;
} else if (tmpAsteroid.x+tmpAsteroid.radius > canvasWidth) {
        tmpAsteroid.x = canvasWidth-tmpAsteroid.radius;
        tmpAsteroid.vX *= -1;
};

if (tmpAsteroid.y-tmpAsteroid.radius < 0) {
        tmpAsteroid.y = tmpAsteroid.radius;
        tmpAsteroid.vY *= -1;
} else if (tmpAsteroid.y+tmpAsteroid.radius > canvasHeight) {
        tmpAsteroid.y = canvasHeight-tmpAsteroid.radius;
        tmpAsteroid.vY *= -1;
};
```

These two conditional statements check the position of each asteroid before it's drawn onto the canvas. If the edge of an asteroid is outside one of the boundaries, then it will be moved back inside of the boundary and its velocity will be reversed to send it in the opposite direction. If you don't move the asteroid back inside then it's possible for it to get stuck on, or escape the boundary completely. As you're using circles for the asteroids, it's important to remember that the (x, y) coordinate position will be in the center, so you will need to either add or subtract the circle's radius to find the *x* or *y* position at the edge.

If you refresh the page, you should now have a bunch of asteroids floating around and bouncing off the sides of the browser window. Now that you have full control over the pesky asteroids, it's time to explore some of the other areas of physics.

Acceleration

As you learned in the introduction to physics, acceleration is the change in velocity over a period of time, which is otherwise known as its increase in speed. Adding acceleration to the asteroids animation is very easy. In fact, it's nearly exactly the same as adding velocity, as acceleration also has a magnitude and direction; the magnitude being the amount of pixels to accelerate the asteroid, and the direction being the *x* and *y* axis of the acceleration.

You're going to let each asteroid have it's own acceleration, so the first thing you need to do is set up the necessary properties in the Asteroid class, and then use those properties when setting up each asteroid. Add the following properties to the Asteroid class:

```
this.aX = aX;
this.aY = aY;
```

Make sure to add the aX and aY arguments to the class function, just like you did for the velocity arguments. The final class should look like this:

```
var Asteroid = function(x, y, radius, vX, vY, aX, aY) {
        this.x = x;
        this.y = y;
        this.radius = radius;

        this.vX = vX;
        this.vY = vY;
        this.aX = aX;
        this.aY = aY;
};
```

The next step is to use these new properties when creating asteroids, so jump into the loop that creates asteroids, and add the following after the velocity variables:

```
var aX = Math.random()*0.2-0.1;
var aY = Math.random()*0.2-0.1;
```

This will give each asteroid an acceleration between –0.1 and 0.1. You'll soon see why it's such a small number.

The last thing to do in the loop is to add the new aX and aY variables as the last arguments in the call to new Asteroid, like so:

```
asteroids.push(new Asteroid(x, y, radius, vX, vY, aX, aY));
```

Nothing will happen as it stands, as you're yet to apply the acceleration to each asteroid. Applying acceleration is as simple as adding it to the current velocity of an object. After all, acceleration is the change in the velocity of an object; that is, it's the difference between the previous velocity and the current velocity.

Apply acceleration to each asteroid by adding the following code within the animation loop. You'll want to place it after where you're adding the velocity to the *x* and *y* position of each asteroid:

```
tmpAsteroid.vX += tmpAsteroid.aX;
tmpAsteroid.vY += tmpAsteroid.aY;
```

All this does is increase the velocity of each asteroid by the amount of acceleration, in pixels. This won't affect the asteroid in the current loop of the animation, but it will mean that the asteroid will have a different velocity on the next loop.

Before you can unleash your accelerated asteroids, you need to add a few lines to the boundary checks. As they stand, the boundary checks invert the velocity when an asteroid hits the edge of the window, which makes it bounce in the opposite direction. The acceleration is not being changed, so when an asteroid changes direction, its acceleration will try and force it back into the direction it was heading originally. If you refresh the browser now you'll see what I mean. It's cool, but nothing like what we want.

Fortunately, fixing this problem is simply a case of inverting the acceleration at the same time as inverting the velocity. Which results in a set of boundary checks, like so:

```
if (tmpAsteroid.x-tmpAsteroid.radius < 0) {
        tmpAsteroid.x = tmpAsteroid.radius;
        tmpAsteroid.vX *= -1;
        tmpAsteroid.aX *= -1;
} else if (tmpAsteroid.x+tmpAsteroid.radius > canvasWidth) {
        tmpAsteroid.x = canvasWidth-tmpAsteroid.radius;
        tmpAsteroid.vX *= -1;
        tmpAsteroid.aX *= -1;
};

if (tmpAsteroid.y-tmpAsteroid.radius < 0) {
        tmpAsteroid.y = tmpAsteroid.radius;
        tmpAsteroid.vY *= -1;
        tmpAsteroid.aY *= -1;
} else if (tmpAsteroid.y+tmpAsteroid.radius > canvasHeight) {
        tmpAsteroid.y = canvasHeight-tmpAsteroid.radius;
        tmpAsteroid.vY *= -1;
        tmpAsteroid.aY *= -1;
};
```

If you refresh the page again, you'll see the acceleration code working like a dream. In fact, the code is working so well that the asteroids will continue accelerating forever, causing them to fly around the screen at near light speed. Not ideal! Stopping the asteroids from continuously accelerating means adding a limit to the maximum velocity of each asteroid – a cosmic speed limit of sorts.

Replace the code that adds the acceleration to the velocity with the following:

```
if (Math.abs(tmpAsteroid.vX) < 10) {
        tmpAsteroid.vX += tmpAsteroid.aX;
};

if (Math.abs(tmpAsteroid.vY) < 10) {
        tmpAsteroid.vY += tmpAsteroid.aY;
};
```

This code only allows acceleration to be applied to an asteroid if its velocity is under ten pixels per loop. A simple check like this means that there is a limit on how fast an asteroid can actually go, resulting in a slightly less insane animation. It's important to note that `Math.abs` turns a number into an absolute number, which basically removes its sign, like you have before a minus number. Using absolute numbers means that you can be sure that you're only dealing with a positive number, which allows you to cut down the number of checks within the conditional statements.

Refresh the page one last time and you should have a bunch of asteroids that have finally been tamed; accelerating slowly up to a maximum velocity. You're now officially one step closer to mastering physics. Nice one!

> Note: I haven't covered forces in detail, but in essence a force is just acceleration in a particular direction. For example, if you wanted to fake gravity, you would create a uniform acceleration in the positive y axis (downwards). Calculating and applying accurate forces is a little too advanced for this book, but I'd highly recommend books like AdvancED ActionScript 3.0 Animation by Keith Peters. It may be about ActionScript, but it's packed to the brim with useful formulas and insights into advanced animation with physics.

Friction

Technically friction is a force, which you could work out super accurately and then apply to an object to reduce its velocity. However, it's at this point that I'm going to let you in on a little secret for using physics in animation: if it's going to be complicated and unnecessarily time consuming to calculate properly, then fake it! Obviously, this approach won't hold true if you're trying to create a perfect simulation of the real world, but in most cases, especially for gaming, faking it will look just as good as the real deal. The main draw to faking physics is that it takes much less time to calculate, and is inherently simpler to understand.

In the case of friction, you want to reduce the velocity of an object. Normally, you'd have to calculate realistic forces based on the friction between one object and the surface that it's passing over, but when faking it you can simply multiply the velocity of an object by a fraction. To the untrained eye, both options will achieve the same effect: calculating the right friction force and applying it to an object will slow it down, and faking it by multiplying the velocity by a fraction will also slow it down. For example, if an object's velocity is 2 pixels, and you then apply a friction of 0.9, the resulting velocity will be the current velocity multiplied by the fraction, which equals 1.8. By applying the same friction fraction on each loop, you'll quickly end up with a velocity of near 0 (assuming that the friction reduces the velocity more than acceleration increases it).

If you wanted to apply friction to the asteroids example, you'll need to add the following just after the acceleration code:

```
if (Math.abs(tmpAsteroid.vX) > 0.1) {
        tmpAsteroid.vX *= 0.9;
} else {
        tmpAsteroid.vX = 0;
};

if (Math.abs(tmpAsteroid.vY) > 0.1) {
        tmpAsteroid.vY *= 0.9;
} else {
        tmpAsteroid.vY = 0;
};
```

This multiplies the velocity of each asteroid by 0.9, which acts as your global friction value. The friction will have the effect of slowing down every asteroid, like if they were rolling along the top of a pool table. The conditional statements are there to stop the friction being applied forever and taking up valuable resources. You do this by setting the velocity to 0 (halting the asteroid) when the velocity is at a very small number – a velocity so small that it looks like the asteroid is still anyway.

If you refresh the page and have a look, you'll notice that the asteroids are moving at a slower speed than they were previously. However, because you're also applying acceleration at the same time, the asteroids will never slow to a complete halt. You can still do that, but you'd have to remove the acceleration entirely.

You've covered quite a lot in this section. Some books are entirely devoted to teaching physics in animation, so you're doing well if it's starting to all make sense. If not, I wouldn't worry; it took me a while to get to grips with physics in code. The trick is to play around with the code, changing values, and seeing what happens. There's absolutely nothing wrong with rereading these past two sections a few times to really let it sink in.

If you're ready, let's press on and explore what else we can do with motion.

Collision detection

Up to this point, you've applied concepts of motion to a set of asteroids that let them float around in a lovely space scene. The annoying thing is that all the asteroids are passing through each other, instead of bouncing off of one another. Fortunately, we can start fixing this right now. This is what's known as collision detection, and it's a fantastic way to introduce some pretty realistic motion effects.

There are two key steps to perform for collision detection to be possible, and I'm going to walk you through them both. The first step is to work out whether two objects (your asteroids) are overlapping (colliding), and the second step is to then work out how to move those objects away from each other in a realistic way. Together, these two steps will allow you to produce an effect that is a little like how pool balls react when they bounce off of each other on a pool table.

Before you start, the first thing to do is to remove the friction code from the last example, and set the acceleration for each new asteroid to 0. The asteroids are in space where there isn't any friction, so it's just going to make the example look unrealistic if we keep it in. Feel free to just comment out the friction code if you don't want to remove it entirely.

Collision detection

In theory, this is simple: two objects are classed as colliding if they are overlapping. It doesn't matter whether the overlap is a single pixel, or many; it's still classed as a collision. It's obvious really. Detecting a collision between objects that are rectangular is relatively simple, and would be achieved in JavaScript like so:

```
if (!(rectB.x+rectB.width < rectA.x) &&
      !(rectA.x+rectA.width < rectB.x) &&
      !(rectB.y+rectB.height < rectA.y) &&
      !(rectA.y+rectA.height < rectB.y)) {
      // The two objects are overlapping
};
```

The first two checks look to see if there is a gap between the rectangles on the left side, and the right side of the chosen rectangle (A) (see Figure 7-3). The last two checks look to see if there is a gap between the rectangles above, and below the chosen rectangle (A) (see Figure 7-4). If any of those checks come back as true, then there must be a gap between the two rectangles somewhere, so they can't be overlapping. In your case, you want to check if they *are* overlapping, so you check for all the rules to be false. It amounts to the same thing.

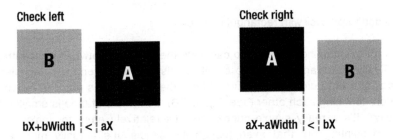

Figure 7-3. Checking for gaps on the left and right

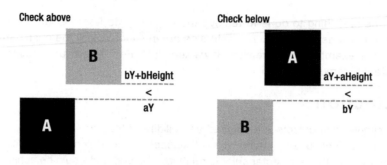

Figure 7-4. Checking for gaps on the top and bottom

You're using circles in the asteroid example, so checking rectangles is not going to work; you'll get false positive results. If you look at Figure 7-5 you'll notice that the rectangles are overlapping, but the circles are not, so a different approach is required.

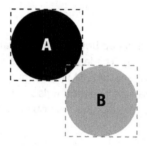

Figure 7-5. Circles don't work well with rectangular checks.

The trick to check for overlapping circles is to calculate the distance between the central points of each circle. More specifically, you want to check to see if the distance between the two circles is smaller than the sum of the radius of both circles. The sum of both the radius gives you the minimum distance the circles can be before touching each other (see Figure 7-6), so if the distance is smaller, then the circles must be overlapping. It's a really simple check, and it's relatively easy to achieve in code as well. Although, it's worth pointing out that even though it's simple, it's actually more expensive to run computationally than the rectangle checks because of the math involved.

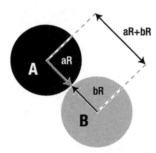

Figure 7-6. Circles touch if the distance between them is less than the radii.

Seeing as the circles that you're checking could be at any position, calculating the distance between the two is going to be a little trickier than simply getting the difference between the *x* and *y* positions. Fortunately, trigonometry is here to save the day. You're going to use Pythagoras' theorem, which is an equation that lets you work out the length of any side of a triangle based on the lengths of the other two sides; it's pretty damn cool. I won't go into the nitty-gritty about the equation, but make sure you read up on it if you want to learn more about it.[2]

When calculating distance between two circles, you're always going to be looking for the hypotenuse of a right angle triangle (see Figure 7-7). To work out the hypotenuse, you first need to calculate the distance between the two circles on the *x* and *y* axis (dX and dY respectfully in Figure 7-7).

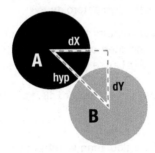

Figure 7-7. Calculating the distance between two points

These two distances correspond to the lengths of the two sides of the triangle that aren't the hypotenuse. Together, these lengths give you enough information to calculate the length of the hypotenuse; you just plug them into the equation for Pythagoras' theorem (see Figure 7-8).

$$hyp = \sqrt{dX^2 + dY^2}$$

Figure 7-8. Pythagoras' equation

It's at this point that it's a good idea to see how to do this in JavaScript, so open up the asteroids code from earlier and move into the animation loop. Add the following code below the declaration of the tmpAsteroid variable:

```
for (var j = i+1; j < asteroidsLength; j++) {
        var tmpAsteroidB = asteroids[j];

        var dX = tmpAsteroidB.x - tmpAsteroid.x;
        var dY = tmpAsteroidB.y - tmpAsteroid.y;
        var distance = Math.sqrt((dX*dX)+(dY*dY));
```

---

[2] http://en.wikipedia.org/wiki/Pythagorean_theorem

```
        };
};
```

This second loop is required so you can make sure that every asteroid is checking every other asteroid to see whether they are overlapping or not. Take note of the j variable in the loop being set to i+1; this is a little trick to cut down on the number of loops that you perform. If j were set to 0, then you'd end up performing checks on asteroids that you already checked in a previous loop, which can get a bit messy.

Calculating the distance is performed within the dX and dY variables, and the distances are then plugged into the Pythagoras' equation in the distance variable. Notice the use of the Math.sqrt method to perform the square root section of the equation. The resulting value in the distance variable will be the true pixel distance between the center of the two asteroids.

Once you have the distance, working out whether the asteroids are touching is child's play. All you need to do is calculate the sum of the radii, and then check to see if the distance is smaller than that value. Place the following code underneath the distance variable in the second loop:

```
if (distance < tmpAsteroid.radius + tmpAsteroidB.radius) {

};
```

And that is as complicated as it gets for calculating whether two circles are overlapping. The fun part is working out what to do with the circles now that you know they're touching, which is exactly what you're going to tackle next.

Bouncing objects away from each other

Now, I'm not going to lie. This section is going to get a little complicated at points, but bear with it. I'd love to spend chapter after chapter explaining all these concepts to you in detail, but unfortunately I wouldn't have time to teach anything about canvas, so we'll have to make do. Rest assured, I'm going to leave you with enough of an understanding of the concepts for you to go out and learn more if needs be. My thinking is that I'd rather show you how to achieve this important concept of motion, even if it does mean skimming over some of the finer details.

> Note: If you want to learn more about collision detection and bouncing objects, you should definitely check out Foundation ActionScript 3.0 Animation by Keith Peters. Just like his other book that I mentioned in the previous section, this one is crammed full of excellent theory and code examples for animating using physics. Even though it's based on ActionScript, there are still plenty of concepts to pick up, and the code can be easily ported to JavaScript.

So far, you already know how to make an object bounce off of a completely straight surface. However, this approach won't work for round objects that are traveling at completely different angles and at different velocities. With a flat surface, you can make an object bounce off of it by reversing the velocity that is perpendicular to the surface, so you reverse the y axis for bouncing off of the top and bottom, and reverse the x axis for bouncing off of the left and right (see Figure 7-9).

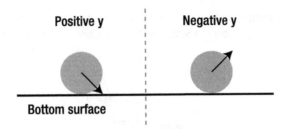

Figure 7-9. Bouncing off of a flat surface

The problem is that this way of doing things will only work in very special circumstances. In fact, it's unlikely that the perfect circumstances would occur between two circles to let you use this method of reversing velocity. For example, the only time this method would work between two circles is if they hit each other perfectly in line, with absolutely no angle between their central points (see Figure 7-10). In the vast majority of cases, the two circles will hit each other at an angle, which won't allow you to simply reverse the velocity (see Figure 7-11). In these cases, you'd expect the circles to bounce off of each other at the correct angle (straight down in the case of the left circle in Figure 7-11). However, with the current method the circles would bounce off of each other at very odd angles, like the left circle in Figure 7-11 bouncing backwards in an unrealistic fashion. It's actually little more complicated than this, but I'm trying to keep things as simple as possible and on a need to know basis.

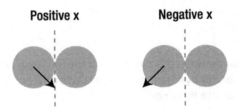

Figure 7-10. A perfect collision between two circles

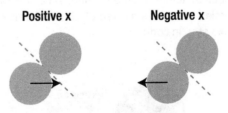

Figure 7-11. An unrealistic collision between two circles

To solve this problem, you need a method that allows you to calculate the position and velocity after a collision with a circle at an unknown angle. The solution is deviously simple in concept, but takes a little while to understand in code. Let me explain.

If two circles have collided, you need to find out the angle between them both before you can do anything (see Figure 7-12). To do that you use the two distance values that you calculated previously (dX and dY), and plug them into the arctangent trigonometric function. This function allows you to work out the angle of a right angle triangle if you already know the length of the opposite and adjacent legs, which correspond to dX and dY respectfully.

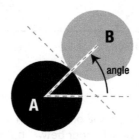

Figure 7-12. Finding the angle between two circles

JavaScript has an arctangent function, but you're not going to use it because it can lead to potential false positive results. Instead, you're going to use `Math.atan2`, which is a slightly more robust function that achieves exactly what you want.

Let's code as we go, so add the following within the empty conditional statement you created above, the one that checks to see whether the circles are colliding:

```
var angle = Math.atan2(dY, dX);
var sine = Math.sin(angle);
var cosine = Math.cos(angle);
```

The first line calculates the angle between the circles, and the following two lines calculate the ratio of dX and dY, compared to the length of the hypotenuse (variable `distance`). You'll be using these values a lot in a moment, so it's useful to calculate them now.

Now you know the angle, the next step is to rotate the velocity of each of the circles in turn, so they appear as if the circles were colliding in the rare and perfect way that I mentioned earlier (refer to Figure 7-10). Doing this will cause the velocities to change from Figure 7-12, to exactly as they look in Figure 7-13, which means that making the circles bounce is a case of simply reversing the velocity. It all sounds so simple in words, so let's create this step in code.

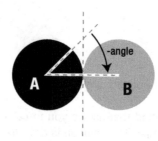

Figure 7-13. Rotating around the around of two circles

The following set of formulas are a bit of a mind bender, but they do everything you need to rotate the position and velocity of each circle. You'll have to take my word for it though, as explaining these formulas will take a fair amount of time and will probably not achieve a great deal. If you really want to know how they work, then I encourage you to go and explore them in more detail at a later date, but don't say I didn't warn you!

Insert the following code below the `cosine` variable that you declared previously:

```
var x = 0;
var y = 0;

var xB = dX * cosine + dY * sine;
var yB = dY * cosine - dX * sine;

var vX = tmpAsteroid.vX * cosine + tmpAsteroid.vY * sine;
var vY = tmpAsteroid.vY * cosine - tmpAsteroid.vX * sine;

var vXb = tmpAsteroidB.vX * cosine + tmpAsteroidB.vY * sine;
var vYb = tmpAsteroidB.vY * cosine - tmpAsteroidB.vX * sine;
```

The resulting values will be the position and velocity of each circle after being rotated so that there is no angle between the circles. I know it can be difficult to grasp, but hold on in there as you're only a few steps away from completing it all.

Reversing the velocity of each asteroid is a simple process. Insert the following below the vYb variable:

```
vX *= -1;
vXb *= -1;
```

You'll then want to move the asteroids apart, to make sure that they don't get stuck together, so insert the following below the code for reversing the velocity:

```
xB = x + (tmpAsteroid.radius + tmpAsteroidB.radius);
```

Finally, you need to rotate the asteroids back to their original positions, each with their new velocity. To do that you basically perform the reverse of the code to rotate the asteroids in the first place.

Insert the following code after reversing the positions and velocities:

```
tmpAsteroid.x = tmpAsteroid.x + (x * cosine - y * sine);
tmpAsteroid.y = tmpAsteroid.y + (y * cosine + x * sine);

tmpAsteroidB.x = tmpAsteroid.x + (xB * cosine - yB * sine);
tmpAsteroidB.y = tmpAsteroid.y + (yB * cosine + xB * sine);


tmpAsteroid.vX = vX * cosine - vY * sine;
tmpAsteroid.vY = vY * cosine + vX * sine;
```

```
tmpAsteroidB.vX = vXb * cosine - vYb * sine;
tmpAsteroidB.vY = vYb * cosine + vXb * sine;
```

And with that, you're done! Refresh the page and take a look at your wildly dynamic asteroid field. I'd be immensely proud of yourself if I were you; you've achieved a whole bunch of stuff in this section.

You might notice that some of the asteroids seem to bounce at quite a fast speed, regardless of the size of the asteroid that they hit. This is because you're reversing the velocity of the asteroids to achieve an effect that looks similar to that of two pool balls bouncing off of each other. Let's take things a step further and quickly take a look at how to conserve the momentum of each asteroid, so that they bounce off of each other at a much more realistic velocity.

Conservation of momentum

In the previous example, asteroids bounce off of each other at the same velocity that they had before the collision; the only difference being that the direction of the velocity reverses. Now this is great and all, but like I just mentioned, it doesn't give the most realistic effect of collision and bouncing. To get that, you'll need to use a process that conserves the momentum of the asteroids.

Conservation of momentum is a process that takes the velocity of one asteroid, and the velocity of another, and uses that when they collide to calculate a new velocity for each asteroid. This allows asteroids with a larger velocity or mass to knock small asteroids out of the way. It also means that asteroids with a similar velocity and mass will appear to stop each other in their tracks if they collide head on, just like when two pool balls collide head on.

However, before you can go any further, you'll need to add mass to the asteroids, as it is a fundamental requirement in calculating momentum.

Add mass to the Asteroid class by replacing it with the following code:

```
var Asteroid = function(x, y, radius, mass, vX, vY, aX, aY) {
        this.x = x;
        this.y = y;
        this.radius = radius;
        this.mass = mass;

        this.vX = vX;
        this.vY = vY;
        this.aX = aX;
        this.aY = aY;
};
```

Then give each asteroid a mass when you create them by changing the loop to the following:

```
for (var i = 0; i < 10; i++) {
        var x = 20+(Math.random()*(canvasWidth-40));
        var y = 20+(Math.random()*(canvasHeight-40));

        var radius = 5+Math.random()*10;
```

```
        var mass = radius/2;

        var vX = Math.random()*4-2;
        var vY = Math.random()*4-2;
        var aX = 0;
        var aY = 0;

        asteroids.push(new Asteroid(x, y, radius, mass, vX, vY, aX, aY));
};
```

Notice the `mass` variable and its addition within the arguments of a new asteroid object.

Now that you have the mass of each asteroid, you can calculate its momentum by multiplying its mass by its velocity. I don't expect this to make complete sense, but it's important to at least be aware of the concepts.

I'm not going to get bogged down with trying to explain all of this in a single section, as it is admittidly a complex topic that would take a while to properly get your head around. My aim here is to show you how to achieve this realistic effect, rather than explaining exactly how the formula works.

With that out of the way, let's crack on and conserve momentum.

The next thing that you want to do is to comment out or remove the code that reversed the velocities of each asteroid after a collision, and then insert the following in its place:

```
var vTotal = vX - vXb;
vX = ((tmpAsteroid.mass - tmpAsteroidB.mass) * vX + 2 * tmpAsteroidB.mass * vXb) /
(tmpAsteroid.mass + tmpAsteroidB.mass);
vXb = vTotal + vX;
```

It looks a bit mental, but that's all there is to it. Refresh the browser and take a look for yourself. Doesn't that look much more realistic now?

What's basically going on is that you're calculating the total, or relative velocity, of the two asteroids (the vTotal variable), and then calculating the new velocity for the first asteroid by utilizing a kinetic energy formula. The new velocity for the second asteroid is calculated by adding the new velocity for the first asteroid to the relative velocity that was calculated earlier.

I wouldn't worry about trying to understand all this, unless you really want to try. I've used this code for a long time now, and even I don't pretend to fully understand it. I leave the crazy math to the clever people.

Summary

This has probably been the hardest chapter yet, so well done on making it through. You've learned about physics and the concepts behind it. You've also learned how to apply those concepts in JavaScript, and how they can be used to create realistic and visually impressive animations. Finally, you've looked at how to create collisions between objects, and how to make those collisions look realistic. You have learned a truly massive amount in this chapter.

The good news is that you've reached the pinnacle of the theory in this book, and from now on you'll be doing nothing but creating awesome games. This is the point at which you start to pull everything together to make something amazing. This is where it gets interesting.

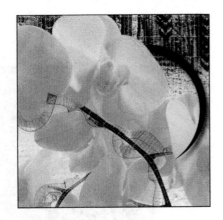

Chapter 8

Creating the Space Bowling Game

You're about to create a space bowling game – presumably your first game in canvas, and perhaps your first game ever. The concept is to tie together the skills that you've picked up from previous chapters to create something that is simple to play, yet fun and addictive at the same time.

I must stress that the focus of this book, particularly within this chapter and the next, is to teach you the fundamental skills required to produce animations and interactive games with canvas. This means that the games this book have been deliberately made to look simplistic. The reason for this is to prevent things from getting overly complicated; there's no reason to spend ages designing an object when you've come to learn how to animate and code it. The beauty of canvas, and the game that you're about to create, is that it's very easy to change things. For example, there is nothing to stop you coming up with a much prettier way of drawing asteroids, and replacing the code in the book with your own. In fact, I would love it if you did that!

You can find all of the code for this chapter available for download on this book's page on the friends of ED website (www.friendsofed.com). You will also find downloads for all the code from the other chapters. It's usefull for checking against your own code to make sure that you're doing things right. Although I recommend typing all the code out by hand, rather than copying and pasting from the downloaded code. You'll learn it better that way.

Overview of the game

The space bowling game consists of a set of stationary asteroids positioned on top of a circular platform, with another bigger asteroid placed further away, acting as a ball that the player can throw (see Figure 8-1). The idea of the game is to throw this bigger asteroid toward the other asteroids, and to knock as many of them off of the platform as possible. You win the game by knocking every asteroid off of the platform, with the score being based on how many attempts (clicks) it took you to knock the asteroids off. It's deviously simple and addictive, probably because it's based on games that have been around for years – ten pin bowling, and marbles.

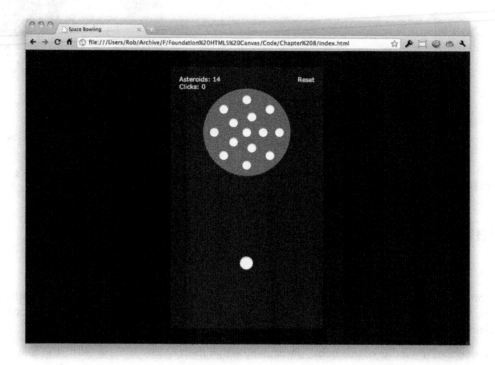

Figure 8-1. The space bowling game

Requirements

Creating this game will require many of the skills you've picked up throughout the book. You'll be using everything you learned about JavaScript, drawing in canvas, animation, and physics. You'll even use a few techniques that haven't been touched on in detail, like constructing a user interface, and using mouse input to control objects drawn on the canvas. This is where you'll really start to see the power that results from combining everything that you've studied up to this point.

I'm sure that you're itching to get started, so let's crack on!

Setting up the core functionality

Before you can get on to the cool stuff, the foundations need to be laid down. In the case of the space bowling game, this is the basic HTML, CSS, and JavaScript code that underpins the more advanced code that you'll add later.

Marking up the HTML

The beauty of creating games in the browser is that you're using technologies that are commonly used for making web sites. This means that the user interface (UI) for the game can be created using HTML. It won't look pretty at the moment, as there is no CSS to style it, but it's the raw structure of the content that matters right now.

Create a new directory on your computer for the game, and insert the following code into a file called *index.html*:

```html
<!DOCTYPE html>

<html>
        <head>
                <title>Space Bowling</title>
                <meta charset="utf-8">

                <link href="game.css" rel="stylesheet" type="text/css">

                <script type="text/javascript"
src="http://ajax.googleapis.com/ajax/libs/➥
jquery/1/jquery.min.js"></script>
                <script type="text/javascript" src="game.js"></script>
        </head>

        <body>
                <div id="game">
                        <div id="gameUI">
                                <div id="gameIntro">
                                        <h1>Space bowling</h1>
                                        <p>This is an awesome game.</p>
                                        <p><a id="gamePlay" class="button" href="">➥
Play</a></p>
                                </div>
                                <div id="gameStats">
                                        <p>Asteroids: <span
id="gameRemaining"></span></p>
                                        <p>Clicks: <span
class="gameScore"></span></p>
                                        <p><a class="gameReset"
href="">Reset</a></p>
                                </div>
                                <div id="gameComplete">
                                        <h1>You win!</h1>
                                        <p>Congratulations, you completed the game
in <span➥
 class="gameScore"></span> clicks.</p>
                                        <p><a class="gameReset button" href="">Play➥
 again</a></p>
                                </div>
                        </div>
                        <canvas id="gameCanvas" width="350" height="600">
                                <!-- Insert fallback content here -->
```

```
                        </canvas>
                    </div>
            </body>
    </html>
```

I'm not going to spend much time explaining all this, as it's relatively simple HTML, but the general idea is that this is everything you need to mark up your game.

Within the head element, you have the code that imports the CSS and JavaScript for the game. And within the body element, you have all the code that describes the game UI and the canvas.

The game UI has been split into separate elements to make it easier to interact with and toggle the visibility of certain areas by using JavaScript. For example, the three main areas of the UI are the introduction screen, the statistics screen, and the game complete screen. In the final game, only one of these areas will be displayed at a single point in time; the intro screen at the beginning, the statistics screen during the gameplay, and the complete screen when the game is finished.

As it stands, the game looks incredibly unexciting, as you can see in Figure 8-2. All you can see at the moment is the raw content for the UI, including the links that we're going to turn into beautiful buttons, and the placeholder text for statistics about the game while it's being played. The canvas element is actually on the page, but it's seemingly invisible at the moment. If you look closely, you'll notice the scroll bar on the right, which indicates that the canvas element is actually there.

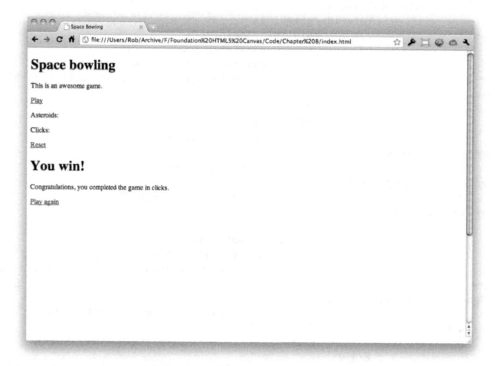

Figure 8-2. Marking up the game with HTML

> Note: It's important to point out that the game UI is marked up before the canvas element; this is because you want to display the UI over the canvas element. If you placed the UI code after the canvas element, it would require some extra CSS fancywork to get the UI to display above the canvas.

Making things pretty

Now that the HTML is sorted out, it's time to put together some CSS to get everything to look more game-like. The CSS that you're going to use is straightforward, but I'll run through it briefly to explain what's happening.

Create a new document called *game.css* and place it in the same directory as the HTML file. Insert the following code into the CSS file:

```
* { margin: 0; padding: 0; }
html, body { height: 100%; width: 100%; }
canvas { display: block; }

body {
        background: #000;
        color: #fff;
        font-family: Verdana, Arial, sans-serif;
        font-size: 18px;
}

h1 {
        font-size: 30px;
}

p {
        margin: 0 20px;
}

a {
        color: #fff;
        text-decoration: none;
}

a:hover {
        text-decoration: underline;
}

a.button {
        background: #185da8;
        border-radius: 5px;
        display: block;
        font-size: 30px;
```

```
        margin: 40px 0 0 45px;
        padding: 10px;
        width: 200px;
}

a.button:hover {
        background: #2488f5;
        color: #fff;
        text-decoration: none;
}

#game {
        height: 600px;
        left: 50%;
        margin: -300px 0 0 -175px;
        position: relative;
        top: 50%;
        width: 350px;
}

#gameCanvas {
        background: #001022;
}

#gameUI {
        height: 600px;
        position: absolute; /* Places UI on top of the canvas */
        width: 350px;
}

#gameIntro, #gameComplete {
        background: rgba(0, 0, 0, 0.5);
        margin-top: 100px;
        padding: 40px 0;
        text-align: center;
}

#gameStats {
        font-size: 14px;
        margin: 20px 0;
}

#gameStats .gameReset {
        margin: 20px 20px 0 0;
        position: absolute;
        right: 0;
        top: 0;
}
```

The first three lines of CSS reset the styling, and set up the HTML document to fit the dimensions of the browser window. Following that are five rules (body, h1, p, a, and a:hover) that are being used to define the background color of the document, as well as the default styling for text and links within the game. The next two rules (a.button and a.button:hover) are used to style the buttons within the game, which you'll see in a moment. You'll notice from the HTML document that you're using classes to define links that are buttons, as it's more economical to use the same style for all the buttons.

All the game HTML code is contained within a single div element. The #game CSS rule is used to give this container specific dimensions, and to center everything within the browser window by using some nifty CSS position and margin tactics. Styling the canvas element is done via the #gameCanvas rule, but it's only changing the background color to a deep blue.

The UI is styled through a variety of CSS rules; #gameUI, #gameIntro, #gameComplete, #gameStats, and #gameStats .gameReset. Each one of these rules affects the styling of the individual UI elements in the HTML. For example, #gameUI uses an absolute position value to effectively move the UI over the top of the canvas element. The rest of the rules are effectively changing text styling, and performing minor positioning changes.

Together, the CSS allows the game to look a little prettier, although it's still not perfect (see Figure 8-3). Everything else will be sorted out within the JavaScript code.

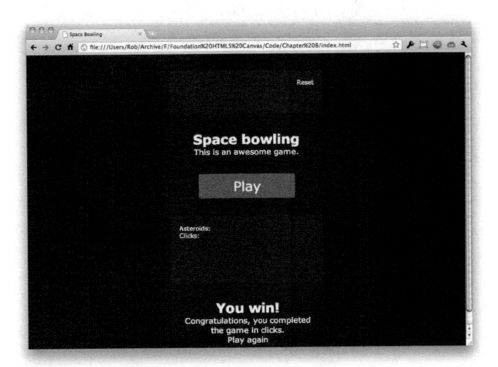

Figure 8-3. Styling the UI with CSS

Setting up the JavaScript

Before you can crack on with the juicy game logic, you need to set up the core functionality of the JavaScript.

Create a new document called *game.js* and place it within the same directory as the HTML and CSS files. Insert the following code within it:

```
$(document).ready(function() {
        var canvas = $("#gameCanvas");
        var context = canvas.get(0).getContext("2d");

        // Canvas dimensions
        var canvasWidth = canvas.width();
        var canvasHeight = canvas.height();

        // Game settings
        var playGame;

        // Reset and start the game
        function startGame() {
                // Set up initial game settings
                playGame = false;

                // Start the animation loop
                animate();
        };

        // Initialize the game environment
        function init() {

        };

        // Animation loop that does all the fun stuff
        function animate() {
                // Clear
                context.clearRect(0, 0, canvasWidth, canvasHeight);

                if (playGame) {
                        // Run the animation loop again in 33 milliseconds
                        setTimeout(animate, 33);
                };
        };

        init();
});
```

None of this should be new to you, apart from the fact that you're using a few extra functions. The first four variables hold the canvas element for the game, access the 2d rendering context, and assign the dimensions of the canvas. The fifth variable, playGame, is declared, but won't have a value assigned to it until later on; it is used to decide whether to run the animation code.

The startGame function is a placeholder that is going to be used to reset and start the game when the player clicks on the "Play," "Reset," or "Play again" links in the UI. As it stands, the function simply sets the playGame variable to false, to prevent the animation from running for now. The function also calls the animate function, which runs a very basic 30 fps timeout, but nothing else yet. The last function is init, which is going to be used to do the entire initial set up of the game when it is loaded for the first time. Right now the function is empty, but it is being called right at the end of the JavaScript in preparation.

Now the core functionality is out of the way, let's move on to the juicy stuff!

Activating the user interface

As it stands, the game is pretty ugly, and the UI doesn't even do anything. Fortunately, fixing this and activating the UI is easy!

Insert the following code above the startGame function:

```
var ui = $("#gameUI");
var uiIntro = $("#gameIntro");
var uiStats = $("#gameStats");
var uiComplete = $("#gameComplete");
var uiPlay = $("#gamePlay");
var uiReset = $(".gameReset");
var uiRemaining = $("#gameRemaining");
var uiScore = $(".gameScore");
```

These are a whole bunch of variables related to the various UI HTML elements; you'll be using them for easy access further on. Right now, they're just shortcuts to the DOM elements for each part of the UI.

To tidy up the initial screen that you see at the moment (see Figure 8-3), you'll want to hide all the unnecessary UI elements and activate the buttons so that you can actually start the game and change screens. Insert the following code inside of the init function:

```
uiStats.hide();
uiComplete.hide();

uiPlay.click(function(e) {
        e.preventDefault();
        uiIntro.hide();
        startGame();
});

uiReset.click(function(e) {
        e.preventDefault();
        uiComplete.hide();
        startGame();
});
```

The first two lines hide the statistics and complete screens of the UI, which instantly makes the game look prettier (see Figure 8-4). Following that are two click event listeners: one for the play button on the first screen and one for the reset buttons that are on the game screen and the screen when the game is finished. Both event listeners hide the relevant screen of the UI, and run the startGame function to kick-start the game.

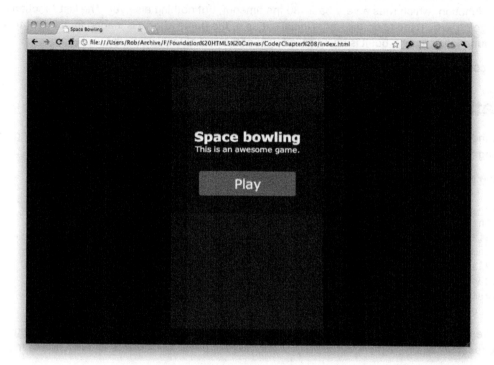

Figure 8-4. Hiding parts of the UI by using JavaScript

You're going to want to show the statistics screen when the game is started, so insert the following code at the top of the startGame function:

```
uiScore.html("0");
uiStats.show();
```

The first line effectively resets the score display by setting it to the string "0". The second line makes sure that the statistics screen is displaying when the game is played (see Figure 8-5). You'll get on to setting the values of and changing other aspects of the UI as you get to them in the game.

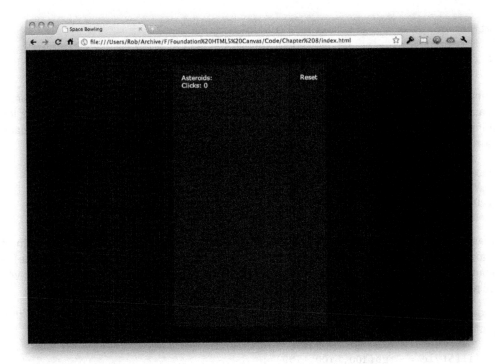

Figure 8-5. Resetting the game score

Creating the game objects

Many games are defined by the objects that give them purpose; whether they are the blocks in Tetris, the pieces in chess, or even Mario in Super Mario. There aren't many computer games around that don't have objects of some sort. In the case of your space bowling game, there are two main objects: you have the asteroids (including the bigger player asteroid) and the platform that the asteroids sit on. It's quite amazing how simple a game can seem when you break it down into its core objects and components.

Particularly when you're going to have multiple objects within a game, it's a good idea to define them as JavaScript classes. This makes sure that they're all based on the same code, and that you can rely on them all to contain the same properties and methods. For your game, you're going to create a class for the asteroids, but not for the platform. This is because the platform is a completely unique object, which will only occur once in the game, so it's not necessary to use a class, which would allow you to create multiple platforms.

Creating the platform

Before you can create the asteroids, you'll need to set up the round platform that they're going to sit on (refer to Figure 8-1). The platform is a circle, and is defined by a few specific variables, which you'll want to place below the playGame variable at the top:

```
var platformX;
var platformY;
var platformOuterRadius;
var platformInnerRadius;
```

These variables will hold the (x, y) origin of the platform, as well as the outer radius (the area of the platform as a whole), and the inner radius (the area the asteroids are actually placed within). As it stands, the platform variables don't have any values, so add the following code under the playGame variable in the startGame function:

```
platformX = canvasWidth/2;
platformY = 150;
platformOuterRadius = 100;
platformInnerRadius = 75;
```

This places the origin of the platform dead centre on the x axis, and 150 pixels from the top of the canvas on the y axis. The outer radius is set to 100 pixels (remember: radius is half the width of a circle), and the inner radius is set slightly smaller so there is some padding between the platform edge and where the asteroids are.

Finally, you want to draw the platform on the canvas, so add the following code underneath the call to clearRect in the animate function:

```
context.fillStyle = "rgb(100, 100, 100)";
context.beginPath();
context.arc(platformX, platformY, platformOuterRadius, 0, Math.PI*2, true);
context.closePath();
context.fill();
```

You can see the platform if you click on the play button on the game UI (see Figure 8-6). It's all very exciting.

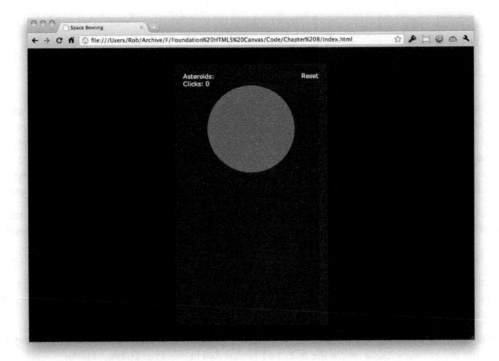

Figure 8-6. Creating the asteroid platform

Setting up the asteroids

The next thing to do is to set up the asteroids code and get them ready to be animated. The majority of the code you need is exactly the same as what you covered in the previous chapter, so I won't spend too much time on it.

You want to be able to remember all of the asteroids for animating and checking for collisions, so declare an asteroids variable under the platform variables at the top of the JavaScript:

```
var asteroids;
```

You'll be using this variable to store an array of all the asteroids within the game environment.

Having an array of asteroids is useless without asteroids, so the next step is to declare the asteroid class, which is based on the same class from the previous chapter. Add the following code above the startGame function:

```
var Asteroid = function(x, y, radius, mass, friction) {
    this.x = x;
    this.y = y;
    this.radius = radius;
    this.mass = mass;
    this.friction = friction;
```

```
        this.vX = 0;
        this.vY = 0;

        this.player = false;
};
```

It's important to note that there are a few differences to this class when compared to the one in the previous chapter. The most notable is the addition of the `friction` and `player` properties, which define the amount of friction that each asteroid experiences, and whether the asteroid is a larger player asteroid. As the majority of the asteroids won't be a larger player asteroid, the default value for `player` is false. You'll also notice that there are no acceleration properties; this is because you'll be using very simple motion within the game, and there is no need to accelerate anything. It will all make sense soon enough.

Before you create all the asteroids and place them on the platform, you'll need to set up the empty asteroids array, so add the following code below the platform variables in the `startGame` function:

```
asteroids = new Array();
```

You're using `startGame` to assign values to these variables because you want them to be fresh and overwritten each time the game is restarted by the player (through winning and playing again, or clicking on the reset link).

Creating all the asteroids in a nice neat set of rings (refer to Figure 8-1) takes a little bit of thinking about to get right. Add the following code below the `asteroids` variable in the `startGame` function:

```
var outerRing = 8; // Asteroids around outer ring
var ringCount = 3; // Number of rings
var ringSpacing = (platformInnerRadius/(ringCount-1)); // Distance between each ring

for (var r = 0; r < ringCount; r++) {
        var currentRing = 0; // Asteroids around current ring
        var angle = 0; // Angle between each asteroid
        var ringRadius = 0;

        // Is this the innermost ring?
        if (r == ringCount-1) {
                currentRing = 1;
        } else {
                currentRing = outerRing-(r*3);
                angle = 360/currentRing;
                ringRadius = platformInnerRadius-(ringSpacing*r);
        };
};
```

I've left in some of the comments, but let me run you through what's going on.

The first three variables declare the amount of asteroids that you want around the outer-most ring, the number of rings that you want, and the distance between each ring, respectively. You'll use these variables when calculating how many asteroids to draw on each ring.

Following those variables is the first loop, which cycles through each ring of asteroids that you want on the platform. Within each loop you set the `currentRing` variable to a default value of 0. This variable is used in the following conditional statement to store the number of asteroids that are to be placed on the current ring. You also set the `angle` and `ringRadius` variables to a default value of 0.

The conditional statement first checks to see whether you're on the last ring of asteroids (the central point) and, if so, sets the number of asteroids to 1. If you're not on the innermost ring, the number of asteroids is calculated by subtracting the number of asteroids around the outer ring by 3 multiplied by the loop number that you're on. It's a fairly arbitrary way of doing things, but it seems to work pretty well. Feel free to change this code if you can come up with a better way. The general concept is that you want the number of asteroids per ring to decrease as you get closer to the central point, otherwise you'll run out of space to put all the asteroids.

Once you have the number of asteroids in the current ring, you want to work out the angle that needs to be between each of them so they are equally spaced around the ring. This is done by dividing the total angle of a circle (360 degrees) by the amount of asteroids that are around the ring (see Figure 8-7). You're using degrees here to make it easy to understand in code, but you could quite easily (and probably should) use radians instead.

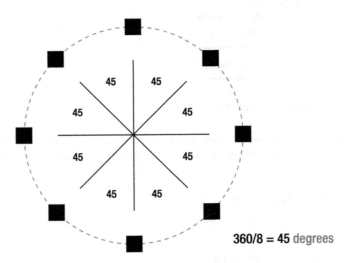

Figure 8-7. Calculating the angle between each asteroid

It's also important to calculate the radius of each ring, as you want them to be equally spaced. You can calculate the radius by using the `platformInnerRadius` variable that you defined earlier, and then subtracting from it the distance between each ring multiplied by the loop number that you're on. This results in each ring getting smaller and smaller, while keeping them equally spaced apart (see Figure 8-8).

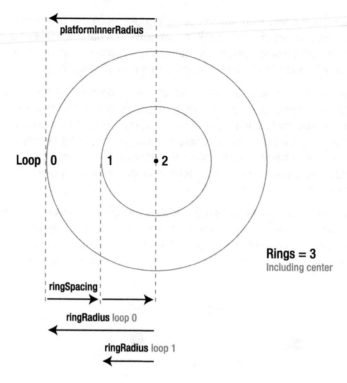

Figure 8-8. Calculating the radius of each ring

You now have everything that you need to create all the asteroids, so the next step involves a second loop that goes through each asteroid in turn. Add the following code below the conditional statement; **within the ring loop**:

```
for (var a = 0; a < currentRing; a++) {
        var x = 0;
        var y = 0;

        // Is this the innermost ring?
        if (r == ringCount-1) {
                x = platformX;
                y = platformY;
        } else {
                x = platformX+(ringRadius*Math.cos((angle*a)*(Math.PI/180)));
                y = platformY+(ringRadius*Math.sin((angle*a)*(Math.PI/180)));
        };

        var radius = 10;
        var mass = 5;
        var friction = 0.95;
```

```
        asteroids.push(new Asteroid(x, y, radius, mass, friction));
};
```

For each asteroid on the current ring, the loop calculates the position of that asteroid with a simple conditional statement. If you're on the innermost ring, then the asteroid needs to be in the centre of the platform, so you can set its (x, y) origin to that of the platform. Otherwise, the asteroid position is calculated by working out its position around the circumference of the current ring. It sounds crazy, but you've already used this code in the animating along a circle section in Chapter 6. The only difference is that instead of increasing the angle by 5, like you did in Chapter 6, you're basing the angle on the one you calculated just a moment ago; the angle needed between each asteroid to make them equally spaced around the ring.

Finally, the radius, mass, and friction of the asteroid is declared, and the asteroid is then added to the asteroids array that you created earlier. Sorted! You'll tackle how to display the asteroids when you animate them in the following section.

Setting up the player asteroid

For now, there is one last object to create, and that is the player asteroid that is used to fling at the other asteroids. It's actually very similar to the other asteroids, but you need to create it separately because it needs to be treated slightly differently. The first thing to do is to set up the variables at the top of the JavaScript, so add the following below the declaration of the asteroids variable:

```
var player;
var playerOriginalX;
var playerOriginalY;
```

You want to use this player variable so you can access the player asteroid separately to the other asteroids within the game. The purpose of playerOriginalX and playerOriginalY will become clear shortly, but for now it's useful to know that these variables will hold the original starting position of the player asteroid.

The next step is to actually create the player asteroid, so add the following code below the asteroids variable in the startGame function:

```
var pRadius = 15;
var pMass = 10;
var pFriction = 0.97;
playerOriginalX = canvasWidth/2;
playerOriginalY = canvasHeight-150;
player = new Asteroid(playerOriginalX, playerOriginalY, pRadius, pMass, pFriction);
player.player = true;
asteroids.push(player);
```

It's all very simple really; you declare the radius (which is larger than the other asteroids), mass (again, larger than the others), friction, and original player position (bottom of the screen), then use that to create a new asteroid object. The difference here is that you assign the new asteroid object to the player variable, so you can access it again at a later stage. You use the player variable straight away to change the player property of the asteroid, as this is the player asteroid (as if it wasn't obvious enough already).

Finally, you add the player asteroid to the `asteroids` array so you can use it in animation and collision detection in the next section.

The player asteroid will be drawn along with the others in the `animate` function, which you'll get on to shortly.

Updating the UI

Now that you've set up all of the asteroids, you should probably update the UI to show the amount of asteroids remaining on the platform. Fortunately, this is as easy as adding one line of code, so insert the following after the loops that you just created:

```
uiRemaining.html(asteroids.length-1);
```

This updates the HTML element assigned to the `uiRemaining` variable with the number of asteroids in the `asteroids` array, minus one because you don't want to include the player asteroid (see Figure 8-9). It's dead simple, although I should probably point out that the asteroids aren't actually visible yet.

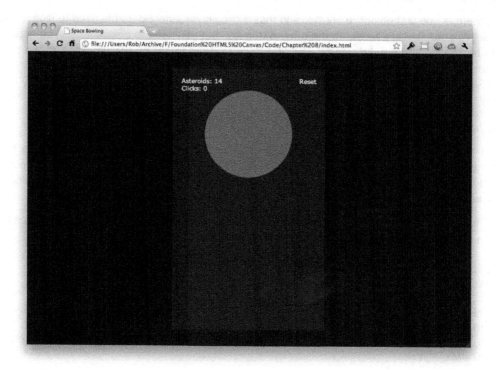

Figure 8-9. Displaying the number of asteroids remaining

Making things move

So far, you've set up all the core functionality for the game, but there are no asteroids or animation yet. It's hardly a game, so let's change that. What's really good is that you already know about everything that you're going to do in this section – it's old hat!

The first step is to set up the two loops that you used in the previous chapter for animation and collision detection of the asteroids. These loops will let the asteroids move and bounce off of each other, which is exactly how you're going to get them to fall off of the platform (by flinging the player asteroid at them).

Insert the following below the code that draws out the platform in the animate function:

```
context.fillStyle = "rgb(255, 255, 255)";

var asteroidsLength = asteroids.length;
for (var i = 0; i < asteroidsLength; i++) {
        var tmpAsteroid = asteroids[i];

        for (var j = i+1; j < asteroidsLength; j++) {
                var tmpAsteroidB = asteroids[j];

        };

        context.beginPath();
        context.arc(tmpAsteroid.x, tmpAsteroid.y, tmpAsteroid.radius, 0, Math.PI*2,
true);
        context.closePath();
        context.fill();
};
```

There's nothing new here apart from setting the fillStyle property to white, as fillStyle was previously set to gray for the platform. If you check out the game in the browser and click play, you'll notice that the asteroids are now showing up (see Figure 8-10). It's starting to look ever so slightly like a game.

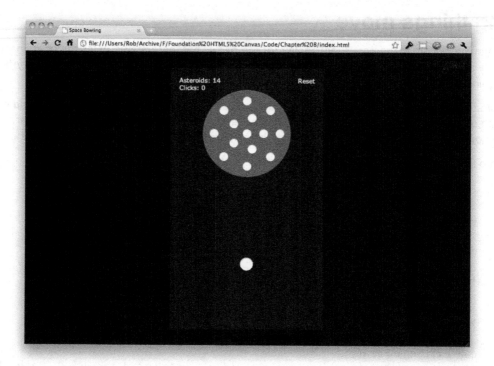

Figure 8-10. Displaying the asteroids

As it stands, there's no movement or animation going on. The first step toward achieving that is to add in the collision detection code from the previous chapter, so add the following below the `tmpAsteroidB` variable:

```
var dX = tmpAsteroidB.x - tmpAsteroid.x;
var dY = tmpAsteroidB.y - tmpAsteroid.y;
var distance = Math.sqrt((dX*dX)+(dY*dY));

if (distance < tmpAsteroid.radius + tmpAsteroidB.radius) {
        var angle = Math.atan2(dY, dX);
        var sine = Math.sin(angle);
        var cosine = Math.cos(angle);

        // Rotate asteroid position
        var x = 0;
        var y = 0;

        // Rotate asteroidB position
        var xB = dX * cosine + dY * sine;
        var yB = dY * cosine - dX * sine;

        // Rotate asteroid velocity
```

```
            var vX = tmpAsteroid.vX * cosine + tmpAsteroid.vY * sine;
            var vY = tmpAsteroid.vY * cosine - tmpAsteroid.vX * sine;

            // Rotate asteroidB velocity
            var vXb = tmpAsteroidB.vX * cosine + tmpAsteroidB.vY * sine;
            var vYb = tmpAsteroidB.vY * cosine - tmpAsteroidB.vX * sine;

            // Conserve momentum
            var vTotal = vX - vXb;
            vX = ((tmpAsteroid.mass - tmpAsteroidB.mass) * vX + 2 * tmpAsteroidB.mass *
vXb) /↩
 (tmpAsteroid.mass + tmpAsteroidB.mass);
            vXb = vTotal + vX;

            // Move asteroids apart
            xB = x + (tmpAsteroid.radius + tmpAsteroidB.radius);

            // Rotate asteroid positions back
            tmpAsteroid.x = tmpAsteroid.x + (x * cosine - y * sine);
            tmpAsteroid.y = tmpAsteroid.y + (y * cosine + x * sine);

            tmpAsteroidB.x = tmpAsteroid.x + (xB * cosine - yB * sine);
            tmpAsteroidB.y = tmpAsteroid.y + (yB * cosine + xB * sine);

            // Rotate asteroid velocities back
            tmpAsteroid.vX = vX * cosine - vY * sine;
            tmpAsteroid.vY = vY * cosine + vX * sine;

            tmpAsteroidB.vX = vXb * cosine - vYb * sine;
            tmpAsteroidB.vY = vYb * cosine + vXb * sine;
};
```

It looks mental, but it's identical to the code from the previous chapter. A quick recap: what it's doing is checking each asteroid to see whether it is overlapping with (colliding with) another asteroid and, if so, changing the velocity of each asteroid so that they bounce apart realistically.

Even if the animation loop was running (which it isn't yet), nothing will move yet, as you haven't updated the position of each asteroid. To do that you'll want to add the position and friction code just before the code that draws each asteroid to the canvas:

```
// Calculate new position
tmpAsteroid.x += tmpAsteroid.vX;
tmpAsteroid.y += tmpAsteroid.vY;

// Friction
if (Math.abs(tmpAsteroid.vX) > 0.1) {
        tmpAsteroid.vX *= tmpAsteroid.friction;
} else {
        tmpAsteroid.vX = 0;
```

```
};

if (Math.abs(tmpAsteroid.vY) > 0.1) {
        tmpAsteroid.vY *= tmpAsteroid.friction;
} else {
        tmpAsteroid.vY = 0;
};
```

Again, this is nothing new. What's happening here is that you're updating the position of each asteroid based on its velocity, and then applying a friction force that is taken into consideration on the next loop of the animation. If the velocity of the asteroid is below 0.1, then you automatically set the velocity to 0 to stop the asteroid from moving any further. This just stops the friction code from running forever.

If you want to see this code at work, you could give the player asteroid a negative *y* velocity when you create it (perhaps something like -25), and also change the playGame value to *true* in the startGame function. What will happen is the player asteroid will fly toward the platform and knock the other asteroids into each other (see Figure 8-11). Cool! Just remember to remove the manually set velocity for the player asteroid, and to change playGame back to *false* once you're done; otherwise you'll run into problems later.

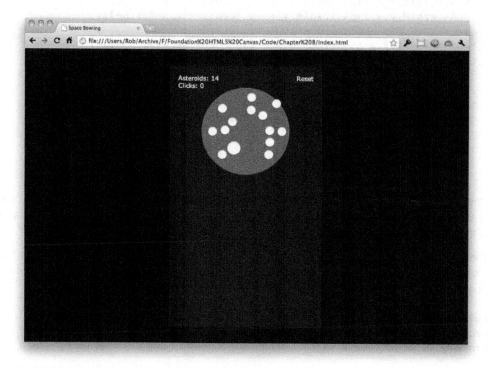

Figure 8-11. Adding physics to and animating the asteroids

That's honestly all there is to it for the animation and collision detection side of things. You still can't win anything, and there is no scoring system, but you'll sort that out in a moment. For now, let's look at how to implement user interaction by detecting mouse input.

Detecting user interaction

As I mentioned previously, the purpose of the game is to throw the player asteroid at the others, with the aim of knocking them off of the platform. In this section, you're going to look at how to detect mouse input and then work out how to use that mouse input to throw the player asteroid around in the game.

The player asteroid is thrown by pressing the left mouse button on it, and then dragging the mouse back behind the asteroid while still holding the mouse button down. When the mouse button is released, the resulting position of the mouse is used to calculate a velocity (further away from the player asteroid equals a bigger velocity) and angle for the player asteroid, making it fly off and hopefully knocking lots of asteroids off of the platform. Figure 8-12 should hopefully clear up the process a little bit.

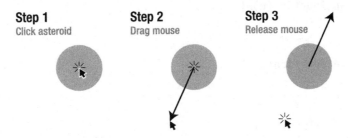

Figure 8-12. User interaction with the player asteroid

Setting everything up

Before you can start calculating mouse positions and velocities, you need to set up the event listeners for the mouse, and also all of the variables that you're going to need.

Add the following variable declarations underneath `playerOriginalY` at the top of the JavaScript file:

```
var playerSelected;
var playerMaxAbsVelocity;
var playerVelocityDampener;
var powerX;
var powerY;
```

Each variable has a specific purpose that will become clear shortly, but here is a quick description of them. The `playerSelected` variable will be used to hold a Boolean *true* or *false* value that lets you know whether the player asteroid is currently clicked on. Velocity settings for the player asteroid are held in `playerMaxAbsVelocity` (to limit how fast the player asteroid can travel) and `playerVelocityDampener` (to fine tune the velocity calculations). The (x, y) position kept in `powerX` and `powerY` is used for determining the velocity of the asteroid, and drawing a line on the canvas to visualize that velocity.

You'll want to set some default values for these variables, so set them up underneath the `asteroids` variable in the `startGame` function:

```
playerSelected = false;
playerMaxAbsVelocity = 30;
```

```
playerVelocityDampener = 0.3;
powerX = -1;
powerY = -1;
```

The velocity values are pretty arbitrary, while powerX, and powerY are set to specific values to effectively reset them (in case the player has already played the game). The two power position variables are set to -1 because it's a value that will never occur with mouse movement; you can't detect mouse movement outside of the element that you're tracking it on. You can't set them to 0 because it's possible that the player could move their mouse to the position (0, 0).

To set up the event listeners, add the following above the call to animate in the startGame function:

```
$(window).mousedown(function(e) {

});

$(window).mousemove(function(e) {

});

$(window).mouseup(function(e) {

});
```

There's quite obviously not much happening here, but these are the three main event listeners that you need to detect when the left mouse button is pressed down (mousedown), moved (mousemove), and when the mouse is released (mouseup).

> Note: You're using the window object for the mouse even listeners and not the canvas element simply because you want to be able to detect movement outside of the visible canvas. If you only detected mouse input on the canvas, and the player moved the mouse outside of the canvas, the game would stop updating the position of the mouse, which can be very annoying for the player.

Selecting the player asteroid

Most of the code that you're going to use to calculate the velocity based on the mouse input is taken from what you've already used when accessing pixel values in Chapter 5. The only difference is that there is some extra logic sprinkled on top.

Add the following code within the mousedown event listener, and I'll explain what it does:

```
if (!playerSelected && player.x == playerOriginalX && player.y == playerOriginalY) {
        var canvasOffset = canvas.offset();
        var canvasX = Math.floor(e.pageX-canvasOffset.left);
        var canvasY = Math.floor(e.pageY-canvasOffset.top);

        if (!playGame) {
                playGame = true;
                animate();
        };

        var dX = player.x-canvasX;
        var dY = player.y-canvasY;
        var distance = Math.sqrt((dX*dX)+(dY*dY));
        var padding = 5;

        if (distance < player.radius+padding) {
                powerX = player.x;
                powerY = player.y;
                playerSelected = true;
        };
};
```

The conditional statement is used to only allow the code to run when the player asteroid isn't already selected, and the player asteroid is in its original starting position. This prevents the player from throwing the asteroid a second time, while it's still moving from the first throw.

Working out the relative position of the player's mouse on the canvas is calculated using the same code from the section on accessing pixel values in Chapter 5; you can see how it works in Figure 5-15.

Within the first conditional statement, there is another conditional statement that checks to see whether the game is currently playing (and animating) and, if not, starts the game and sets the animation loop running. This means that you won't be wasting precious resources animating the game when nothing is moving on the screen.

The last set of code works out the distance between the player asteroid and the mouse. If the distance is less than the radius of the player asteroid, then it's safe to assume that the player has clicked on it – practically the same method as used for collision detection. The padding is used to make it harder to miss the asteroid, and can be increased if you want to make it even easier to click on. When it's known that the player has clicked on the asteroid, you then set powerX and powerY to that of the origin of the player asteroid (to zero the velocity, which you'll calculate later), and set the playerSelected variable to *true*, to let other areas of the game know that the asteroid has been selected.

Increasing the power

The player can change the power and angle of the asteroid's velocity by moving the mouse after clicking on it. The majority of the code to achieve this is very similar to that of the mousedown event listener that you just created.

Add the following code within the mousemove event listener:

```
if (playerSelected) {
        var canvasOffset = canvas.offset();
        var canvasX = Math.floor(e.pageX-canvasOffset.left);
        var canvasY = Math.floor(e.pageY-canvasOffset.top);

        var dX = canvasX-player.x;
        var dY = canvasY-player.y;
        var distance = Math.sqrt((dX*dX)+(dY*dY));

        if (distance*playerVelocityDampener < playerMaxAbsVelocity) {
                powerX = canvasX;
                powerY = canvasY;
        } else {
                var ratio = playerMaxAbsVelocity/(distance*playerVelocityDampener);
                powerX = player.x+(dX*ratio);
                powerY = player.y+(dY*ratio);
        };
};
```

The first thing that you'll notice is the conditional statement that checks for playerSelected to be true. This means that the following code will only run when you know that the player has clicked on the asteroid and is currently in the process of dragging the mouse afterward.

Within the conditional statement are three lines of code that work out the relative position of the mouse on the canvas.

Like with the mousedown event listener, you then work out the distance that the mouse is away from the origin of the player asteroid. In this case, you want to use it to work out how powerful to make the velocity (its magnitude). To do that you first need to dampen the distance value by using the playerVelocityDampener variable from earlier (see Figure 8-13). This allows the player to drag quite far (to visually see the power line that you'll be drawing later), but reduces the resulting velocity to something more realistic.

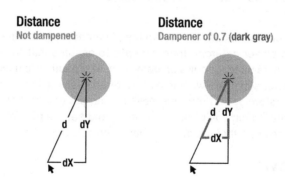

Figure 8-13. Dampening the velocity

If the resulting dampened value is lower than the maximum velocity magnitude set in `playerMaxAbsVelocity`, then it's safe to set the `powerX` and `powerY` values to the (*x*, *y*) position of the mouse on the canvas. Otherwise, the velocity magnitude is beyond the maximum allowed, so you need to reduce it to the maximum, while still keeping the correct angle. You can achieve this by calculating the ratio between the maximum velocity magnitude, and the current velocity magnitude (`distance`), then using that to shrink the `dX` and `dY` values (the distance on each axis between the mouse and the player asteroid), and adding that to the (x, y) origin of the asteroid.

Letting go

You now have all the pieces needed to complete the velocity puzzle. All that's left now is to use the `powerX` and `powerY` values to calculate the final velocity and apply it to the player asteroid. Simple.

Add the following code to the `mouseup` event listener:

```
if (playerSelected) {
        var dX = powerX-player.x;
        var dY = powerY-player.y;

        player.vX = -(dX*playerVelocityDampener);
        player.vY = -(dY*playerVelocityDampener);
};

playerSelected = false;
powerX = -1;
powerY = -1;
```

This is much simpler than the code in the other mouse event listeners. All you're doing here is working out the distance between the power position and the player asteroid (to convert from a coordinate position to a velocity), then using that to apply a *negative* velocity on the player asteroid, affected by the velocity dampener. You want to use a negative velocity because you want the asteroid to go in the opposite direction to where you're dragging, like how a catapult works (see Figure 8-12).

The last thing to do is to set `playerSelected` as *false*, because the asteroid is not selected any longer, and reset the `powerX` and `powerY` coordinate values.

Visualizing the user input

Everything up to this point will now work, but it's not very user-friendly. In fact, the player will have no idea about how much velocity they're giving the asteroid and at what angle it's going to travel. To do that you want to indicate the velocity using a simple line.

Add the following code after drawing the platform in the `animate` function:

```
if (playerSelected) {
        context.strokeStyle = "rgb(255, 255, 255)";
        context.lineWidth = 3;
        context.beginPath();
        context.moveTo(player.x, player.y);
```

```
        context.lineTo(powerX, powerY);
        context.closePath();
        context.stroke();
};
```

This effectively draws a line from the player asteroid to the position of the velocity (or at least the visual representation of the velocity). The line is only drawn when the player asteroid is selected because of the conditional statement checking for playerSelected to be *true*. You can see how communication between various functions and areas of the game code allows for some pretty cool stuff to happen.

Refresh the game in the browser and you'll now have a fully interactive game that lets you fling the player asteroid wherever you want. You won't be able to rack up a score yet, but give it a go and knock the asteroids off of the platform. It's fun!

As it stands, you can only fling the player asteroid once, and the asteroid can disappear off of the edge of the canvas. That's not fun, so let's sort that out by resetting the state of play after each throw and implementing some boundary detection on the player asteroid.

Resetting the player

To reset the state of play after each throw you need to move the player asteroid back to the start position, and reset it's velocity to 0, so that it doesn't move until the player clicks on it again. You'll be resetting the player in a few places, so it's useful to wrap it all up in one function.

Add the following code before the startGame function:

```
function resetPlayer() {
        player.x = playerOriginalX;
        player.y = playerOriginalY;
        player.vX = 0;
        player.vY = 0;
};
```

There's not much to explain here really, it's just the code version of what I described previously – you reset the position, and set the velocity to 0.

The only time you want to reset the player asteroid is when it leaves the visible canvas, or when it stops moving after being thrown. Fortunately, now that you have the reset code tucked away within a function, you can achieve this by adding the following code above where each asteroid is drawn in the animate function:

```
if (player.x != playerOriginalX && player.y != playerOriginalY) {
        if (player.vX == 0 && player.vY == 0) {
                resetPlayer();
        } else if (player.x+player.radius < 0) {
                resetPlayer();
        } else if (player.x-player.radius > canvasWidth) {
                resetPlayer();
        } else if (player.y+player.radius < 0) {
```

```
            resetPlayer();
    } else if (player.y-player.radius > canvasHeight) {
            resetPlayer();
    };
};
```

This set of conditional statements first checks to see whether the player asteroid has actually moved from its original position, by checking to see whether the original position and current position are different. If the asteroid *has* moved, then a further set of conditional statements is used to perform a variety of checks. The first checks to see whether the asteroid velocity has reduced to 0, and therefore the asteroid has stopped moving. The others check to see whether the asteroid has moved beyond the boundaries of the canvas. If any of the checks turn up true, then the player asteroid is reset so the player can take another throw.

> Note: You could probably combine the conditional statements for the player reset into one giant one, but I'll leave that decision up to you. I wouldn't want to confuse matters.

Give it a go. You'll notice that once you've taken your first throw, the player asteroid will reset and move back to its original position (see Figure 8-14).

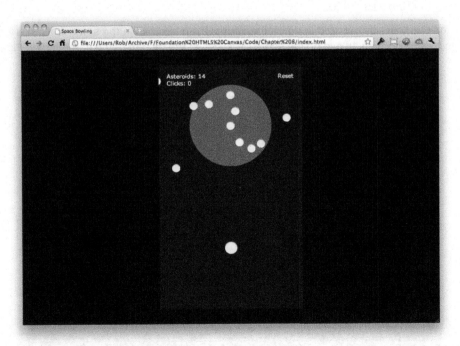

Figure 8-14. Resetting the player asteroid

Letting the player win

Right now, the game is pretty pointless because you simply can't win; to fix that, you need to implement a scoring system of some description. In the case of this game, the scoring system is based on the amount of attempts (clicks) it takes the player to knock all of the asteroids out of the platform. This requires you to know how many asteroids have been knocked out of the platform, and how many clicks have been made (the score). After every click you then update the UI to show the player the current score. Once all of the asteroids have been knocked out, you end the game and show the player their final score – they win.

Updating the score

The first step is to set up the variable that will hold the score, so add the following declaration underneath the powerY variable at the top of the JavaScript:

```
var score;
```

And set the default score to 0 by adding the following code underneath the powerY variable at the top of the startGame function:

```
score = 0;
```

You want to update and display the score every time the player clicks, so add the following under player.vY in the mouseup event listener:

```
uiScore.html(++score);
```

This increases the score by one and updates the score UI element, all at the same time. You'll see this by trying the game and keeping an eye on the score ("Clicks") at the top left of the canvas (see Figure 8-15).

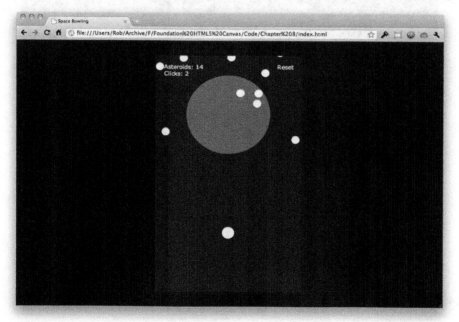

Figure 8-15. Updating the score on each click

Removing asteroids from the platform

To win the game you have to knock all of the asteroids off of the platform, so you need a method of actually working out whether all the asteroids have left the platform. There are two steps to this, the first being a simple check that looks at each asteroid to see whether it's still on the platform, and the second being a routine that keeps track of the number of asteroids still on the platform. When the second step returns a value of 0 (no asteroids left), then you know the game is over and you can move on to the next screen of the game.

There are probably a few ways that you could track the number of asteroids that are still on the platform. The way that you're going to use involves removing any asteroid from the asteroids array if it falls off of the platform. That way you will always know how many asteroids are left by just checking the length of the asteroids array.

However, there is a problem: you can't just remove an asteroid from the array straight away because it will screw up the asteroid loops within the animate function. This is because the loop is running for a set number of times (the amount of asteroids), so if you remove one mid-loop, then there will become a point where you're looping more times than there are asteroids. Not good.

To overcome this you need to create a new temporary array that holds all of the asteroids that have fallen off of the platform in one animation loop, and then use that array at the very end of the animation loop to remove the asteroids from the original asteroids array. This will make more sense when illustrated with code.

Add the following code above the asteroidsLength variable in the animate function:

```
var deadAsteroids = new Array();
```

This is the temporary array that is going to hold all of the asteroids that have fallen off of the platform and died. Morbid, but useful. The next step is to actually check to see whether the current asteroid in the loop has fallen off of the platform.

Add the following beneath the friction code in the animate function:

```
if (!tmpAsteroid.player) {
        var dXp = tmpAsteroid.x - platformX;
        var dYp = tmpAsteroid.y - platformY;
        var distanceP = Math.sqrt((dXp*dXp)+(dYp*dYp));
        if (distanceP > platformOuterRadius) {
                if (tmpAsteroid.radius > 0) {
                        tmpAsteroid.radius -= 2;
                } else {
                        deadAsteroids.push(tmpAsteroid);
                };
        };
};
```

There are a few key steps in this bit of code. The first is the initial check to make sure that the current asteroid isn't actually the player asteroid (that's being thrown); you don't want to remove that one. Second are the calculations that work out the distance between the asteroid and the centre of the platform. Third is the check to see whether the centre of the asteroid is outside of the platform edge.

Within the third check is another set of code that deals with the asteroid now that you know that it's not on the platform. It would be a shame to just make the asteroid disappear out of the blue, so why not make it shrink and look like it's falling off of a real platform? You do this with a simple check. If the asteroid has a radius above 0, then it's obviously still visible, so reduce the radius by two pixels. This will happen on each loop of the animation and ultimately cause the effect of shrinking the asteroid quite quickly. Once the asteroid radius is at or below 0 (after a few loops), you can then safely assume that it's dead and add it to the deadAsteroids array.

Give the game a go and you'll see that the asteroids now shrink and seems to disappear when they fall off of the platform (see Figure 8-16).

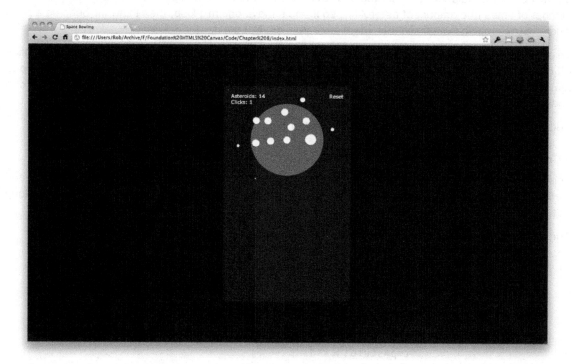

Figure 8-16. Making the asteroid disappear when they leave the platform

The next task is to remove the dead asteroids from the original asteroids array, and let the player know that the game is over when there are no asteroids left.

Add the following code at the end of the animate function, but above the conditional statement with the call to setTimeout in:

```
var deadAsteroidsLength = deadAsteroids.length;
if (deadAsteroidsLength > 0) {
        for (var di = 0; di < deadAsteroidsLength; di++) {
                var tmpDeadAsteroid = deadAsteroids[di];
                asteroids.splice(asteroids.indexOf(tmpDeadAsteroid), 1);
        };
};
```

This section of code runs outside of the asteroid loops, so it runs after every asteroid has been updated, collision detected, and moved. The first thing it does is check to see whether there are any dead asteroids to deal with. If so, you're free to start doing the fun stuff and letting the player get one step closer to winning the game.

If there are dead asteroids to deal with, you loop through them all and assign each one to the temporary tmpDeadAsteroid variable. Because the asteroid object in the deadAsteroids array is the same one that's in the asteroidsArray, you can use a special array method called indexOf to work out the index of the dead asteroid in the original asteroids array, which ultimately allows you to remove it. This is a little confusing, so it's important to get your head around. In the previous code listing, you added the asteroid held in the tmpAsteroid variable to the deadAsteroids array. The asteroid in deadAsteroids is not a copy, it's actually pointing to the asteroid in the original asteroids array. I honestly don't expect this to make complete sense; it's a bit of a mind bender. It's just important to bear in mind.

To remove the asteroid from the asteroids array, you need to use the splice method of the Array object. This allows you to remove one or more elements from an array, starting at the index defined in the first argument, and continuing for as many elements as defined in the second argument.

You need the start index to be the index of the asteroid that you want to remove; so to do that you need to use the indexOf method of the Array object. This effectively searches through an array for a particular item, and returns its index position within the array if it can find it. In this case, you want to find the asteroid, so you pass in the tmpDeadAsteroid variable as the argument in indexOf. You know you only want to remove one asteroid, so the second argument of the call to splice can be left as 1.

Together, this gives you enough information to remove the correct dead asteroid from the original asteroids array.

The very last thing to do is update the UI with the number of asteroids left, and to actually let the player win the game when there are no asteroids left on the platform.

Add the following after the for loop in the previous section of code:

```
var remaining = asteroids.length-1; // Remove player from asteroid count
uiRemaining.html(remaining);

if (remaining == 0) {
        // Winner!
        playGame = false;
        uiStats.hide();
        uiComplete.show();

        $(window).unbind("mousedown");
```

```
        $(window).unbind("mouseup");
        $(window).unbind("mousemove");
};
```

The first line declares a variable that holds the number of asteroids remaining on the platform. Notice how you need to reduce the number by 1, because you don't count the player asteroid. You then use that variable to update the game UI with the remaining asteroids in the game.

To see whether the player has won or not, you simply perform a conditional statement that checks for the number of remaining asteroids to be 0. If so, you stop the game, hide the game statistics UI, and show the game complete screen. The final three lines just remove the mouse event listeners, as you won't need them again unless the player wants to play again.

Refresh the game and give it a go (see Figure 8-17). My best score is two clicks, although that took me ages!

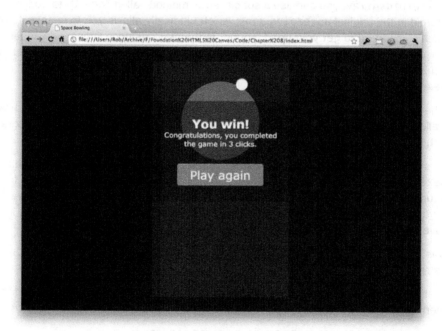

Figure 8-17. The finished game

Summary

So you actually just finished your first game in canvas. Pretty awesome, isn't it? I'd definitely be proud if I were you. In fact, I'm proud *for* you. It wasn't the easiest chapter in the world, but my hope is that you now know enough about putting together various parts of a game to produce something interactive and exciting to play. If you didn't already, I bet you appreciate the effort that goes into games programming.

The key aspects that you learned in this chapter are detecting user input with a mouse, creating and manipulating a user interface, and constructing a scenario in which a player can win the game. You'll be using these aspects and more when you construct the next game, except this time the player will be controlling a rocket with their keyboard. Cool!

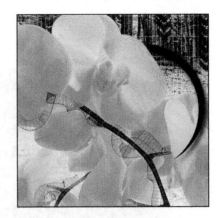

Chapter 9

Creating the Asteroid Avoidance Game

This time around you're going to create an asteroid avoidance game; a game that's going to build from the lessons learnt in previous chapters, while also teaching you a few new skills at the same time. The game is also going to be very different in gameplay from the previous game, with much more control from the player.

The two most important lessons that you'll take from this chapter are how to detect keyboard input with JavaScript, and also how to use and control HTML5 audio for sound within a game. Enjoy!

Overview of the game

The goal of the asteroid avoidance game should be fairly obvious, I hope (it's kind of in the name). For those who are still unsure, the aim of the game is to fly a rocket around and survive for as long as possible while asteroids hurtle towards you (see Figure 9-1). If you hit an asteroid then it's game over, with the score being based on how many seconds you managed to survive for. It may not be a blockbuster, but it leads to some surprisingly addictive gameplay, just like the bowling game.

The asteroid avoidance game will differ wildly from the space bowling game that you made in the previous chapter. The main difference is that this will be a side-scrolling game, or at least it will feel like one. Whereas the previous game was very much static, this new game will have a prominent feeling of movement.

Another major difference between the two games is that of player input. In the bowling game the player input came from the mouse; in this game the player input will be achieved through various keys on the keyboard. It's possible that this game could also be controlled with the mouse, but I feel that it's important for you to explore other ways to interact with a game.

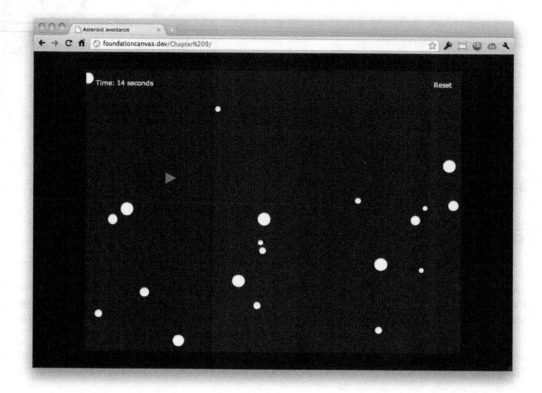

Figure 9-1. The asteroid avoidance game

Requirements

Most of the core logic from the previous game will be reused within this game; things like the animation loop, some game objects, and the main functions. The HTML and UI will also be fairly similar to the previous game, apart from obvious changes specific to the asteroid avoidance game.

New skills that you'll learn through this chapter include the detection of keyboard input, and the use of HTML5 audio for sound effects within the game. You'll be tying in these new skills with most of the others that you've learnt within this book, like drawing in canvas, animation, physics, and game logic.

Setting up the core functionality

As I mentioned previously, most of the core logic within this game will be based on the bowling game logic. This may seem lazy, but it's this kind of code reuse that speeds up development, and allows you ultimately to create a robust engine that you can use as a foundation for future games. You'd be hard pushed to find a game that requires entirely unique functionality that's never been attempted before. Why reinvent the wheel?

Marking up the HTML

Nearly all the HTML is the same for this game, so let's jump right in. Create a new directory on your computer for the game, and insert the following code into a document called *index.html*:

```html
<!DOCTYPE html>

<html>
        <head>
                <title>Asteroid avoidance</title>
                <meta charset="utf-8">

                <link href="game.css" rel="stylesheet" type="text/css">

                <script type="text/javascript"
src="http://ajax.googleapis.com/ajax/libs/jquery/1/jquery.min.js"></script>
                <script type="text/javascript" src="game.js"></script>
        </head>

        <body>
                <div id="game">
                        <div id="gameUI">
                                <div id="gameIntro">
                                        <h1>Asteroid avoidance</h1>
                                        <p>Click play and then press any key to start.</p>
                                        <p><a id="gamePlay" class="button"
href="">Play</a></p>
                                </div>
                                <div id="gameStats">
                                        <p>Time: <span class="gameScore"></span> seconds</p>
                                        <p><a class="gameReset" href="">Reset</a></p>
                                </div>
                                <div id="gameComplete">
                                        <h1>Game over!</h1>
                                        <p>You survived for <span class="gameScore"></span>
seconds.</p>
                                        <p><a class="gameReset button" href="">Play
again</a></p>
                                </div>
                        </div>
                        <canvas id="gameCanvas" width="800" height="600">
                                <!-- Insert fallback content here -->
                        </canvas>
                </div>
        </body>
</html>
```

Nothing scary here. The only things that have changed are the title of the page, some wording of the content, and the dimensions of the canvas. Apart from that it's very much similar to what you had before (see Figure 9-2).

Figure 9-2. Marking up the game with HTML

Making things pretty

Create a new document called *game.css* and place it in the same directory as the HTML file. Insert the following code into the CSS file:

```
* { margin: 0; padding: 0; }
html, body { height: 100%; width: 100%; }
canvas { display: block; }

body {
        background: #000;
        color: #fff;
        font-family: Verdana, Arial, sans-serif;
        font-size: 18px;
}

h1 {
        font-size: 30px;
}

p {
        margin: 0 20px;
```

```
}

a {
        color: #fff;
        text-decoration: none;
}

a:hover {
        text-decoration: underline;
}

a.button {
        background: #185da8;
        border-radius: 5px;
        display: block;
        font-size: 30px;
        margin: 40px 0 0 270px;
        padding: 10px;
        width: 200px;
}

a.button:hover {
        background: #2488f5;
        color: #fff;
        text-decoration: none;
}

#game {
        height: 600px;
        left: 50%;
        margin: -300px 0 0 -400px;
        position: relative;
        top: 50%;
        width: 800px;
}

#gameCanvas {
        background: #001022;
}

#gameUI {
        height: 600px;
        position: absolute; /* Places UI on top of the canvas */
        width: 800px;
}


#gameIntro, #gameComplete {
        background: rgba(0, 0, 0, 0.5);
        margin-top: 100px;
        padding: 40px 0;
        text-align: center;
}

#gameStats {
```

```
        font-size: 14px;
        margin: 20px 0;
}

#gameStats .gameReset {
        margin: 20px 20px 0 0;
        position: absolute;
        right: 0;
        top: 0;
}
```

Much the same as the HTML, the CSS has barely changed; the only differences are a change in dimensions for the CSS rules #game and #gameUI. These changes tweak the visual styling of the UI to be positioned correctly within the bigger canvas (see Figure 9-3).

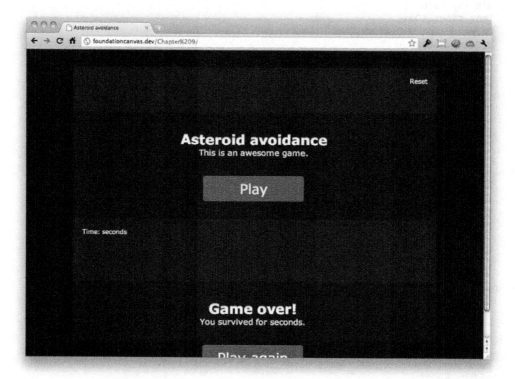

Figure 9-3. Styling the UI with CSS

Setting up the JavaScript

The last stage in the set up is to add in the JavaScript, just as you did with the bowling game. Create a new document called *game.js* and place it within the same directory as the HTML and CSS files. Insert the following code within it:

```
$(document).ready(function() {
        var canvas = $("#gameCanvas");
```

```javascript
var context = canvas.get(0).getContext("2d");

// Canvas dimensions
var canvasWidth = canvas.width();
var canvasHeight = canvas.height();

// Game settings
var playGame;

// Game UI
var ui = $("#gameUI");
var uiIntro = $("#gameIntro");
var uiStats = $("#gameStats");
var uiComplete = $("#gameComplete");
var uiPlay = $("#gamePlay");
var uiReset = $(".gameReset");
var uiScore = $(".gameScore");

// Reset and start the game
function startGame() {
        // Reset game stats
        uiScore.html("0");
        uiStats.show();

        // Set up initial game settings
        playGame = false;

        // Start the animation loop
        animate();
};

// Inititialize the game environment
function init() {
        uiStats.hide();
        uiComplete.hide();

        uiPlay.click(function(e) {
                e.preventDefault();
                uiIntro.hide();
                startGame();
        });

        uiReset.click(function(e) {
                e.preventDefault();
                uiComplete.hide();
                startGame();
        });
};

// Animation loop that does all the fun stuff
function animate() {
        // Clear
        context.clearRect(0, 0, canvasWidth, canvasHeight);

        if (playGame) {
```

```
            // Run the animation loop again in 33 milliseconds
            setTimeout(animate, 33);
        };
    };

    init();
});
```

Although slightly scary looking, this is practically the same as the core logic from last chapter. The only difference is that the core UI logic has been included now, rather than adding it all in a separate chapter later on. Regardless, the UI code is the same as before, so it should all make sense to you.

Give the game a whirl in your favorite browser and you should have a much tidier UI (see Figure 9-4). You should also be able to click on the play button to reach the main game screen, although it looks mighty boring at the moment (see Figure 9-5).

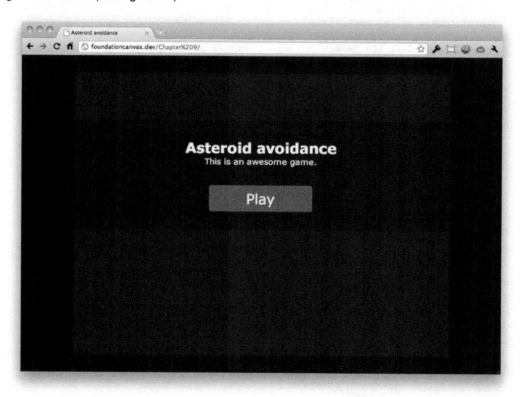

Figure 9-4. Hiding parts of the UI by using JavaScript

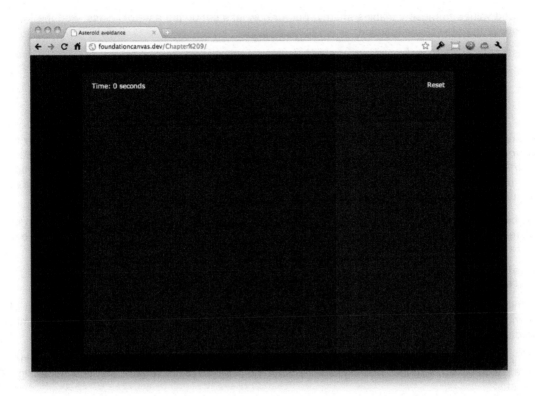

Figure 9-5. Viewing the currently empty main game screen

Creating the game objects

The asteroid avoidance game is going to have two main objects: the asteroids and the player rocket. Each of these objects are going to be created as JavaScript classes. You might be wondering why you're going to use a class for the player when there is only one of them. The short answer is that it's possible that you might want to add multiple players into your game, in which case it's going to make things much easier if the player is created with a class.

Setting up the asteroids

Using classes for your game objects means it's dead easy to reuse and repurpose them in another game. For example, in the asteroid avoidance game you're going to use the same asteroid class as the bowling game, with just a few changes.

The first step is to declare the main variable that will be used to store all the asteroids within, as well as another variable which you're going to use to work out how many asteroids should be in the game. Add the following code underneath the `playGame` variable at the top of the JavaScript:

```
var asteroids;
var numAsteroids;
```

You'll add values to these variables shortly, but for now let's set up the asteroid class. Add the following code above the startGame function:

```
var Asteroid = function(x, y, radius, vX) {
        this.x = x;
        this.y = y;
        this.radius = radius;
        this.vX = vX;
};
```

You'll recognize this from the previous game, although it should look a lot shorter. The reason for this is that you won't be using as much physics to animate the asteroids this time, so you don't need any properties for mass or friction. You'll also notice that there is only one velocity property; this is because the asteroids will only be moving from right to left, which is the x velocity. There is no need to have a y velocity, so it has been left out.

Now, before you can start creating all the asteroids, you need to set up the array to store them in and declare the amount of asteroids to actually use. Add the following code below the playGame variable within the startGame function:

```
asteroids = new Array();
numAsteroids = 10;
```

You might think ten asteroids is a small number, but you'll be recycling them when they move off of the screen, so it will actually seem like there is an unlimited number of them. Try to think of the number of asteroids as the total amount that can possibly exist on the screen at a single time.

Setting up the asteroids is simply a case of creating a loop that cycles for the number of asteroids that you've just declared. Add the following code beneath the numAsteroids variable that you just assigned a value to:

```
for (var i = 0; i < numAsteroids; i++) {
        var radius = 5+(Math.random()*10);
        var x = canvasWidth+radius+Math.floor(Math.random()*canvasWidth);
        var y = Math.floor(Math.random()*canvasHeight);
        var vX = -5-(Math.random()*5);

        asteroids.push(new Asteroid(x, y, radius, vX));
};
```

In an effort to make each asteroid slightly different and to make the game look a little more interesting, you're setting the radius to a random value between 5 and 15 pixels (5 plus a random number between 0 and 10). The same can also be said about the x velocity, although this value is being set between -5 and -10 (-5 minus a number between 0 and 5). You're using a negative velocity because you want the asteroids to travel from right to left, meaning that their x position decreases over time.

The calculation for the x position for each asteroid looks a bit complex, but it's actually very simple. It looks a little weird to have all of the asteroids suddenly appearing on the screen when you start the game, so it's much better to have them positioned off to the right of the screen, and then letting them move across as the game progresses.

To do this you first set the x position as the width of the canvas element, and then add the radius of the asteroid. This means that if you drew the asteroid now it would be positioned just off the right hand edge of the screen. If you left it like this then all the asteroids would appear in a line, so the next step is to add a random value onto the *x* position that is between 0 and the canvas width (see Figure 9-6). In comparison, the *y* position is simple; it's just a random value between 0 and the height of the canvas.

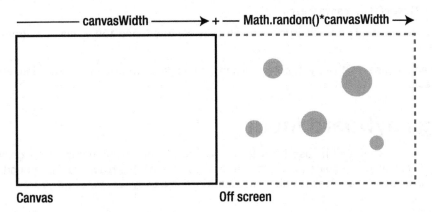

Figure 9-6. Storing the asteroids offscreen

What this achieves is effectively a box the same size as the canvas which is full of randomly positioned asteroids that will move across the visible canvas when the game starts. Trust me, it's not as complicated as it sounds.

The last thing to do is to push a new asteroid into the array of asteroids, ready to animate and draw.

Setting up the player rocket

In the last game the player was just a simple asteroid. That's boring. In this game the player is going to control a freaking rocket ship; that's much cooler!

Let's jump right in and declare the initial variables that will be used to set up the player. Add the following code below the `numAsteroids` variable at the top of the JavaScript:

```
var player;
```

This variable is going to hold a reference to the player object, which hasn't actually been defined yet; let's change that. Add the following code beneath the `Asteroid` class:

```
var Player = function(x, y) {
        this.x = x;
        this.y = y;
        this.width = 24;
        this.height = 24;
        this.halfWidth = this.width/2;
        this.halfHeight = this.height/2;

        this.vX = 0;
        this.vY = 0;
};
```

You'll recognize some of this from the `Asteroid` class, namely the position and velocity properties. The rest of the properties describe the dimensions of the player rocket, both in full and at half size. You'll be using these dimensions when drawing out the rocket and performing collision detection.

The last step is to create a new player object, so add the following code below the `numAsteroids` variable within the `startGame` function:

```
player = new Player(150, canvasHeight/2);
```

This will place the player at an *x* and *y* position vertically centered, and 150 pixels away from the left edge of the canvas.

You won't be able to see anything yet, but you'll sort that out later on when you move onto animating all of the game objects.

Detecting keyboard input

In the bowling game you used mouse input to control the player; in this game you're going to use the keyboard. Specifically you're going to use the arrow keys to move the player rocket around. How do you achieve this? Is it harder than dealing with mouse input? No, it's easy. Let me show you.

Key codes

The first thing to understand when dealing with keyboard input is how to work out which key is being used. In JavaScript, every single button on a regular keyboard has been assigned a specific key code. It's this code that lets you know the exact key that has been pressed down, or released. You'll see exactly how to use this key code shortly, but for now it's just important to know that each key has a number attached to it.

For example, the keys *a* to *z* (regardless of case) have key codes of 65 to 90, respectively. The arrow keys have the key codes 37 to 40; left 37, up 38, right 39, and down 40. Space bar has a key code of 32.

> I'd advise you to check out this article on the QuirksMode website for more information about key codes [www.quirksmode.org/js/keys.html].

It's the arrow keys that you're most interested in for the asteroid avoidance game, so add the following code beneath the `player` variable at the top of the JavaScript:

```
var arrowUp = 38;
var arrowRight = 39;
var arrowDown = 40;
```

What you're doing here is assigning the key code for each arrow to a variable that describes it. This is called enumeration, which is the process of giving a value a name. It basically makes things a lot easier later on, as you'll be able to easily work out which arrow key you're referring to.

Notice how you've not declared a variable for the left arrow. This is because you're not going to let the player move backwards manually; instead you're going to move the player backwards whenever they aren't pressing a key. This will make more sense later on.

Keyboard events

Before you can get to the juicy part of adding keyboard interaction to the game, you need to work out when the player has pressed and released a key. To do this you'll need to utilize the keydown and keyup event listeners, which are very similar to the mousedown and mouseup event listeners you used in the previous game.

Add the following code above the call to the animate function within the startGame function (below the loop in which you're creating all the asteroids):

```
$(window).keydown(function(e) {

});

$(window).keyup(function(e) {

});
```

Looks similar to the mouse event listeners you used last chapter, doesn't it? The first listener triggers when a key is pressed down, and the second triggers when a key is released. Simple.

You'll fill those event listeners with useful code in a moment, but first let's make sure that the listeners are removed when the game is reset, which will prevent the game from being inadvertently started by pressing a key. Add the following code above the call to startGame in the uiReset.click event listener:

```
$(window).unbind("keyup");
$(window).unbind("keydown");
```

Next up, you need to add some properties to help when animating the player. Add the following code at the bottom of the Player class:

```
this.moveRight = false;
this.moveUp = false;
this.moveDown = false;
```

These properties will let you know which direction to move the player, and they will be set depending on which key has been pressed. Is it all starting to make sense now?

Now it's time to add some logic into the keyboard event listeners. Firstly, add the following code within the keydown event listener:

```
var keyCode = e.keyCode;

if (!playGame) {
        playGame = true;
        animate();
};

if (keyCode == arrowRight) {
        player.moveRight = true;
} else if (keyCode == arrowUp) {
        player.moveUp = true;
} else if (keyCode == arrowDown) {
        player.moveDown = true;
};
```

And the following within the `keyup` event listener:

```
var keyCode = e.keyCode;

if (keyCode == arrowRight) {
        player.moveRight = false;
} else if (keyCode == arrowUp) {
        player.moveUp = false;
} else if (keyCode == arrowDown) {
        player.moveDown = false;
};
```

It should be fairly obvious as to what's going on here, but let me clarify it for you. The first line in both listeners assigns the key code of the key to a variable. You then use this key code within a set of conditional statements to work out if an arrow key has been pressed and, if so, exactly which one. From there it's a case of enabling (if the key is being pressed down), or disabling (if the key is being released) the respective property on the player object.

For example, if you press the right arrow key then the `moveRight` property of the player object will be set to *true*. If you release the right arrow key then the `moveRight` property will be set to *false*.

> You should be aware that if the player holds down a key then multiple keydown events will be fired. It's important to make sure that your code can handle keydown events being fired multiple times; there won't always be a keyup event after each keydown event.

Also, notice how in the `keydown` event listener that you've got a conditional statement that checks to see whether the game is currently playing. This is to stop the game running without the player being ready; it will only start once they press down a key on the keyboard. Simple, but effective.

That's pretty much it for keyboard input for the game; in the next section you'll be using this input to animate the player in the right direction.

Making things move

You've now got absolutely everything prepared to start animating the game objects. This is the fun bit, when you actually get to see stuff. Hooray!

The first step is to update the position of all the game objects. Let's start with the asteroid objects, so add the following code beneath the call to the canvas `clearRect` method in the `animate` function:

```
var asteroidsLength = asteroids.length;
for (var i = 0; i < asteroidsLength; i++) {
        var tmpAsteroid = asteroids[i];

        tmpAsteroid.x += tmpAsteroid.vX;

        context.fillStyle = "rgb(255, 255, 255)";
        context.beginPath();
        context.arc(tmpAsteroid.x, tmpAsteroid.y, tmpAsteroid.radius, 0, Math.PI*2, true);
        context.closePath();
        context.fill();
};
```

This is all straightforward, and is nothing new from what you did in the last chapter. Basically what's happening is that you're looping through each asteroid, updating its position based on the velocity, and then drawing it to the canvas.

Refresh the browser and have a look (remember to press a key to start the game). You should be able to see an asteroid field float past the screen (see Figure 9-7). Notice how they disappear off the left hand side of the screen; you'll learn how to stop that in the following section on side-scrolling.

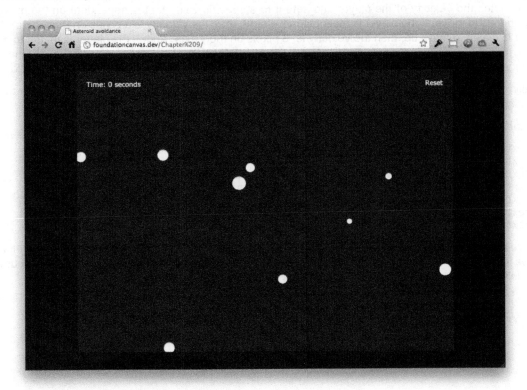

Figure 9-7. Drawing and animating the asteroid field

For now, let's imagine that those asteroids are doing everything that you want them to do. It's time to update and visualize the player!

Add the following code beneath the asteroid code that you just added in the `animate` function:

```
player.vX = 0;
player.vY = 0;

if (player.moveRight) {
        player.vX = 3;
};

if (player.moveUp) {
        player.vY = -3;
};
```

```
if (player.moveDown) {
        player.vY = 3;
};

player.x += player.vX;
player.y += player.vY;
```

This updates the velocity of the player and sets it to a specific value that is dependent on the direction that it needs to move. If the player is meant to move right, then the velocity is 3 pixels on the *x* axis. If the player is meant to move up, then the velocity is -3 pixels on the *y* axis. And, if the player is meant to move down, then the velocity is 3 pixels on the *y* axis. Simple stuff so far. Also, notice how you're resetting the velocity values at the beginning; this causes the player to stop if no arrow keys are being pressed down.

Finally, you update the *x* and *y* position of the player, based on the velocity. You won't be able to see anything yet, but you now have everything that you need to draw the rocket on the screen.

Add the following code directly beneath the code you just added:

```
context.fillStyle = "rgb(255, 0, 0)";
context.beginPath();
context.moveTo(player.x+player.halfWidth, player.y);
context.lineTo(player.x-player.halfWidth, player.y-player.halfHeight);
context.lineTo(player.x-player.halfWidth, player.y+player.halfHeight);
context.closePath();
context.fill();
```

Can you work out what's going on here? It's obvious that you're drawing a filled path, but can you tell what shape it is from the way that you're drawing it? You could just cheat and have a look at Figure 9-8, but that wouldn't be much fun! Okay, okay. It's a triangle. Happy now?

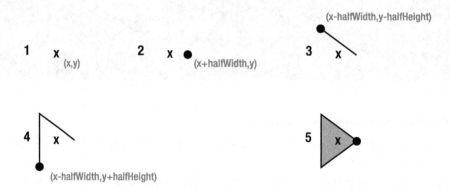

Figure 9-8. Drawing a triangle for the player rocket

If you take a proper look at Figure 9-8 then you'll be able to see how the dimensional properties from the player object come into play. By knowing the half width and height of the player object, you're able to construct a dynamic triangle that could grow and shrink if the dimension values ever changed. Simple, but cool.

Check out the game in the browser now and you should be able to see the player rocket (see Figure 9-9). Try pressing the arrow keys. See the rocket moving? Now that's pretty awesome.

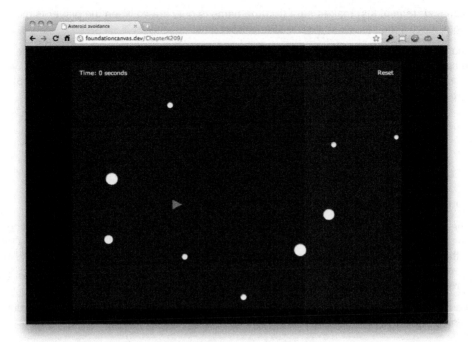

Figure 9-9. Drawing and animating the player rocket

You could just leave the movement logic there, but that wouldn't be any fun. Let's add an animated flame to the rocket! Add the following code at the end of the `Player` class:

```
this.flameLength = 20;
```

You'll be using this to decide how long the flame is, but more on that later. For now, add the following code just before you draw the rocket in the `animate` function:

```
if (player.moveRight) {
        context.save();
        context.translate(player.x-player.halfWidth, player.y);

        if (player.flameLength == 20) {
                player.flameLength = 15;
        } else {
                player.flameLength = 20;
        };

        context.fillStyle = "orange";
        context.beginPath();
        context.moveTo(0, -5);
        context.lineTo(-player.flameLength, 0);
        context.lineTo(0, 5);
        context.closePath();
        context.fill();

        context.restore();
};
```

The conditional statement just makes sure that the flame is only drawn when the player is moving right; it would just look weird if the flame was visible at any other time.

You're going to utilize the canvas `translate` method to draw the flame, so to save some time later you're saving the canvas drawing state with a call to `save`. Now you have the original state stored, you can call the `translate` method and move the origin of the 2D rendering context to the left edge of the player rocket (the translated origin is marked with an x in Figure 9-10).

Figure 9-10. Drawing the rocket flame

Now that the origin of the canvas has been moved, the rest is easy. All you're doing is cycling the value stored in the `flameLength` property of the player object (making it seem to flicker), changing the fill color to orange, then beginning a path and drawing out a triangle that is the same length as the `flameLength` property (see the right side of Figure 9-10). The last thing that you want to do is call `restore`, to push the original drawing state back onto the canvas.

Refresh the browser and take a look at your handy work; the rocket should now have a flickering flame whenever you press down the right arrow key (see Figure 9-11).

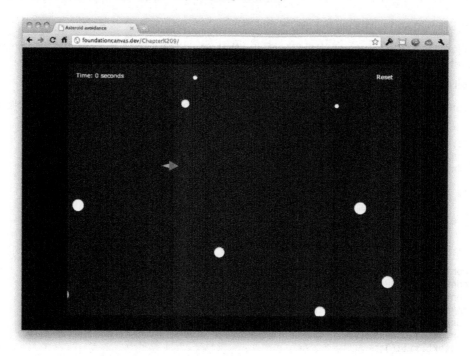

Figure 9-11. Drawing and animating the rocket flame

That's pretty much it for movement. You're not doing any advanced physics in this game (it doesn't always make a game more awesome), so you're now ready to move onto making this game a true side-scroller.

Faking the side-scrolling effect

Did I say faking? So I did! Yes, although this game will look like a side-scroller, you're not actually traveling through the game world. Instead, you're going to recycle all the objects that fall off of the screen and make them reappear on the other side. This gives the effect that you're travelling through an endless game world. A bit of a trick, but it's still a side-scroller.

Recycling the asteroids

Making the game look like your flying through a field of endless asteroids is actually not all that hard. In fact, it's easy! Jump into the `animate` function and add the following code just above where you draw out each asteroid:

```
if (tmpAsteroid.x+tmpAsteroid.radius < 0) {
        tmpAsteroid.radius = 5+(Math.random()*10);
        tmpAsteroid.x = canvasWidth+tmpAsteroid.radius;
        tmpAsteroid.y = Math.floor(Math.random()*canvasHeight);
        tmpAsteroid.vX = -5-(Math.random()*5);
};
```

That's literally all you need to do. What's happening here is that you're checking to see whether the asteroid has moved outside the left edge of the canvas and, if so, resetting it and moving it back over to the right hand side. You've recycled the asteroid, yet it looks and feels like a completely new one.

Adding boundaries

At the moment the player can quite happily fly out of the game and potentially get stuck (try flying off the right hand side). To fix this you need to put some boundaries in place. Add the following code above where you draw out the player flame (just below when you set the new player position):

```
if (player.x-player.halfWidth < 20) {
        player.x = 20+player.halfWidth;
} else if (player.x+player.halfWidth > canvasWidth-20) {
        player.x  = canvasWidth-20-player.halfWidth;
}

if (player.y-player.halfHeight < 20) {
        player.y = 20+player.halfHeight;
} else if (player.y+player.halfHeight > canvasHeight-20) {
        player.y = canvasHeight-20-player.halfHeight;
};
```

You can probably guess what's going on here. Basically you're performing some standard boundary checks, just like you did in the previous game. These checks look to see whether the player is within twenty pixels of the edge of the canvas and, if so, stops them from moving any further in that direction. The twenty pixel padding is there because I felt that it looked a little better, but feel free to change it so the player can move right up to the very edge.

Giving the player constant movement

As it stands, if the player isn't pressing down any keys then the rocket stops moving. This looks a little bit weird with all the asteroids floating by, so to add a bit of extra movement to the game let's try moving the player backwards when they aren't moving forward.

Change the piece of code that changes the player vX property in the `animate` function to the following:

```
if (player.moveRight) {
        player.vX = 3;
} else {
        player.vX = -3;
};
```

What you've done here is simply add an extra part to the conditional statement that sets the player vX property to -3 if the player isn't meant to be moving right. As with most game logic when you boil it down; it's simple.

Give it a go in your browser. It's really starting to look like a proper game now!

Adding sound

This is probably the coolest part of the game, as it's something that we didn't cover in the bowling game. It's amazing how much some simple sound can add to a game; it just feels more immersive and interesting. You'd think adding audio to a game would be hard, but with HTML5 audio it's a breeze! Let me show you.

The first thing you need to do is declare all the HTML5 audio elements in the game HTML. Jump into the *index.html* file and add the following beneath the `canvas` element:

```
<audio id="gameSoundBackground" loop>
        <source src="sounds/background.ogg">
        <source src="sounds/background.mp3">
</audio>
<audio id="gameSoundThrust" loop>
        <source src="sounds/thrust.ogg">
        <source src="sounds/thrust.mp3">
</audio>
<audio id="gameSoundDeath">
        <source src="sounds/death.ogg">
        <source src="sounds/death.mp3">
</audio>
```

If you understood the section on HTML5 audio in Chapter 1, then this should all make sense to you. If not, then don't worry; it's easy. All your doing is declaring three separate HTML5 audio elements, and giving each a unique id attribute that you'll be using later. For the sounds that you want to loop, you also give them a loop attribute.

> *Note that at the time of writing, the* loop *attribute does not work in all browsers. It is part of the spec, so should eventually be included across the board. If you need a workaround, you can add an event listener for when the end of the track is reached and play the track again at that point.*

The three sounds are the background music, a thruster sound for when the rocket is moving, and finally a deep booming sound for when the player dies. Each sound requires two versions of the file to be compatible with the most amount of browsers, so two `source` elements are included; one for an mp3 version, and the other for an ogg version.

> Remember that you can download all the code and assets for this book from the Friends of ED website. This includes the sound files for the asteroid avoidance game.

That's all you need to do for the HTML side of things, so jump back into the JavaScript file and add the following beneath the `uiScore` variable at the top of the file:

```
var soundBackground = $("#gameSoundBackground").get(0);
var soundThrust = $("#gameSoundThrust").get(0);
var soundDeath = $("#gameSoundDeath").get(0);
```

These variables are using the `id` attributes that you declared in the HTML to grab each `audio` element, just like how to grab the `canvas` element for the game. You'll be using these variables to access the HTML5 audio API and control the sounds.

There's no point hanging around, so jump into the `keydown` event listener and add the following code after setting `playGame` to *true*:

```
soundBackground.currentTime = 0;
soundBackground.play();
```

You've just added and successfully controlled HTML5 audio in your game. Cool, huh? What's going on here is that you're accessing the HTML5 `audio` element associated with the background sound, and then directly controlling it through the HTML5 audio API. This allows you to reset the playhead of the audio to the beginning, by changing the `currentTime` property, and also to play the audio, by calling the `play` method. Did you think it was going to be hard?

Load up the game and give it a go, you should now have some lovely background music playing once you start moving the rocket.

> All the audio used within this game is from FreeSound. The background music is by the user asdftekno [www.freesound.org/samplesViewSingle.php?id=48546], the thrust sound is by the user nathanshadow [www.freesound.org/samplesViewSingle.php?id=22455], and the death sound is by the user HerbertBoland [www.freesound.org/samplesViewSingle.php?id=33637]. Creative Commons initiatives for the win!

The next step is to control the thrust sound for when the player is moving the rocket. As I hope you've already guessed, this is just as easy as implementing the background sound.

Add the following code beneath setting the `moveRight` property of the player object in the `keydown` event listener:

```
if (soundThrust.paused) {
        soundThrust.currentTime = 0;
        soundThrust.play();
};
```

265

The first line basically checks to see whether the thrust sound is actually playing and, if so, stops the game from playing it a second time. This prevents the sound from being cut out mid-flow, as the key down event is fired many times a second, and you don't want the thrust sound to play absolutely every time that it occurs (that would be a nightmare).

You probably don't want the thrust sound to continue playing when the player stops moving, so add the following code beneath setting the moveRight property of the player object in the keyup event listener:

```
soundThrust.pause();
```

That's really it; the API is a joy to use because it allows you to access and manipulate audio in such a simple way.

Before we move on (you'll add in the death sound in the next section), it's a good idea to make sure that the sounds are stopped if the player resets the game. Add the following code above the call to startGame in the uiReset.click event handler in the init function (that was a bit of a mouth full):

```
soundThrust.pause();
soundBackground.pause();
```

Those two lines will make sure that both the thrust and background sound are stopped when the game is reset. You don't need to worry about the death sound because it doesn't loop and you want it to play over the game over screen.

Ending the game

The game is starting to really shape up now. In fact, it's practically finished; the only thing left to do is implement some kind of scoring system and a method that causes the game to end. Let's tackle the scoring first, I'll show you how to end the game in a moment.

Scoring

As the gameplay is entirely different to the last game, you need to come up with a different metric to base the scoring on. Seeing as you're trying to survive for as long as possible, then surely the amount of time that you've survived for is a good metric. Right? Good, I'm glad that you agree with me on that.

What you need is a method that lets you work out the number of seconds that have passed since the game was started. This is the perfect job for a JavaScript timeout, but before we set that up you'll want to declare a couple of variables. Add the following code beneath the player variable at the top of the JavaScript:

```
var score;
var scoreTimeout;
```

These variables will store the score (the number of seconds that have passed), and a reference to the timeout operation so you can access it and stop it when needed.

It's also going to be a good idea to reset the score whenever the game is started or reset, so add the following code beneath the numAsteroids variable near the top of the startGame function:

```
score = 0;
```

To manage the score timeout, let's create a dedicated function called timer. Place the following code above the animate function:

```
function timer() {
        if (playGame) {
                scoreTimeout = setTimeout(function() {
                        uiScore.html(++score);
                        timer();
                }, 1000);
        };
};
```

This won't run yet, but what it's doing is checking to see whether the game is playing and, if so, setting a timeout for 1 second and assigning it to the `scoreTimeout` variable. Within the timeout you're increasing the `score` variable and updating the score UI at the same time, just like how you updated the score in the bowling game. The timeout then calls the `timeout` function itself to repeat the entire process, which means that the timeout will stop when the game has stopped playing.

The `timer` function is useless right now as it's not being called yet. You want it to start when the game starts, so add the following code beneath the call to `animate` in the `keydown` event listener:

```
timer();
```

This will cause the timer to kick into action as soon as the player starts the game. Check it out in your browser now and watch the score increase in the top left corner (see Figure 9-12).

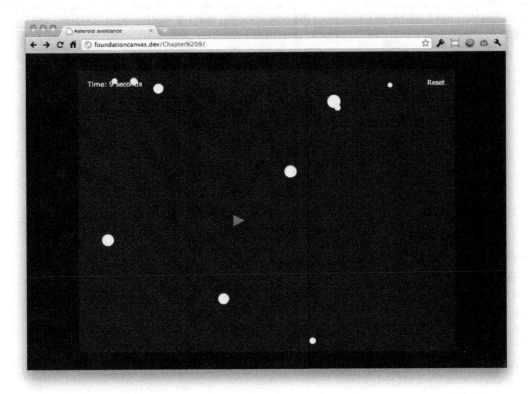

Figure 9-12. Adding a timer to the game

267

But alas, there is a problem; if you reset the game then the score sometimes changes to show 1 second. This is because the score timeout is still running when the game is reset, but it doesn't actually run until after the reset happens (changing the reset score of 0 to 1). To fix this you need to clear the timeout when the game is reset, and fortunately there is a specific function in JavaScript to help you do this.

Add the following code above the call to `startGame` in the `uiReset.click` event listener in the `init` function:

```
clearTimeout(scoreTimeout);
```

It's pretty self-explanatory really, but this lonely little function takes the score timeout that you assigned to the `scoreTimeout` variable and stops it from running. Try out the game now and watch how the annoying bug has been successfully squashed with a single line of JavaScript.

Killing the player

There's no point avoiding asteroids if they can't harm you, so let's add in some functionality to kill the player if they touch an asteroid. You're going to base the logic for the asteroid collision on the logic that you've used over the over in the previous chapters; circle collision detection.

Noticed the glaring issue here? How can you perform circle collision detection when the rocket is a triangle? Well, the short answer is you can't, at least not easily. You're going to cheat a little bit here, which means that there will be small areas of the player rocket that will register as a collision (see Figure 9-13), when in reality, and with a little bit of luck, you might have been able to avoid it.

I think that this is a fair sacrifice for much simpler code. After all, you're not aiming for super realism here, just an enjoyable and easy to play game.

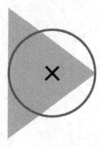

Figure 9-13. Using circle collision detection on a triangle

With that disclaimer out of the way, add the following code just above where you draw each asteroid in the `animate` function:

```
var dX = player.x - tmpAsteroid.x;
var dY = player.y - tmpAsteroid.y;
var distance = Math.sqrt((dX*dX)+(dY*dY));

if (distance < player.halfWidth+tmpAsteroid.radius) {
        soundThrust.pause();

        soundDeath.currentTime = 0;
        soundDeath.play();
```

```
        // Game over
        playGame = false;
        clearTimeout(scoreTimeout);
        uiStats.hide();
        uiComplete.show();

        soundBackground.pause();

        $(window).unbind("keyup");
        $(window).unbind("keydown");
};
```

You'll recognize the distance calculations straight away; they're exactly the same as the ones that you've used time and time again in the previous chapters. You're using them to work out the pixel distance between the player rocket and the current asteroid in the loop.

The next step is to work out whether the rocket and the asteroid have collided, which you can do by checking to see whether the distance is less than the radius of the asteroid plus the radius of the arbitrary collision circle for the rocket. At the moment the rocket collision circle has a radius that is half the width of the rocket, but you can change it to anything you want.

If the two are colliding then it's time to kill the player. Killing the player and ending the game is a fairly simple process, but let's walk through it line by line.

The first three lines stop the thrust sound and reset and play the death sound. Once the death sound is started you then stop the entire game by setting playGame to *false*, and stop the score timeout by using the same clearTimeout function call that you used previously.

At this point all the game logic has stopped, so you can hide the statistics UI, and bring up the game completed UI. This is exactly the same as with the bowling game.

Once the game completed UI is displaying, you then stop the background sound, and finally unbind the keyboard event handlers to prevent the game from being inadvertently started by pressing a key.

Still with me? Try it out in the browser and deliberately fly into an asteroid. I believe you've just finished your second game; well done (see Figure 9-14)!

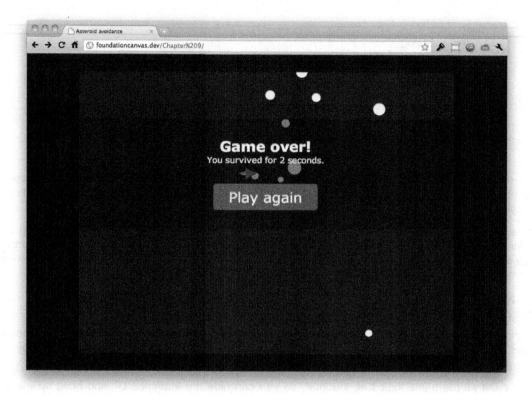

Figure 9-14. The finished asteroid avoidance game... or is it?

Increasing the difficulty

Okay, so I lied about finishing the game. Let's add one more feature into the game; one that makes the game more difficult to play the longer you survive for. That sounds like fun.

Jumping straight in again, add the following code beneath uiScore.html in the timer function:

```
if (score % 5 == 0) {
        numAsteroids += 5;
};
```

Looks like a normal conditional statement right? Wrong. Check out that random percentage symbol. For the initiated, that's the modulus sign, for the uninitiated, that's the modulus sign.

Modulus allows you to calculate whether one number is fully divisible by another number, it returns the remainder from dividing the two numbers. For example, 2 % 2 is 0 (2 divided by 2 is 1, no remainder), and 4 % 2 is 0 (4 divided by 2 is 2, no remainder). On the other hand, 5 % 2 is 1 (5 divided by 2 is 2, with a remainder of 1).

You can use modulus in this way to make things happen at a regular interval, like every 5 seconds. You can do this because you can apply modulus 5 to a number and if it returns 0, then it must be divisible by 5. It might sound complicated, but it's really straightforward once you get your head round it.

In the case of the game you're using modulus to make sure that a piece of code is run only every 5 seconds. The piece of code in question adds 5 more asteroids to the game, every 5 seconds. Actually, it doesn't add them yet, it just increases the number of asteroids that should be in the game.

Getting those new asteroids added to the game is simple. Add the following code beneath where you draw the player rocket in the `animate` function:

```
while (asteroids.length < numAsteroids) {
        var radius = 5+(Math.random()*10);
        var x = Math.floor(Math.random()*canvasWidth)+canvasWidth+radius;
        var y = Math.floor(Math.random()*canvasHeight);
        var vX = -5-(Math.random()*5);

        asteroids.push(new Asteroid(x, y, radius, vX));
};
```

This code checks the number of asteroids on every loop and, if the number is wrong, it adds the required number of new asteroids to the game until the numbers match up. You're using a `while` loop here, which is a different JavaScript loop that continues going until the condition between the brackets is false. In your case the `while` loop will continue until the length of the asteroids array is equal to or greater than the `numAsteroids` variable.

Kick up the game in the browser again and give it a go. Notice how more and more asteroids appear the longer that you survive (see Figure 9-15)? Now you're definitely finished. I promise!

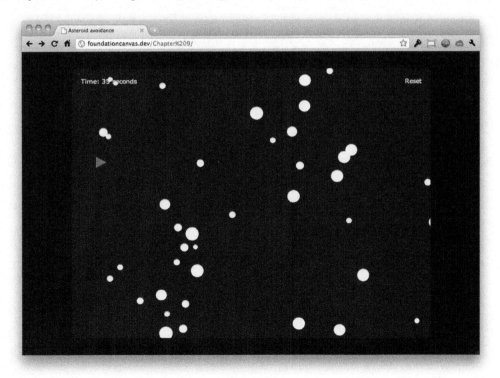

Figure 9-15. Definitely the finished asteroid avoidance game

Summary

This game may not have been as complicated as the previous one, but it certainly taught you some valuable skills for making games in JavaScript and HTML5. The most valuable of these have been learning how to detect keyboard input, and also how to use and manipulate HTML5 audio for sound within the game.

You've finished two games now, both of which are incredibly different in gameplay. I hope that they've shown you how fun and addictive games can be created by building up simple code and splitting it into logical sections. I also hope that the asteroid avoidance game has shown that you don't always have to use complex physics to make a game interesting.

Well done for getting this far. Let's take things down a level and have a look at the future of canvas.

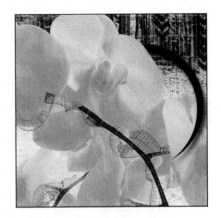

Chapter 10

Taking Things Further and the Future of Canvas

In this last chapter, I'll walk you through some of the ways to take things further with animation and game development. I'll also highlight some of the issues surrounding canvas and it's future, like the comparison with Flash and other technologies.

Canvas and SVG

Back in Chapter 1, I mentioned that SVG is often considered part of HTML5, when in reality it's actually a completely different technology. It's massively important to be aware of SVG, as it provides functionality that is very similar to that of canvas. It's also important to know the difference between SVG and canvas, as these differences will decide which of the two technologies you should be using.

SVG is another 2d drawing platform that is available within the browser, and that doesn't require plug-ins like Adobe Flash. As I mentioned in Chapter 1, SVG stands for Scalable Vector Graphics, which sort of gives away its major feature – vector graphics. In comparison, canvas uses bitmap graphics, but I'll explain the difference in more detail shortly.

Graphics are created in SVG by utilising the DOM, and everything that is drawn is created within a separate DOM element. For example, the following is the definition of a rectangle in SVG:

```
<svg xmlns="http://www.w3.org/2000/svg" version="1.1" height="100" width="200">
        <rect x="50" y="50" width="200" height="100" fill="#000000"/>
</svg>
```

Notice how all the attributes of the shapes are defined within the DOM element? This is a massive difference to canvas, in which everything is drawn within a single element, using JavaScript instead of the DOM.

There are many benefits to drawing shapes in the DOM like this, but one of the most valuable is that it allows you to access and edit a shape after you've drawn it. This is something that you can't do in canvas, as you'd need to wipe the canvas clean and redraw the shape again. In SVG there is nothing to wipe clean; you just edit the properties of each shape in the DOM, and it will update automatically.

A good way to compare to two technologies is by thinking of canvas as Microsoft Paint back in the day, where the only way that you can edit or change anything is by erasing it all and starting again. In comparison, SVG is more like Adobe Illustrator, where shapes are selectable and editable, and infinitely resizable.

> *Note: It's worth mentioning that inline SVG support is pretty lacking in browsers at the moment. Fortunately all the major manufacturers seem to be working on supporting it, so watch this space. I'd certainly keep an eye on the "When can I use" web site for more up to date information* http://caniuse.com/#feat=svg-html5.

Accessibility

Another huge benefit to SVG is that it's accessible. In canvas, everything that you draw is created using pixels, so the canvas is completely unaware of what's actually on it. For example, you might draw a circle using the arc method, but as far as the canvas is aware you've just changed the color of a specific area of pixels, even though they happen to look like a circle to the human eye. With SVG, you can access every shape and its data by traversing through the DOM. This allows you to pull data back out of SVG, and to also be aware of the kind of shapes that have been drawn and their properties (like size, position, and so on).

Bitmap vs. vector

As I mentioned previously, SVG is vector graphics, and canvas is bitmap graphics. What does this actually mean? In short, a lot!

Bitmap graphics (a.k.a. raster graphics) are stored as pixels in a 1-to-1 format (see Figure 10-1). What this means is that if you draw a one pixel square in bitmap, it will only ever exist as one pixel. If you tried to change that pixel, like resizing it, the single pixel would become pixellated and distorted. This is because the bitmap graphic has absolutely no idea about the type of shape that it represents. If you enlarged the one pixel square to say five pixels square, that single pixel would be stretched to five times the size, causing the new five pixel square to look fuzzy. I'm sure that you've noticed this effect before, perhaps when resizing a JPEG image.

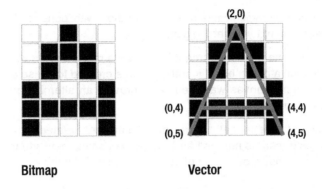

Bitmap   **Vector**

Figure 10-1. Bitmap vs. vector

On the other hand, vector graphics are stored as coordinates that describe the shape that you want to draw (again, see Figure 10-1). The benefit to this method is that pixels don't get involved until you actually want to visualize the vector graphic on a screen. This means that you can resize a vector graphic as much as you want and the resulting output in pixels will stay crisp and clean. The process going on here is simple; the coordinates of the shape are resized, but keep the same relationship between each other, then the new coordinates are converted into pixels to be displayed.

There are both massive pros and cons to canvas and SVG. For example, SVG is great for accessibility and for visualizing data that you want to be able to insert and pull out of the drawing at a later date (because it uses the DOM). Canvas, on the other hand, is fast and perfect for detailed pixel-level drawing, like manipulating images and video. It's worth weighing up the options before deciding which technology that you want to use. I wouldn't worry too much about it though; it's not a life-or-death decision.

> *Note: If you want to start playing with SVG then I'd highly recommend trying out the Raphaël JavaScript library at http://raphaeljs.com. It's a painless way to experiment with SVG without getting too caught up in setting everything up and creating all the individual DOM elements.*

Canvas and Flash

It seems that you can't go anywhere these days without someone claiming that canvas is a Flash killer, or that Flash is better than canvas. It's actually quite annoying, because there really isn't a battle between the two technologies; they serve completely different purposes!

Flash was created many years ago, and has evolved to solve some of the issues surrounding animation and multimedia on the Web. At the time, there were no native methods of drawing 2d graphics within the browser, or embedding video and audio. Flash solved these problems by providing a plugin that worked consistently across most, if not all browsers and platforms. It was a lifesaver!

Since then, Flash has evolved into something much bigger. In fact, Flash has matured into a solid platform that lets you produce fast animated graphics, encode video, and create complicated games. It also does a lot more, including network communications and integration with peripheral devices. Obviously I'm leaving out many of its features, but you get the gist.

Canvas was created to solve the problem of requiring a native method of drawing 2d graphics within the browser, without depending on a plugin being installed. It was created to utilise existing technologies like HTML and JavaScript. In short, canvas was created to provide an alternative solution for drawing and animating graphics within a browser. Simple!

I suppose what I'm getting at here is that canvas and Flash were created for different purposes. They solve different problems, and there is no need for there to be conflict between them. In my opinion, they shouldn't be compared, and it should be a case of using the right tool for the job.

JavaScript developers can learn from Flash

My friend, Seb Lee-Delisle, helped me put Flash and canvas into perspective. He said that canvas is at a stage of development that Flash was at many years ago (which is true), and that JavaScript developers can learn from the Flash developers that have gone through all this before.

He's absolutely right. Canvas is still not mainstream, and therefore not many people develop with it. The state of canvas means that JavaScript developers are still experimenting with it, trying to push it as far as possible to learn what can actually be done with it. The truth is that these experiments and the resulting lessons learned are very similar to the ones learned by the developers who pushed Flash to its limits all those years ago.

Seb's message is simple: stop trying to differentiate yourselves from each other, have a hug, and share your knowledge. If you can do that, then I can guarantee you that canvas will have a much brighter future.

Canvas doesn't have a user-friendly editor like Flash

One argument on the side of Flash is that it's difficult to use canvas because it doesn't have an application that makes it easy to work with, like the Flash IDE. Fortunately, this is no longer true.

There is a whole host of options available to canvas developers that help make the process of producing animations and games much easier. Some of these options are Radi (`http://radiapp.com`), which is a dedicated application to create HTML5 animation (see Figure 10-2), and ai2canvas, an Adobe Illustrator plug-in.

In all honestly, I wouldn't be surprised if Flash itself offers an option to export directly to canvas; I know Adobe are definitely toying with the concept.

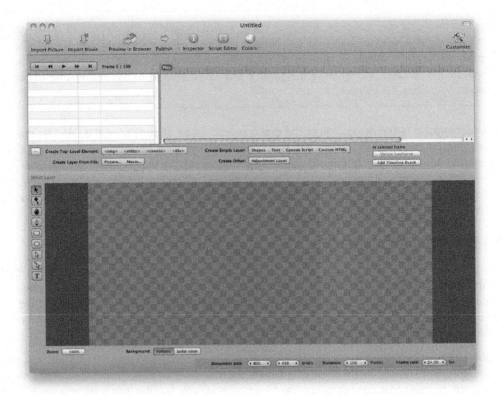

Figure 10-2. The Radi HTML5 animation application

In general, there is rarely an argument raised about Flash and canvas that can't be brushed aside with a little bit of sensible thinking. So next time someone asks you why they should use canvas instead of Flash, consider telling them that they shouldn't. That'll surprise them!

Canvas and performance

One of the most obvious limitations of canvas at the moment is that of performance. I'm not going to lie to you, it's pretty shocking at the moment. The reason for this is because most browsers use the CPU to render the canvas, which means that the processor quickly gets overwhelmed and the canvas grinds to a halt. Admittedly, this only happens when you're trying to create a complicated animation, or draw lots and lots of objects, but it's still a problem.

The good news is that there is a solution, and it's called hardware acceleration. The even better news is that the solution is available for you to experiment with today. What's surprising is that IE9 is one of the forerunners in canvas hardware acceleration, with a few other browsers in Windows following suit. Unfortunately, no browser on the Mac supports proper hardware acceleration just yet, but I'm sure that this will change soon.

> *Note: Interestingly, although IE9 is a major improvement to the Microsoft range of browsers, it won't be available on Windows XP. This means that users of those older versions of Windows will be without the amazing new Web technologies that are on the horizon. However, it's arguable that they should really be thinking about upgrading from XP by now.*

Hardware acceleration is the delegation of the drawing processes of canvas to the GPU on the graphics card. This frees up the CPU and allows the GPU to do what it does best: crunching through hardcore graphics-related tasks. The difference that hardware acceleration brings about is immense, and it's immediately obvious. I'd encourage you to play a canvas animation through on a browser that isn't hardware accelerated, and then again on a browser that is. If anything, the accelerated browser will probably feel a lot smoother.

Testing for performance

Hardware acceleration is definitely not a magic bullet; it can't solve all performance related problems. Some of the most common issues with performance can be solved quite simply. For example, too many loops in collision detection routines can cause all sorts of headaches. Another example would be using overly complicated mathematical calculations when you could achieve the same effect with an arbitrary number (like how you achieved friction in Chapter 7).

This is where the lessons from experienced Flash developers come into play. These are the guys that have gone through the hardships involved with squeezing every ounce of performance out of an animation loop. These are the guys that can teach you the tricks of the trade, like the little performance tips that add up to create some pretty noticeable gains.

If you want to do your own testing with performance, then I'd definitely check out jsPerf (`http://jsperf.com`). This benchmarking tool allows you to test various methods that achieve the same end goal; ultimately letting you work out if one is faster than the other. It's not foolproof, but it's certainly a great way of quickly finding out whether you can squeeze a bit more out of your code.

Canvas gaming and animation libraries

As far as what you've learned in this book, you should now have all the basic knowledge to go out and start creating your own games and animations from scratch. But what if you don't want to create them from scratch all the time? What if you want the everyday tasks like animation loops taken care of for you? This is where the influx of new animation and gaming libraries for HTML5 come in.

These libraries, like Impact (`http://impactjs.com`, shown in Figure 10-3), allow you to put together games and animations without having to worry about the nitty gritty. In essence, these libraries work in exactly the same way as jQuery; they abstract away the complexities, which allow you to worry about *what* you're making, instead of *how* you're making it.

Figure 10-3. The Impact game library

At the time of writing, there are numerous libraries to choose from (`https://github.com/bebraw/jswiki/wiki/Game-Engines`). Aside from Impact, another of the most prominent libraries is Easel (http://easeljs.com, shown in Figure 10-4). This is less of a dedicated gaming library, and more of a general helper library for animating with the canvas element.

If you're a Flash developer, then you'll notice straight away that Easel uses a lot of concepts from ActionScript; like display objects, and a stage. This isn't by accident. The developer, Grant Skinner, is well known for his Flash skills and says himself that Easel is "loosely based on Flash's display list, and should be easy to pick up for both JS and AS3 developers."

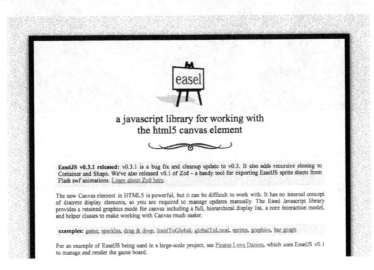

Figure 10-4. The Easel animation library

These libraries are good, but it's impossible for them to provide absolutely everything that you'll need. I'd recommend not jumping in and relying on them to do all the work for you. If you first learn the core concepts of animation and game development, then you'll have a solid standing for tackling issues, and attempting unique tasks that the libraries might not support.

Going into the third dimension

So far everything that you've created within the canvas has been two-dimensional. If this bores you, then you'll be mighty excited to know that three-dimensional graphics are coming to canvas under the guise of a technology called WebGL. It's not supported in all browsers (only Chrome and development versions of Webkit and Firefox at the time of writing), but it's still pretty cool.

If you'd like to try it today then I'd highly recommend giving the three.js library by Mr.doob a go (`https://github.com/mrdoob/three.js`). This library tries to lower the barrier for entry to WebGL (which is admittedly quite high) by making it as easy as possible to create awesome 3d graphics with as little code as possible (see Figure 10-5).

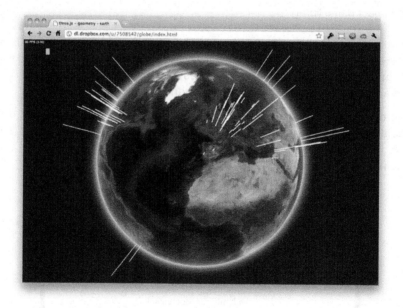

Figure 10-5. Mr.doob's 3d globe created using three.js

I'd be lying if I said 3d graphics in canvas wasn't complicated, but it doesn't make it any less fun. I'd certainly take a look at it, even if you don't plan to use it.

Integration with peripheral devices

A major area that browsers haven't cracked yet is that of interfacing with connected peripheral devices, like webcams and microphones. This is an area that Flash is particularly experienced in, and is one that is only just starting to see the light of day in a format that uses no plug-ins.

There's actually a group of people whose sole job is to come up with the specification for this communication between a browser and connected devices. The group is called the Device and APIs Policy Working Group, or DAP for short, and their work on the Media Capture API is what's most interesting, in my opinion.

It would be the Media Capture API that allows JavaScript developers to access images from a webcam and to then manipulate them or use them in some way. For example, you could build in face detection, a simple set of filters (like Photo Booth on the Mac), or perhaps even video streaming through something like WebSockets? Who knows. The possibilities are endless.

You should definitely check out the official website for the DAP group; it's very interesting to see the kind of stuff that's being worked on (www.w3.org/2009/dap/).

Project Rainbow

So far, there isn't much to show from the DAP, but at the time of writing Mozilla have already started experimenting with accessing the webcam and microphone through JavaScript. This experiment is called Rainbow (https://mozillalabs.com/rainbow/), and it's beginning to look really promising. As it stands, you can access a webcam and microphone, and then record them to an open format video file. The resulting file can then be accessed through JavaScript so you can manipulate it, or even upload it to a server. It's really cool!

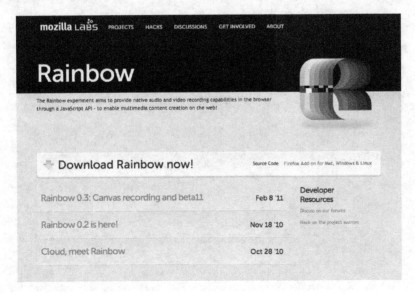

Figure 10-6. The project Rainbow web site

One of the coolest, most interesting features of Rainbow is its ability to record the contents of the canvas. What this allows you to do is record an animation, or perhaps a gaming session, and save it as a video file. It basically removes the need to use applications that record your entire desktop.

Multiplayer with WebSockets

Both of the games that you've created in this book are single player. Although, they could quite easily be made multiplayer by adding some simple logic for more than one player, like using a different set of keys for player two to move another rocket in the last game. However, this would still require both players to be playing on the same computer, and both using the same keyboard. WebSockets would allow you to make your game truly multiplayer over a network, like the Internet.

WebSockets aren't actually anything to do with games; they're a method of communicating data back and forth in realtime, as described at the end of Chapter 1. On their own, WebSockets aren't that exciting, but that excitement grows infinitely when you start to combine WebSockets with other technologies, like canvas.

Being able to tie the data being sent back and forth via WebSockets to a visual display (the canvas) unlocks a whole host of possibilities. For example, you could send the (x, y) coordinate position of a player to a server, using WebSockets, and then have that position sent by the server to every other player connected to the game, using WebSockets. That (x, y) position could then be used to display all the other players in the game. This is a really basic example of multiplayer, but it's exactly how I started with Rawkets (http://rawkets.com), my own multiplayer game that uses canvas and WebSockets (see Figure 10-7).

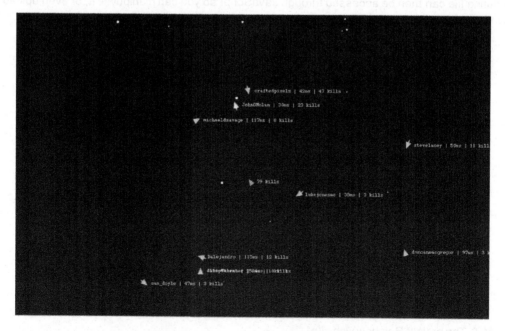

Figure 10-7. My multiplayer canvas and WebSockets game, Rawkets

As with everything else in this section, WebSockets aren't super easy, but that doesn't meant that you shouldn't go off and learn about them. I encourage you to explore what WebSockets can do for you, and to experiment with creating your own multiplayer game. This is another section that I could write an entire book about, but I hope that I've given you enough to get excited about WebSockets enough to consider them in the future.

Inspiration

Before I leave you, I thought it would be a good idea to give you some inspiration in the form of great HTML5 games that have been created during the writing of this book. Enjoy!

Sketch Out

This is a fantastically immersive space-based game that throws you feet first into an epic battle with another planet-type entity. Your job is to draw defenses around your planet and protect it from being hit. The music is great as well; so atmospheric. Check it out at `http://sketch-out.appspot.com/`.

Figure 10-8. Sketch Out by Fi

Z-Type

This is a weirdly addictive game, based on words. That's right, the entire game is based around typing in the words that appear on the screen, with each correct letter landing a direct shot on your opponent. Cool! Check it out at `www.phoboslab.org/ztype/`.

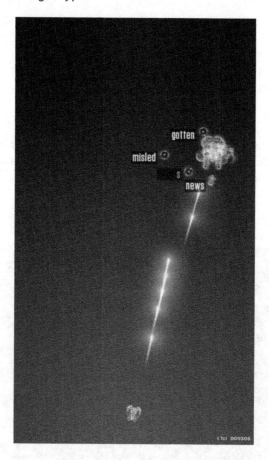

Figure 10-9. Z-Type by Dominic Szablewski (image from Mozilla Labs)

Sinuous

This is a pretty cool game, and it's very similar in functionality to the asteroid avoidance game that you made in the previous chapter. In fact, Sinuous is much more advanced and it a great example of exactly what can be achieved when you use the techniques from this game alongside some time and effort. Check it out at `http://sinuousgame.com/`.

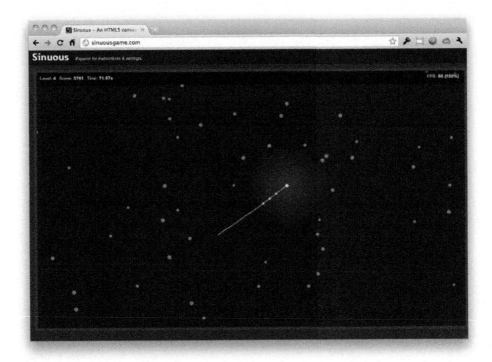

Figure 10-10. Sinuous by Hakim El Hattab

Summary, and farewell

In this chapter I've explored some of the areas relating to canvas and it's future for animation and gaming. I've also highlighted some of the technologies that canvas is often compared to, hopefully allowing you to make an educated decision about which one to use for your projects.

Some of these topics could perhaps have come earlier in the book, but I felt that together they combined to shed some light on the future of canvas. Overall, canvas has a massively bright future, and you should be excited to be around during its development. Learn how to use canvas today, and who knows what kind of cool stuff you'll be able to create in the near future!

But really, we're only at the beginning of canvas' journey. Technologies like hardware acceleration and WebGL are still yet to be supported cross-platform. It's these technologies that are really going to shape how canvas is used in the future; they're going to help define its purpose.

All in all, canvas is a massively awesome addition to your toolkit, especially when combined with WebSockets, and other HTML5 technologies, like video and audio. I hope that this book has inspired you to experiment with it, even if it's just to see what can actually be achieved.

I'd love to hear about the kind of stuff that you get up to. So what are you waiting for? Go forth and be amazing!

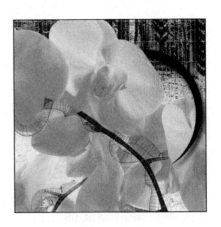

Index

CPSIA information can be obtained
at www.ICGtesting.com
Printed in the USA
LVOW03s1731081216

516414LV00002B/10/P